Get the eBook FREE!

(PDF, ePub, Kindle, and liveBook all included)

We believe that once you buy a book from us, you should be able to read it in any format we have available. To get electronic versions of this book at no additional cost to you, purchase and then register this book at the Manning website.

Go to https://www.manning.com/freebook and follow the instructions to complete your pBook registration.

That's it!
Thanks from Manning!

Testing Vue.js Applications

Testing Vue.js Applications

EDD YERBURGH

MANNING
SHELTER ISLAND

For online information and ordering of this and other Manning books, please visit
www.manning.com. The publisher offers discounts on this book when ordered in quantity.
For more information, please contact

    Special Sales Department
    Manning Publications Co.
    20 Baldwin Road
    PO Box 761
    Shelter Island, NY 11964
    Email: orders@manning.com

♾ Recognizing the importance of preserving what has been written, it is Manning's policy to have
the books we publish printed on acid-free paper, and we exert our best efforts to that end.
Recognizing also our responsibility to conserve the resources of our planet, Manning books
are printed on paper that is at least 15 percent recycled and processed without the use of
elemental chlorine.

Manning Publications Co.
20 Baldwin Road
PO Box 761
Shelter Island, NY 11964

Development editor:	Toni Arritola
Production editor:	Tiffany Taylor
Copy editor:	Pam Hunt
Proofreader:	Keri Hales
Technical proofreader:	Cody Sand
Typesetter and cover designer:	Marija Tudor

ISBN 9781617295249
Printed in the United States of America
1 2 3 4 5 6 7 8 9 10 – SP – 23 22 21 20 19 18

brief contents

contents

CONTENTS xi

12 Writing snapshot tests 193

12.1 Understanding snapshot tests 194

Writing snapshot tests for components 196 ▪ Writing snapshot
tests for static components 196 ▪ Writing snapshot tests for
dynamic components 198

12.2 Adding snapshot tests to your workflow 200

13 Testing server-side rendering 203

13.1 Understanding server-side rendering 204

The advantages of SSR 204 ▪ The disadvantages of SSR 206

13.2 Testing server-side rendered components 207

Using Vue Server Test Utils 208 ▪ Traversing server-side rendered
markup with render 210

13.3 Testing status codes with SuperTest 211
13.4 Testing SSR implicitly 214

14 Writing end-to-end tests 216

14.1 Understanding end-to-end tests 217

Using end-to-end tests effectively 217 ▪ Understanding
Nightwatch and WebDriver 218

14.2 Adding Nightwatch to a project 219

Installing dependencies 219 ▪ Configuring Nightwatch 220
Adding a sanity test 221 ▪ Writing an end-to-end test script 222

14.3 Writing end-to-end tests with Nightwatch 224

Deciding which end-to-end tests to write 224 ▪ Writing
end-to-end tests for routes 224 ▪ Writing end-to-end tests
for dynamic data 226

14.4 Running end-to-end tests in multiple browsers 228
14.5 Where to go from here 229

appendix A Setting up your environment 231
appendix B Running the production build 237
appendix C Exercise answers 239

index 243

preface

When I began writing tests for frontend applications I had a lot of questions. What should I test? How should I write tests? Where should tests fit into the workflow? Most of the resources on testing that I could find were written about backend applications, and often the advice didn't translate well to the frontend.

That was many years ago now, and since then the frontend testing scene has blossomed. But there's still a lack of good resources, and I know many people have the same questions I once had.

This book is my chance to answer those questions. I've worked hard to include all the information you need to test a large Vue application from start to finish. By the end of the book, you'll have the tools to write tests for lots of different situations. I look forward to sharing my experience testing Vue components and to teaching the techniques I use every day.

acknowledgments

I wrote this book while working a full-time job, maintaining open source projects, and speaking at conferences. I can honestly say I've worked harder this year than any other time in my life, and I couldn't have done it without the help of family, friends, and co-workers.

First, I want to thank Bláithín, who supported me throughout this process. Thank you so much for being patient and understanding on those weekends I spent hunched over my laptop, writing. I couldn't have done this without you.

I want to thank the people at Manning who made this book possible: publisher Marjan Bace and everyone on the editorial and production teams. In particular, I'd like to thank Toni, my editor, who helped me through the entire process. Her guidance has been invaluable.

I'd also like to thank the reviewers who took the time to read my manuscript at various stages during its development and who provided invaluable feedback: Dane Balia, Gabriele Bassi, Julio Biason, John Farrar, Tamara Forza, George Gaines, Jon Guenther, Foster Haines, Clive Harber, Reka Horvath, Roman Kuba, Alberto Luis, Tom Madden, Viktor Nemes, Ubaldo Pescatore, Julien Pohie, Dan Posey, Fernandez Reyes, Jim Schmehil, Vishal Singh, and Yuxi (Evan) You.

about this book

This is a book about writing automated tests for Vue applications. Most of the book is focused on unit testing, because the techniques for unit testing components are the most specific to Vue. I also spend a chapter explaining snapshot testing and a chapter explaining end-to-end testing.

The aim of the book is to teach you how to write a robust suite of automated tests to verify that your Vue applications work correctly. I'll teach you the techniques and the approach to testing that I've found most effective.

Who should read this book

Testing Vue.js Applications is written for Vue developers who want to improve their testing skills. The book is intended for both experienced Vue developers and beginners, although developers with no Vue experience should learn the basics before picking up this book.

How this book is organized

This book is organized into 14 chapters:

- Chapter 1 introduces automated testing and the Vue framework.
- Chapter 2 introduces unit testing. In this chapter, you'll set up Jest to compile Vue single-file components and write your first unit test.
- Chapter 3 discusses writing unit tests to check component output.
- Chapter 4 explains how to test methods. You'll learn how to use stubs to test component methods, how to test code that uses timer functions, and how to test components that import complex functions from other modules.

- Chapter 5 discusses testing events. It covers testing native DOM events and custom Vue events.
- Chapter 6 introduces Vuex. Vuex is a complicated topic, so this chapter is a primer for the next chapter, where you'll learn how to test Vuex.
- Chapter 7 is about testing Vuex. It covers testing a Vuex store, and testing components that interact with a Vuex store.
- Chapter 8 discusses using factory functions to improve test-file structure.
- Chapter 9 covers Vue Router and how to add it to a project.
- Chapter 10 examines how to test components that use Vue Router.
- Chapter 11 discusses testing mixins and filters, as well as testing components that use them.
- Chapter 12 examines snapshot testing.
- Chapter 13 describes how to test code in server-side rendered apps.
- Chapter 14 finishes the book by teaching end-to-end testing, to finish your tests.

The book is best read cover-to-cover, although I've made sure each chapter can be read as a standalone. The book teaches testing by building a Hacker News application from the ground up, so you'll learn the process of testing a large application from scratch. If you follow the book sequentially, you'll be able to see the entire process of writing tests and code for an application. But I've included the code for each chapter, and the code listings are written so they make sense without the wider context of the Hacker News application.

About the code

This book contains many examples of source code, both in numbered listings and inline with normal text. In both cases, source code is formatted in a `fixed-width font like this` to separate it from ordinary text.

In this book, you'll build a Hacker News application from start to finish; only chapter 5 uses a different code base. All of the code is available from the book's website: www.manning.com/books/testing-vue-js-applications. It's also available from GitHub; you can find the repository by following the instructions in appendix A. Each chapter has a Git branch with the current code, so you can use the branches to see what the Hacker News code from the previous chapter should look like.

GitHub uses Git, so you'll need that installed to be able to read the repository. You'll need Node to run the tests and application code. You'll also need Java installed to run the end-to-end tests. I've included details on installing Node and Java in appendix A.

Online resources

Need additional help? The Vue Discord channel is a useful place to get help with Vue-related problems. In addition, the Vue tag on StackOverflow (http://stackoverflow.com/questions/tagged/vue) is a great place to ask more complex questions.

Book forum

Purchase of *Testing Vue.js Applications* includes free access to a private web forum run by Manning Publications where you can make comments about the book, ask technical questions, and receive help from the author and from other users. To access the forum, go to https://forums.manning.com/forums/testing-vuejs-applications. You can also learn more about Manning's forums and the rules of conduct at https://forums .manning.com/forums/about.

Manning's commitment to our readers is to provide a venue where a meaningful dialogue between individual readers and between readers and the author can take place. It is not a commitment to any specific amount of participation on the part of the author, whose contribution to the forum remains voluntary (and unpaid). We suggest you try asking the author some challenging questions lest his interest stray! The forum and the archives of previous discussions will be accessible from the publisher's website as long as the book is in print.

about the author

EDD YERBURGH is a JavaScript developer and Vue core team member. He's the main author of the Vue Test Utils library and is passionate about open source tooling for testing component-based applications.

about the cover illustration

The figure on the cover of *Testing Vue.js Applications* is captioned "Habit of a Tartarian Woman of Schouvache subject to Russia in 1768." The illustration is taken from Thomas Jefferys' *A Collection of the Dresses of Different Nations, Ancient and Modern* (four volumes), London, published between 1757 and 1772. The title page states that these are hand-colored copperplate engravings, heightened with gum arabic.

Thomas Jefferys (1719–1771) was called "Geographer to King George III." He was an English cartographer who was the leading map supplier of his day. He engraved and printed maps for government and other official bodies and produced a wide range of commercial maps and atlases, especially of North America. His work as a mapmaker sparked an interest in local dress customs of the lands he surveyed and mapped, which are brilliantly displayed in this collection. Fascination with faraway lands and travel for pleasure were relatively new phenomena in the late 18th century, and collections such as this one were popular, introducing both the tourist as well as the armchair traveler to the inhabitants of other countries.

The diversity of the drawings in Jefferys' volumes speaks vividly of the uniqueness and individuality of the world's nations some 200 years ago. Dress codes have changed since then, and the diversity by region and country, so rich at the time, has faded away. It's now often hard to tell the inhabitants of one continent from another. Perhaps, trying to view it optimistically, we've traded a cultural and visual diversity for a more varied personal life—or a more varied and interesting intellectual and technical life.

At a time when it's difficult to tell one computer book from another, Manning celebrates the inventiveness and initiative of the computer business with book covers based on the rich diversity of regional life of two centuries ago, brought back to life by Jeffreys' pictures.

Introduction to testing Vue applications

1

This chapter covers

- What testing is
- Why testing is useful
- The difference between unit tests, end-to-end tests, and snapshot tests
- Core Vue concepts

As a developer, you want to ship bug-free code. Nothing is worse than finding out on Monday morning that your Friday changes broke the live application! The only way you can make sure your application works correctly is by testing it, so it's vital that you learn how to test applications thoroughly.

A good testing approach speeds up development, improves code quality, and limits the bugs in your app. A poor testing approach cripples a project. This book will teach you to test Vue applications effectively to make sure you get the benefits of testing and avoid the pitfalls. By the end of the book you will have become a Vue testing master, ready to test any Vue application you encounter.

To learn the techniques to test a Vue application, you're going to write a test suite for a Hacker News clone from start to finish. The Hacker News application

1

will use Vue, Vuex, Vue Router, and server-side rendering—just like most large Vue applications.

As well as teaching you the techniques, I want to teach you the mindset and approach to testing that I've developed over the years. Throughout the book I'll give you advice to hone your testing skills.

This first chapter is a primer on testing Vue applications. I'll give you a high-level overview of testing in general, the different types of tests you'll learn in this book, and the Hacker News app you'll write. Finally, I'll explain some core Vue concepts, to make sure we're speaking with the same vocabulary.

The first thing to do is to define testing.

1.1   Defining testing

Any academic paper worth its salt defines the concepts it uses before discussing them in depth. So, like a good academic, I'll define what I mean *by testing an application* before I teach you about different testing techniques.

A simple definition is that testing an application is *the process of checking that an application behaves correctly.* It's a no-brainer that you should verify your application behaves correctly, but the topic gets more interesting when you talk about the different testing techniques.

There are two main approaches to testing: manual testing and automated testing. Manual testing is where you check that an application works correctly by interacting with it yourself. Automated testing is the practice of writing programs to perform the checks for you.

Most of this book is about automated testing. But to understand the benefit of automated testing, you need to understand manual testing.

1.1.1   Manual testing

Every employable developer tests code manually. It's the next logical step after writing source code, like how the next step after chewing food is to swallow it.

Imagine you're creating a sign-up form. When you finish writing the code, you don't just close your text editor and tell your boss that you've finished the form. No, you'll open the browser, fill out the form, and make sure it completes the sign-up process correctly. In other words, you'll test the code *manually.*

Manual testing works great for small projects. If you have a TODO list app that you can check manually in two minutes, you don't need automated tests. But when your app grows to a certain size, relying on manual testing becomes a burden.

Let me tell you about the first large JavaScript application I worked on. The application was a mess. You've heard of spaghetti code? This code was spaghetti, tagliatelle, and linguini code rolled into one. It was very difficult to follow the application logic, and there weren't any automated tests. Needless to say, the code had bugs. In an attempt to stop bugs, we would manually test the application before releasing it. Every Wednesday we would pour some coffee, open a list of *user journeys* to test, and hunch over our laptops for four hours to work through the set of instructions. It was *painful.*

DEFINITION A user journey is a list of steps that a user can take through an application. For example—*open application, fill out form, click submit.*

Considering we spent 10% of our development time manually testing the app, you would have thought we would stop any bugs reaching production. Nope. The application was riddled with them. The reason is that manually testing hundreds of features is difficult—it's all too easy to lose concentration and forget to check something.

One time when working through a user journey, I accidentally forgot to check that clicking a button would display the metadata of a music track. The other developers must have forgotten to test that feature too, because the bug was live for months!

Although some of our manual testing time was spent testing new features, most was taken up testing old features to check they still worked. This kind of testing is known as *regression testing*. Regression tests are difficult tasks for us humans to do—they're repetitive, they require a lot of attention, and there's no creative input. Put simply, they're boring. Luckily, computers are great at tasks like these, and that's where automated testing comes in!

1.1.2 Automated testing

Automated testing is the process of using programs to check that your software works correctly. In other words, you write extra code to test your application code. After the test code is written, you can test your app as many times as you want with minimal effort.

You can use lots of different techniques to write automated tests. You can write programs to automate a browser, call functions in your source code directly, or compare screenshots of your rendered application. Each of the techniques has different benefits, but they all have something in common: they save you time over manual testing.

In the previous section, I spoke about an untested application I worked on. One of the problems with the application was that we had a four-hour manual testing process every time we wanted to release a new version of the app. Soon after I joined the team, the CTO decided that we should write automated tests to do this work for us. Over time, we reduced the testing time from four hours of manual work to 20 minutes of automated work.

After that experience, I've always written automated tests for large projects from the start. It's easier to domesticate a horse that's lived with humans from birth than it is to tame a wild horse in captivity. In this book you'll learn to create a tame application by writing tests right from the application's conception.

Automated tests are great for checking that your application still works. They also make it easier to review code changes to an application. Let's take a look at a real-world example of using automated tests—testing pull requests on GitHub.

1.1.3 Testing pull requests on GitHub

GitHub is a website that hosts Git repositories. A lot of open source projects like Vue are hosted on GitHub, and most of the companies I've worked for keep their code in private GitHub repositories.

DEFINITION   Git is a version-control system. I'm going to assume you've used it before and are familiar with the concepts of merging, branching, and committing. If you haven't, check out the Git docs: https://git-scm.com.

Pull requests are part of the GitHub workflow. They give developers the chance to review code changes made on separate branches before they are merged into the master branch.

NOTE   if you aren't familiar with the GitHub flow, read *Understanding the GitHub Flow*—https://guides.github.com/introduction/flow.

Without tests, when you review a pull request you need to pull code changes to your machine, run the app, and test the code manually to verify that it still works. This is time-consuming, and you won't be surprised to hear some people skip this process entirely when they review pull requests.

Automated tests make this process much easier. When you have automated tests in a project, you can set up a service to download the pull request branch, run the test suite, and report back whether the tests passed or failed (figure 1.1). As long as you trust the tests, there's no need to check the code on your own machine.

Figure 1.1   A pull request that passed the tests; the tick appears when the tests have passed.

Webpack src alias ✓

#7 by Austio was merged on 13 Jun

NOTE   Most open source projects require developers to write new tests when they add new functionality. Vue accepts only pull requests that include tests for the new code.

As well as making pull requests easier to review, automated tests make modern workflows like continuous integration and continuous delivery possible. If you're interested in these workflows, you can read about them on Martin Fowler's blog (http://mng.bz/nxVK).

Now that I've defined automated testing and manual testing, it's time to get more specific. The next section provides an overview of automated testing techniques, and how you can use them to check your applications.

NOTE   Just as *the Facebook* dropped *the* to become *Facebook*, it's time to drop the *automated* from *automated testing*. From now on, I'm going to refer to automated testing simply as *testing*.

1.2   *Testing overview*

So far, I've spoken about tests at a high level. Now it's time to talk about the specific types of tests you can write. In this book you're going to learn to write three types of tests for frontend applications—unit tests, snapshot tests, and end-to-end tests.

1.2.1 Overview of end-to-end tests

End-to-end tests are the most intuitive type of test to understand. In frontend applications, end-to-end tests automate a browser to check that an application works correctly from the user's perspective.

Imagine you're writing a calculator app and you want to test that it sums two numbers correctly. You could write an end-to-end test that opens a browser, loads the calculator app, clicks the 1 button, clicks the plus (+) button, clicks the 1 button again, clicks equals (=), and checks that the screen displays the correct result (2). You can see an example of what that might look like as code in the next listing.

> **Listing 1.1 An end-to-end test to check that a calculator sums two numbers**

```
function testCalculator(browser) {
  browser
    .url('http://localhost:8080')        Navigates in the browser to the
                                         application running locally
    .click('#button-1')
    .click('#button-plus')               Clicks the
    .click('#button-1')                  calculator buttons
    .click('#button-equal')
    .assert.containsText("#result", "2")   Asserts that the calculator
    .end();                                displays the correct result
}
```

End-to-end tests are powerful time-savers. After you've written an end-to-end test, you can run it as often as you want. Imagine how much time a suite of hundreds of these tests could save!

At first, end-to-end tests seem like the only testing tool you need. But they have a few problems. First, end-to-end tests are slow. Launching a browser can take several seconds, and websites can be slow to respond. It's common for a suite of end-to-end tests to take 30 minutes to run, and if you relied purely on end-to-end tests, your test suite would take *hours* to run.

Another problem with end-to-end tests is that debugging them can be difficult. To debug an end-to-end test, you need to open a browser and step through the user journey to reproduce the bug yourself. This is bad enough when you're running end-to-end tests locally, but if your tests fail on your CI server and not on your local machine, you're going to have a bad time.

> **NOTE** One way to avoid the reproducibility problem is to run end-to-end tests in a reproducible environment, like a Docker container. Docker containers are outside the scope of this book, but you should consider looking into them to run end-to-end tests to make sure you avoid the problem of failures on different machines.

There's another problem with end-to-end tests—they can be *flaky*. Flaky tests are tests that frequently fail even though the application they are testing is working. Maybe the code took too long to execute or an API was temporarily down. Like a flaky friend, you will stop taking a flaky test seriously. "Oh no, the tests failed! Let me have a look. … Oh, it was *that one*. The one fails all the time—nothing to worry about." Flaky tests make your test suite less useful, but they're difficult to avoid when you write end-to-end tests!

If you made a list of everything developers complain about, I would put money on end-to-end tests being in the top three. Although they are useful, they shouldn't be your only type of test.

In this book, only one chapter is dedicated to end-to-end tests, partly because of the downsides of end-to-end tests, and partly because end-to-end tests are framework agnostic—they work whether your application is written using Vue or MooTools.

End-to-end tests automate the kind of testing that you would do manually. You can set them up to run against a live website at regular intervals or run them against code before it's merged into a master branch.

End-to-end tests don't give you a new approach to testing code—you just get faster manual testing. Unit tests, on the other hand, provide you with a new tool that you don't get from testing code manually.

1.2.2   *Overview of unit tests*

Unit testing is the process of running tests against *the smallest parts of an application* (units). Normally the units you test are functions, but in Vue apps, *components* are also units to test (more on those later).

Remember the calculator application? In the code, the application uses a sum function to calculate the sum of two numbers.

If you edited the function to make it easier to read, you would want to test that the function still works correctly. You *could* run an end-to-end test, but if the end-to-end test failed, you wouldn't know whether the problem was with the sum function or with a different part of the source code. The only way you could know for sure that it was the sum function that was broken would be to run the function in isolation. You can do this with unit tests.

Unit tests are functions that call functions in your source code in isolation and assert that they behave correctly. Take a look at the next listing. It's a simple program that imports a sum function, runs it, and throws an error if sum does not return 2.

Listing 1.2   A basic unit test

```
// sum.js
export default function sum(a, b) {          ⟵⎤ The function
  return a + b                                 ⎦ to test
}

// sum.spec.js                    ⎤ Imports the sum function
import sum  from '../sum'    ⟵⎦ into the test file

function testSum() {                          ⎤ Throws an error if sum
  if (sum(1,1) !== 2) {             ⟵⎦ does not return 2
    throw new Error('sum(1,1) did not return 2')
```

```
    }
  }
testSum()        ◁──┐  Runs
                    │  the test
```

Because unit tests run against an isolated unit, when a well-written unit test fails, it acts as a flashing neon sign pointing you toward the problem code.

Unlike end-to-end tests, unit tests are fast. They run in a few seconds, so you can run unit tests each time you make a code change to get quick feedback on whether the change broke existing functionality.

A happy side effect of unit tests is that they provide documentation. If a new developer starts on a project and needs to know how a unit of code behaves, they can look at the tests to see exactly how a unit behaves.

I spoke earlier about flaky end-to-end tests—tests that regularly fail even though the application is working correctly. Well-written unit tests don't suffer from this problem. As long as the unit test is deterministic, you can run it a thousand times, and it will pass every time.

So far, I've had nothing but good things to say about unit tests—I'm making them blush. But I don't want to mislead you. Like end-to-end tests, unit tests have their own problems.

A big problem with unit tests is that they make it difficult to *refactor* code. People don't often talk about this problem, but it's one I encounter a lot.

> **DEFINITION** Refactoring is the process of rewriting code—normally to improve the quality of it (but that depends on who's doing the refactoring!).

If you have a complicated function with unit tests and decide to split the function into two separate functions, you need to change the unit tests as well as the code. This can make refactoring a lot less appealing. At times I've been unwilling to change the structure of my code because it required too much extra work to update the unit tests. There's not an easy solution here, but it's something extra to consider when you decide whether the tests you write will save you time in the long term.

Another problem with unit tests is that they check only individual parts of an application. You can test that the individual parts of a car work correctly, but if you don't check that they work when they're fitted together and then the engine doesn't turn on, your tests were useless. Unit tests suffer from this problem. They make sure units of code behave as expected, but they don't test that the units interact with each other correctly. That's why you need to supplement unit tests with end-to-end tests.

So far I've given you an overview of end-to-end tests and unit tests. The final tests that you'll learn in this book are snapshot tests.

1.2.3 Snapshot testing

Have you played Spot the Difference? Spot the Difference is a game where you have two pictures of the same thing with small differences between them. The aim of the game is to identify the differences.

Snapshot tests are similar to Spot the Difference. A snapshot test takes a picture of your running application and compares it against previously saved pictures. If the pictures are different, the test fails. This test method is a useful way to make sure an application continues to render correctly after code changes.

Traditional snapshot tests launch an application in a browser and take a screenshot of the rendered page. They compare the newly taken screenshot to a saved screenshot and display an error if differences exist. These types of snapshot tests have problems when differences between operating systems or browser versions cause tests to fail even though the snapshot hasn't changed.

In this book, I'll teach you how to write snapshot tests with the Jest testing framework. Instead of comparing screenshots, Jest snapshot tests can compare any *serializable* value in JavaScript. You can use them to compare the DOM output from Vue components. You'll learn about snapshot tests in detail in chapter 12.

> **DEFINITION**   Serializable means any code that can be converted to a string and then back into a value. In reality, it refers to a V8 method, but there's no need to go into those details!

Now you've seen each of the test types you're going to write. It's time to talk about how you can combine these different test types to write effective test suites.

1.2.4   Combining test types effectively

If you combine sugar, flour, and butter in the correct quantities, you get tasty cookie dough. If you use the wrong quantities, you get floury milk. You need to combine different types of tests together in the correct quantities to make sure you have a robust test suite, rather than a mess of test code.

In figure 1.2, you can see the frontend testing pyramid. This represents the proportion of the different types of tests that should make up your frontend testing suite. From my experience, this is the best way to structure a testing suite for a frontend Vue application.

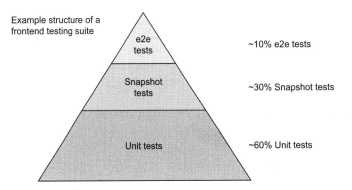

Figure 1.2   The testing pyramid. Most of your tests should be unit tests.

Most of the pyramid consists of unit tests—they provide quick feedback when developing the application. Snapshot tests also run quickly, but they cover more ground than unit tests, so you don't need as many snapshot tests as unit tests.

As I said earlier, end-to-end tests are great for checking an app, but they can be slow and flaky. The best way to avoid flaky tests is to not write them, so the frontend testing pyramid contains only a few end-to-end tests.

> **No integration tests**
>
> If you're an experienced developer, you might have heard of integration tests. Integration tests are another type of tests that are often used in combination with unit tests and end-to-end tests.
>
> I don't recommend writing integration tests for frontend code. Integration tests on the frontend are difficult to define, difficult to write, and difficult to debug.
>
> People define integration tests differently, especially on the frontend. Some think tests that run in a browser environment are integration tests. Some think any test that tests a unit with module dependencies is an integration test. Some think that any fully rendered component is an integration test.
>
> In chapter 13 I'll teach you how to write server-side integration tests (using my own definition) to make sure a server responds with the correct HTTP requests. But for the frontend tests in this book, you won't write any integration tests.

In this book you'll create a test suite that's structured following the frontend testing pyramid. I'm going to teach you how to write the test suite by following a test-driven development workflow. It's important that you understand the test-driven workflow to understand how the code in this book is structured.

1.2.5 *Test-driven development*

Test-driven development (TDD) is a workflow where you write a failing test before you write the source code. Before you write code in a component, you write a test to makes sure the component behaves correctly.

A popular TDD approach is *red, green, refactor.* Red, green, refactor is where you write a failing test (red), make the test pass (green), and then refactor the code to make it more readable.

Developing applications like this offers some benefits. First, you write source code only for the functionality that's tested, which keeps the source code small. Second, it forces you to think about component design before you start writing code.

> **NOTE** I appreciate that TDD isn't for everyone, and I'm not trying to sell you on it. You don't need to join the temple of TDD to benefit from this book. The main reason I use TDD in this book is because it places the test code before the source code, and in the context of this book, test code is more important than the source code.

TDD comes in a lot of flavors—vanilla, lime, cherry, orange. I'm kidding, of course, but there are different ways of approaching TDD. This book follows a frontend-focused version of TDD.

Some TDD advocates write all test code before the source code. I don't follow TDD that strictly. I write the unit test code before the source code, but I add end-to-end tests and snapshot tests after the code is written. My general approach to writing a Vue component follows:

1 Decide the components I need.
2 Write unit tests and source code for each component.
3 Style the components.
4 Add snapshot tests for the finished components.
5 Test the code manually in the browser.
6 Write an end-to-end test.

In real life, sometimes I don't write unit tests for components, and sometimes I write the component code before I write tests. TDD advocates might clasp their faces in horror, but I find that a rigid approach to TDD can slow development.

A common saying is that *life is about the journey, not the destination.* Although this may be true about life in general, in the context of developing applications it's the opposite. As long as you write valuable tests that save you time, how you wrote them is irrelevant.

For most of the book I will tell you what you're going to test, show you the test code, and then show you the source code that would make the test pass. Expect that the tests will fail when you run a test before you add the source code that follows.

So far, I've told you about the benefits of automated testing, but before you get overexcited and create an automated-test-appreciation society, there's a disclaimer. Automated testing is not always necessary.

1.2.6 *Learning when not to test*

When I started to write automated tests I wanted to test *all the things.* I had experienced the pain of an untested application firsthand, and, like a middle-aged man with a hangover, I was determined not to do it again. But I soon learned another lesson. *Testing can slow development.*

When you write tests, it's important to keep in mind the reason that you're writing them. Usually, *the purpose of tests is to save time.* If the project you're working on is stable and will be developed for a long time, then tests pay off in dividends.

But if tests take longer to write and maintain than the time they save you, then you shouldn't write the tests at all. Of course, it's difficult to know before you write code how much time you will save by having tests—you'll learn this over time—but, for example, if you're creating a prototype, working on a short-term project, or iterating on an idea at a startup company, you probably won't benefit from writing tests.

Even when a project benefits from tests, it probably doesn't need as many tests as you might think. Let me tell you about the fallacy of 100% code coverage.

1.2.7 *The fallacy of 100% code coverage*

Code coverage is a measurement of how many lines in your codebase are run by your automated tests. Normally code coverage is measured as a percentage: 100% code coverage means every line of code runs during the execution of tests; 0% code coverage means that no lines are executed. It's a fun measurement, but it can lead to some dire consequences.

Tests provide diminishing returns. It's like going to the gym. When you first go to the gym, you build muscle quickly. You can lose your beer belly and look toned in a few months with only three hours of gym a week. But the bigger you get, the more time you need to spend to grow any bigger. The more hours you spend in the gym, the less benefit you get from each extra hour.

The same principle applies to tests. You can write simple tests that cover your applications' core features in a few hours. After you've written those tests, increasing your code coverage gets progressively more difficult. If you aim for 100% code coverage (the holy grail for some developers), it will feel like wringing the final drops of water from a towel. It's hard work.

Most of the time, 100% code coverage is not something to aim for. Sure, if you were working on a mission-critical payment app where bugs can cost millions, then 100% code coverage would benefit you. But in my experience, most apps do not benefit from 100% code coverage.

In the last few years, I've worked on projects with 0% code coverage, 100% code coverage, and coverage somewhere in between. Having 0% code coverage makes development a struggle. But 100% code coverage can make development slower and more painful than a slug climbing a sand dune.

Not only is it time-consuming to reach the fabled 100% code coverage, but even with 100% code coverage, tests do not always catch bugs. Sometimes you make the wrong assumptions. Maybe you're testing code that calls an API, and you assume that the API never returns an error; when the API *does* return an error in production, your app will implode.

You don't become a test master by striving for 100% code coverage on every app. Like a good MMA fighter who knows when to walk away from a fight, a true testing master knows when to write tests and when not to write tests.

In the next chapter you'll write your first unit test and get started on the Hacker News application. Before that chapter, I want to give you a high-level overview of what the Hacker News app will look like.

1.3 *Writing a Hacker News application*

When I first learned to test frontend applications, the tutorials I read taught me how to write tests for small apps. They were useful for learning techniques, but they didn't answer any questions I had about problems I had testing large real-world applications. I was left to answer those questions myself. In this book, I want to teach you how to test an application from start to finish, so you're going to write tests for a real-world Hacker News clone.

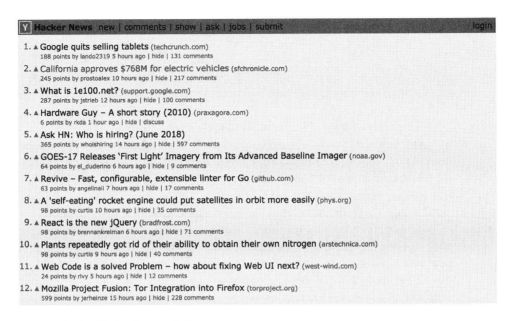

Figure 1.3   The Hacker News website

Hacker News is a social news website. It has a dynamic feed of items—like news stories, blog posts, and job listings (figure 1.3). Users can upvote an item to improve its score and downvote an item to decrease its score. If you've used Reddit, you'll be familiar with the concept.

> **NOTE**   The best way to understand Hacker News is to visit the site yourself—https://news.ycombinator.com.

In this book you're not going to implement the voting system. That level of complexity goes beyond the remit of testing Vue applications. What you will do is create an app that displays items, comments, and user profiles using real data from the Hacker News API.

The Hacker News clone will use Vue for the view part of the application, Vuex for state management, and Vue Router for client-side routing. Don't worry if you haven't used Vuex or Vue Router before. I'll cover them in detail later in this book.

A Hacker News clone is a great app to teach how to test Vue applications. It's complex enough for you to learn advanced testing techniques but simple enough to avoid getting bogged down in design details.

Now that you know what you're building, it's time to talk about Vue. For a book about testing Vue, we've gotten pretty far without mentioning it!

1.4   *Vue testing overview*

This book is about *testing* Vue applications, not *developing* Vue applications. I'm not going to teach you how to use Vue from the ground up. If you're a complete beginner with no Vue experience, you should spend time outside this book to learn the basics of Vue if you want to get the most out of this book.

> **NOTE** To learn Vue from the ground up, I recommend *Vue.js in Action* by Erik Hanchett with Benjamin Listwon (Manning, 2018, www.manning.com/ books/vue-js-in-action). Alternatively, the Vue docs are some of the best I've ever read. You can check them out at https://vuejs.org/v2/guide.

That said, throughout the book I will explain features of Vue briefly and link you to resources so you can learn about them in more detail if you need to, and two chapters in this book are devoted to learning the more-complex topics of Vuex and Vue Router.

Although I'm not going to teach Vue 101, I'll teach you some basic concepts before the next chapter, to make sure we're speaking the same language. The first term to add to your vocabulary is the *Vue instance*.

1.4.1 *The Vue instance*

Vue applications are made up from *Vue instances*. Every application contains at least one Vue instance, and when you write unit tests for a component, you will create a Vue instance with the component under test.

In listing 1.3, you can see a simple example of a Vue application. To start the application, you create a `new` Vue instance with an options object. Vue uses the `el` option to find a DOM node into which to render the nodes generated from the `template` string.

> **NOTE** I'm going to assume you're familiar with the DOM. If you're not familiar with the DOM, you can read an introduction to it on MDN (http://mng.bz/k5iQ).

Listing 1.3 Creating a Vue instance

```
new Vue({
  el: '#app',                              ◁──── Selector used to find the DOM
  template: '<div>{{message}}</div>',           element into which to render
  data() {                                 ◁──── Template string used
    return {                                     to generate DOM nodes
      message: 'Hello Vue.js!'             ◁──── Data used in the
    }                                            template string
  }
})
```

Creating a Vue instance that generates DOM nodes is known as *mounting an instance*. If you've written a Vue app before, you will have mounted a Vue instance to start the application running.

> **NOTE** If you're still confused by what a Vue instance is, you can read about it in the Vue docs (https://vuejs.org/v2/guide/instance.html).

The example in listing 1.3 uses a template string to describe the DOM nodes that Vue should generate. You can use a few different ways to describe the DOM nodes that Vue should render, so let's take a look at them now.

1.4.2   *Templates and render functions*

Vue gives you a way to declaratively render the DOM. In other words, you describe the DOM nodes that Vue should render.

You can describe the DOM nodes in two main ways: templates and render functions. Templates use an HTML syntax to describe a DOM, as shown in the following code.

Listing 1.4   A template string

```
new Vue({
  // ..
  template: '<div>{{message}}</div>',      ◁──── Template string that renders
  // ..                                            a message property
})
```

For Vue to use to generate DOM nodes from a template, it needs to convert the template into *render functions*—known as *compiling* the template. As shown in the next listing, you can use render functions directly in the Vue options instead of using a template string.

Listing 1.5   Using a render function

```
new Vue({
  // ..
  render(createElement) {
    return createElement('div', this.message)
  },
  // ..
})
```

Vue runs render functions to generate a virtual DOM—which is a JavaScript representation of the real DOM, shown in the following code. It then compares the virtual DOM against the real DOM, and updates the real DOM to match the virtual DOM.

Listing 1.6   Simple example of a virtual DOM

```
{
  tag: 'div',
  children: [
    {
      text: 'Hello Vue.js'
    }
  ]
}
```

NOTE If you want to learn more about render functions or the virtual DOM, you can read about them in the Vue docs http://mng.bz/dP7N and http://mng.bz/VqwP.

Render functions are more difficult to read than templates. You should write most of your components with templates, but when you do so, you should be aware that Vue needs to compile the template into render functions.

Templates make code easier to read, but large templates can be difficult to understand. Vue contains a component system that you can use to split templates into self-contained units, which makes code easier to read and maintain. A lot of this book is about unit testing Vue components, so you need a good understanding of what Vue components are.

1.4.3 Understanding the Vue component system

Components are self-contained modules of code that you can use in Vue templates. They abstract away logic and make templates easier to read. If you've used a frontend framework like React or Angular, you'll be familiar with the concept of components. If not, you can think of components as the building blocks of an application. For large Vue applications, it's components all the way down.

The easiest way to explain components is to show you some code. You can see an example of a `<custom-title>` component in the next code sample. Notice that after you *register* a component with Vue, you can use it in your code like an HTML tag.

Listing 1.7   Registering a component globally in Vue

```javascript
// JavaScript
Vue.component('hello-vue', {
  template: '<div>Hello Vue.js!</div>'       ◁——————  Defines the hello-vue
})                                                    component

// HTML
  <div>
    <hello-vue />         ◁——————  Uses hello-vue in
  </div>                           the template
```

You could define components in a few different ways, but in this book I'll have you write single-file components (SFCs).

NOTE All the techniques in this book will work the same way for any correctly defined Vue component.

Vue SFC files can be identified by their .vue extension. SFCs can contain a `<template>` block (similar to a template string), a `<script>` block, `<style>` blocks, and custom blocks (listing 1.8).

NOTE You won't use any custom blocks in this book, but you can read about them in the vue-loader docs at http://mng.bz/xJBW.

The object that's exported in the `<script>` block is known as a *component options object*. It accepts most of the options that a root Vue instance can take.

Listing 1.8 A single-file component (SFC)

```
<template>
  <div>{{message}}</div>          ⊲──┐   Template block
</template>                       ⊲──┘

<script>                                            ⊲──┐
  export default {        ⊲──┐  Component               │
    data: {                   │  options object          │
      message: 'Hello Vue.js!'                          │   Script block
    }                                                    │
  }                                                      │
</script>                                           ⊲──┘

<style>                    ⊲──┐
  div {                        │
    color: red;                │   Style block
  }                            │
</style>                   ⊲──┘
```

SFCs are not valid JavaScript or HTML. You can't run them in the browser, so you need to compile SFCs before you send them to the client.

A compiled SFC becomes a JavaScript object with the template converted to a render function. You can see an example in the next listing.

Listing 1.9 A compiled SFC

```
Module.exports = default {
  render() {                    ⊲────────┐   Generated
    var _vm = this;                      │   render function
    var _h = _vm.$createElement;
    var _c = _vm._self._c || _h;
    return _c('p', [_vm._v("I'm a template")])
  },
  name: 'example-template'
}
```

I hope that code didn't scare you. Compiled SFCs aren't designed to be human readable. You don't need to concern yourself with compiled render functions; that's the job of the Vue framework. The main takeaway here is that an SFC compiles into an object with a render function.

This gives you a good idea of what part of a component you should test.

1.4.4 Unit testing components

Deciding what unit tests to write is important. If you wrote tests for every property of a component, you would slow development and create an inefficient test suite.

One method for deciding what parts of a component should be tested is to use the concept of a *component contract*. A component contract is the agreement between a component and the rest of the application.

When you start a new job, you sign a contract with your employer. You agree that you'll spend 40 hours a week working in exchange for a salary. Because you've agreed to work 40 hours as part of a contract, your employer can safely assume they can use you to produce 40 hours of work a week as long as they pay your salary.

In the same vein, when you write a component to be used in the rest of the application, you are defining a contract for how it should behave. Other components can assume the component will fulfill its contractual agreement and produce the agreed output if it's provided the correct input.

The idea of input and output is important in component contracts. A good component unit test should always trigger an input and assert that the component generates the correct output (figure 1.4). You should write tests from the perspective of a developer who's using the component but is unaware of how the component functionality is implemented.

A common input for a component is a user action, like when a user clicks a button. The most common output is the DOM nodes generated by the render function, but lots of other inputs and outputs exist for Vue components. For example, the input could be

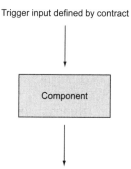

Figure 1.4   **Triggering an input and asserting an output in a component unit test**

- Component props
- User actions (like a button click)
- Vue events
- Data in a Vuex store

Forms of output for a Vue component could be

- Emitted events
- External function calls

NOTE   Don't worry if you don't know what emitted events or data in a Vuex store are. You'll learn about them later in the book.

Imagine you have an `AuthorizedStatus` component. The `AuthorizedStatus` component accepts an `authorized` prop. If the `authorized` prop is `true`, it renders "you're authorized" inside a `<div>` element. If it is `false`, it renders "you're not authorized."

DEFINITION   A prop is a piece of data passed to a component. Props are a way to pass data from parent components to child components. You can read more about props in the Vue docs at http://mng.bz/A2Dz.

You can see the `AuthorizedMessage` component next.

Listing 1.10   AuthorizedMessage.vue

```
<template>
  <div>
    {{authorized ? 'you're authorized' : 'you're not authorized'}}     ◁──┐
  <div>
</template>                                                        Conditionally
                                                                   rendered text
<script>
  export default = {
    name: 'loader',              A prop
    props: ['authorized']   ◁──┘ declaration
  }
</script>
```

When you use this component in an app, you expect that it will output "you're authorized" if you pass it an `authorized` prop set to `true`. If `authorized` is `false`, or not passed in, you expect it to be render "you're not authorized." This is its component contract, and it is the functionality that you should write unit tests for. In this book I'll use the idea of a component contract to show you what tests you should write for components.

Now that you've got a high-level overview of testing, you're on your way to becoming a testing master. In the next chapter, you'll create a test script and write your first unit test!

Summary

- There are two types of testing—automated testing and manual testing.
- A frontend testing suite that follows the frontend testing pyramid is made up of unit tests, snapshot tests, and end-to-end tests.
- Testing is not always beneficial. If a test doesn't save you time, then it's not worth writing.
- Vue applications are made up from Vue instances that use template strings or render functions to describe the DOM.
- Single-file components compile into objects with a render function.
- You can use component contracts to define what unit tests to write for Vue components.

Creating your first test

This chapter covers
- Writing npm scripts
- Catching formatting errors with ESLint
- Writing unit tests with Jest
- Writing unit tests for Vue components with Vue Test Utils
- Debugging Jest tests with the Chrome Debugger

A journey of a thousand miles begins with a single step, and every great test suite begins with a single test. This chapter is about writing that first test. By the end of the chapter you will have a test script that checks the project for formatting errors and runs a unit test against a Vue component.

To follow along with this chapter you need to install the correct programs and set up your environment. You can find the installation and setup instructions in appendix A. Follow the instructions to install the project and check out the chapter-2 branch, then return to this chapter.

The first part of this chapter is about the project structure. You'll learn how to use npm to manage dependencies and run scripts, and then set up Jest to run a simple unit test.

After Jest is set up, you'll write your first unit test for a Vue component. To do that, you'll learn how to compile components with Jest and use the official Vue test library—Vue Test Utils.

The last section of this chapter is about debugging. Specifically, I'll show you how to debug test code running in Jest using the Node Debugger and Chrome Developer tools. By the end of this chapter, you will be up to speed on the test setup and ready to test Vue component output in chapter 3.

The first thing to do is investigate a Vue project structure.

2.1   Understanding a Vue project structure

Common conventions make our lives easier. For example, when you want to use an unfamiliar tool, you can be pretty sure that the green button powers it on and the red button powers it off.

In a similar way, directory structure conventions make a code base easier to navigate for developers who are new the project. In this section you'll learn about a common Vue project structure that the Hacker News app you write will follow.

Vue projects use build tools to compile code. These build tools shape the conventions of Vue projects, so it's important to understand the build tools that Vue projects use.

2.1.1   Understanding build tools

As a developer, you have been gifted with the power to automate. You can automate routers to direct traffic across the internet, you can automate cars to park themselves in a garage, and, most excitingly, you can automate tools to compile JavaScript.

In this book, you're going to write code that uses Vue single-file components (SFCs) and modern JavaScript features like ES modules. Older browsers don't support ES modules, and you can't use SFCs in a browser, so you need to run a program to compile and bundle the source code into JavaScript that runs in a browser. These programs are called *build tools*.

The most popular JavaScript build tool is webpack. Webpack is a module bundler. Its main purpose is to bundle JavaScript files written as modules into a single file for use in a browser, but it's also capable of transforming, bundling, or packaging other assets, like Vue SFCs.

> **NOTE** If you're interested in learning more about webpack, read the webpack docs (https://webpack.js.org).

Under the hood, the Hacker News project uses webpack to bundle the code. Like most popular projects, webpack gets a lot of criticism. The common complaint is that webpack is difficult to configure. To avoid this pain point, this book comes with webpack preconfigured by Vue CLI.

2.1.2 Using Vue CLI to generate a project

Lighting is useful in a house, but if you do the wiring yourself you could get electrocuted. Build tools are like lighting. They're vital for a modern project, but they require wiring up. Instead of learning to wire them yourself, you can hire a professional to do it for you so that you can focus on writing application code.

The Hacker News project that you will work on is built with the Vue command-line interface (CLI). The Vue CLI *scaffolds* Vue projects—it generates a boilerplate project with build tools already configured, so you don't need to configure them yourself.

> **NOTE** If you want to use the Vue CLI to generate your own future projects, check out the GitHub page (https://github.com/vuejs/vue-cli). Vue CLI also includes a unit test plugin, which you can use to add a test setup for you, but in this chapter you'll learn how to set up unit tests without using the plugin.

Vue CLI uses a package called the Vue CLI service to run common tasks like bundling a file and starting a development server. The Vue CLI service assumes that some files are in a standard location, so that it can compile the code correctly without any configuration. Let's take a look at that structure now.

2.1.3 Understanding directory structure

Because Vue CLI relies on a directory structure to configure the build tools correctly, the file structure followed by Vue CLI has become a convention for Vue projects. The Hacker News app that you'll work on was built with Vue CLI, so it follows this structure. I'll talk you through the important directories and files now. You might want to open up the project to follow along with this explanation, but you can see a condensed directory tree in figure 2.1.

The src directory contains the main application code. src stands for *source code*. Everything in the src directory is bundled by webpack during the build process. You'll see what that looks like later in the chapter. The src directory is where you'll write most of the application code.

In the src directory you'll see a main.js file. Webpack uses this file as the entry point for the bundle it produces. Webpack recurses through the files imported by main.js to find the files it should process before including them in the final bundle.

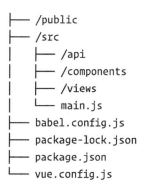

Figure 2.1 A common Vue project directory structure

In src, you'll see a components directory, which contains Vue components, as well as a views directory, which also contains components.

> **NOTE** The distinction between views and components will become clear when you get to chapter 10, but for now just think of views as top-level components.

The src/api directory contains functions that interact with the Hacker News API. You'll use these prewritten functions to fetch the Hacker News data—you won't write any API code in this book.

The public directory contains public assets, like a favicon (the image displayed in a browser tab). This directory is for images, icons, videos, or any other assets that you want to include in your application, but you don't want webpack to process.

The public directory also includes an index.html file. This file is the HTML template used by webpack to generate an index.html file for distribution. You'll see what that looks like later in this chapter.

Now that you're up to speed on the directory structure, it's time to look at npm and how to use npm in this project.

2.1.4   *Understanding npm*

npm is the Node package manager. It's a program that manages the installation of Node dependencies, known as node modules. Your project will use lots of node modules to run tests and build the code, so it's important to understand how npm works at a high level.

> **DEFINITION**   A node module is a directory that contains a package.json and at least one JavaScript file. You can use node modules to perform tasks, like starting a development server, optimizing images, or mining cryptocurrency.

The best way to learn about npm is to use it. Open the terminal and run the following command in the command line to run a development server:

```
npm run serve
```

> **NOTE**   Read appendix A if you're unsure how to run a command in the command line.

> **DEFINITION**   A development server is a server that runs a development build of an application locally.

In the output, you'll see the following error:

```
vue-cli-service: command not found
```

This error is because you haven't installed the project dependencies yet. The project is empty, like an unfurnished house. If you open the package.json file and search for vue-cli-service, you will see that it's listed in a devDependencies field. This field defines development dependencies—modules that are used for development tasks but aren't included in the production code.

You need to install the node module dependencies before you can start the development server. Open the command line, and run the following command:

```
npm install
```

This command instructs npm to download all the node module dependencies listed in package.json to the project. npm downloads modules from the npm registry, which is like a database of npm packages. You can see a diagram of this in figure 2.2.

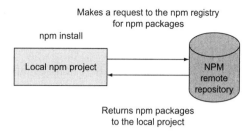

Figure 2.2   Downloading packages from the npm remote repository

The installation can take some time. You could go and make yourself a cup of oolong tea while you wait for the modules to finish downloading.

After the `npm install` command has finished, you'll have a new directory in your project: node_modules. The node_modules directory contains all the node modules your project uses. Open it up and look at its structure. There are hundreds of directories! It can be overwhelming, but don't worry—the node_modules directory is managed by npm. You rarely need to look at or edit the files inside.

Now you have the dependencies installed, run the dev server script again with the following command in the terminal:

```
npm run serve
```

This time the source code will be compiled, and you'll get a notice that a development server is started, with a URL on which the server is running. Open a browser and navigate to the URL. This is your development server.

Now webpack will watch for file changes and perform *hot module replacement* to update the app without you needing to refresh the page.

In the browser, open the Chrome inspector window and navigate to the Console.

> **NOTE**   You can find instructions for opening the Chrome Console window in appendix A if you are unsure how.

In the Console, type the following code and press Enter:

```
items
```

The Console will log a large array of items. This is the data you'll use in the next chapter to render a news items feed. Notice that it's globally available in the browser. Now return to the terminal, and cancel the script by pressing Ctrl-C.

The main use of npm is coordinating dependencies. It does this using the package.json file, so let's look at it in detail.

2.1.5   *Understanding the package.json file*

A package.json file is an npm configuration file. It includes details of project dependencies, as well as information used for publishing a package to the npm repository. In this project, you're going to use it to track dependencies and to define *npm scripts.*

In a text editor, open the package.json file and scroll to the `dependencies` field. Dependencies are the packages that the application uses in production. So far, Vue and Firebase are the only dependencies of this project.

> **NOTE** Firebase is used to access the Hacker News API. You won't be working with Firebase directly in this project; it's managed for you by code in the api directory.

The other section to look at in the package.json file is the `scripts` field. This is where you define project-specific scripts. In this project, you're going to use npm scripts to run your tests.

Scroll to the `scripts` field in package.json. You'll see a few script definitions there already. Let's look at the `serve` script, which you ran earlier. As you can see, the script runs the `vue-cli-service` command with a `serve` parameter:

```
"serve": "npm run build && node scripts/serve"
```

This project uses the Vue CLI service to compile code and run other build jobs. This way, you get the latest features by updating the Vue CLI Service package.

Most node projects use npm scripts to run development tasks. A common task people use npm scripts for is linting code; let's look at what linting is and then add your own linting script.

2.1.6 *Linting files with ESLint*

Linting is the process of checking code for potential errors and formatting issues. Linting is like getting a pedantic colleague to read over every line of your code and warn you when your code doesn't meet the project's style guide.

In your project, you'll use the Vue CLI service `lint` command to run linting. Under the hood, the Vue CLI service uses a library called ESLint.

ESLint is a configurable linting library. You can specify the rules it should look for and what files it should check. In the Hacker News application there's an `eslint Config` field in package.json to configure the rules that ESLint should follow. If you look in the `eslintConfig` object in package.json, you'll see an `extends` property, set to `plugin:vue/essential` and `@vue/standard`. These are sets of ESLint rules that the project follows. You can read the full set of Vue rules on the GitHub page: https://github.com/vuejs/eslint-plugin-vue.

Now let's run ESLint to check whether the project files are formatted correctly. There's already a `lint` script defined in the package.json `scripts` field as follows:

```
"lint": "vue-cli-service lint",
```

At the command prompt, run the command `npm run lint`. You'll get an error telling you that `api` is defined but never used in src/components/ItemList.vue. Remove the `import` statement from ItemList.vue to fix the error, and rerun the lint script to ensure that it's fixed:

```
npm run lint
```

Linting is a useful way to enforce code style on a project. You should use linting as part of a testing process, to make sure the code matches the project's style guide.

Now it's time to write a script of your own: the famous *test script*.

2.1.7 *Writing a test script*

The test script is a powerful script. By the end of the book it will run all the tests in your project and display an error if any test fails. A passing test script is a seal of approval. It's a big green check mark stamped on your project to say that the app is ready for production. On the other hand, a failing test script lets you know that there's a problem in your code.

Right now, you haven't written any unit tests, snapshot tests, or end-to-end tests to run in your test script. But you do have a linting script.

Linting often gets overlooked in the testing world. It's hard to make a case that catching a trailing comma is as important as stopping a bug from entering production. But linting is still an important part of a testing pipeline.

In the `scripts` field of package.json, add the following line:

```
"test": "npm run lint"
```

The test script is so common that npm has an alias for it. You can run the test script with the following command:

```
npm t
```

By the end of the book, this test script will run hundreds of tests against your application source code. You can use it with the npm install alias, `npm i`, to make your install and test script super concise, as follows:

```
npm it
```

Before you roll your sleeves up and add a unit test, let's look at one more script—the `build` script.

2.1.8 *Building the project*

The purpose of a web application is to serve it over the internet to a user. Right now, your project is just source code. There isn't anything you can send to the user. To produce the production code, you need to compile the source code into a JavaScript bundle.

As you saw in the previous section, there's a `build` script in the package scripts. Run that script as follows:

```
npm run build
```

The script takes a few seconds to complete while webpack processes the files. When the build finishes, you'll get some output saying "Build complete" in the terminal. If you look back at the project, you'll notice a shiny new dist directory has appeared. This is the distribution directory, which contains the finished application files.

> **NOTE** The dist directory is ignored by Git. This is a common convention: it means fewer files exists in the source code to be stored in the Git repository, so the Git repository will be smaller.

In the dist directory you'll see an index.html file and a public directory containing JavaScript files; later, when you add CSS to the project, the build script will generate CSS files in the dist directory as well. These are the files you need to serve the application in a browser. You can learn how to serve the files in appendix B.

By now you should have a good understanding of the project and how you are going to use npm scripts to run tests. The next step is to add a unit test to the project.

2.2 Introduction to Jest

Frameworks are tools to make writing software easier. You're going to use a framework called Jest to make it writing unit tests easier.

Jest includes a lot of features that improve unit testing. You'll encounter them throughout this book, but the most important feature is that Jest runs unit tests and reports back to you whether they passed or failed.

> **NOTE** Although this book uses Jest as the test runner, you can use most of the techniques with a different test runner. The underlying concepts are the same, and the syntax is similar to any spec runner like Mocha or Jasmine.

The first step when you set up a testing system is to write a simple test to check that the system is set up correctly. This is known as a sanity test.

2.2.1 Writing a sanity test

Have you ever spent hours debugging a website only to realize you were viewing a cached version? I have, and it was incredibly frustrating. Now, whenever I test code in an old browser, I add a console log in my code to make sure I'm running the latest version. The console log is a little *sanity test* that stops me from spending hours debugging something that was never broken.

My console log trick has saved me from testing cached content on Internet Explorer many times. You should add a similar sanity check when you write unit tests. A failing test will lead you on a debugging spree, and it would be very annoying to find out that it was actually the test setup that was broken rather than the source code.

A *sanity test* is a test that always passes. If the sanity test fails, you know there is a problem with the test setup.

First, you need to install Jest. Run the following command from the command line to install Jest and save it as a development dependency in the package.json file:

```
npm install --save-dev jest
```

If you open the package.json file, you'll see Jest has automatically been added to the `devDependencies` object by npm.

You'll use an npm script to run unit tests in Jest. It's useful to separate different types of tests into their own scripts, so that you can run only one type of test if you need to.

Open the package.json file in a text editor, and add the following line to the `scripts` object:

```
"test:unit": "jest"
```

> **NOTE** If you're using Windows, you should add a `no-cache` flag to the `jest` command to avoid potential errors. The full script will look like `"test:unit": "jest --no-cache"`.

Now you can add the unit test script to the test script. Tests are about quick feedback. Like a startup company, if a test is going to fail, it should fail fast. It would be annoying to wait 30 seconds for your unit tests to run, only to find your tests fail in the lint script because of a trailing comma. To avoid this, you should arrange the scripts in your test script from the quickest to the slowest.

Update the test script as follows to also run the unit tests after linting:

```
"test": "npm run lint && npm run test:unit",
```

Now run the unit test script by entering the following command in the command line:

```
npm run test:unit
```

You'll see a Jest error. It couldn't find any matching files! If you look at the error output, you'll see the following line:

```
testMatch: **/__tests__/**/*.js?(x),**/?(*.)(spec|test).js?(x)
```

This is the default *glob* pattern Jest uses to find test files in the project. For non-glob speakers, this pattern means that Jest matches .js and .jsx files inside __tests__ directories, as well as all files with a .spec.js or .test.js extension.

> **DEFINITION** Globs are the patterns used to match files. Jest uses the Node glob module to match files. You can read more about globs in the glob primer section of the glob npm page at www.npmjs.com/package/glob#glob-primer.

You're going to write your tests using a .spec.js file extension, so the test file for Item.vue file will be named Item.spec.js.

> **NOTE** Here, *spec* stands for specification, because unit tests are specifications for how your code should behave. Each test specifies a result to expect when the function you are testing is called.

Create a directory called __tests__ in the same directory as the component you're testing, and create a file named Item.spec.js inside the __tests__ directory. The file path from the root of your project will be src/components/__tests__/Item.spec.js.

TIP   It's good practice to keep unit tests as close to the code they're testing as possible. It makes it easier for other developers to find the test files for components or modules.

To define a unit test in Jest you use the `test` function. The `test` function takes two parameters: the first parameter is a string that identifies the test in the test report. You'll see what I mean by *the test report* when you run Jest in a second.

The second parameter to `test` is a function that contains the test code. Jest parses each test function in a test file, runs the test code, and reports back whether the test passed or failed.

A test fails if the `test` function throws an error. You can imagine Jest running the tests in a big `try/catch` statement. If the `catch` statement runs, Jest reports the test as failed.

In src/components/__tests__/Item.spec.js, add the next code to define a sanity test.

Listing 2.1   Sanity test

```
test('sanity test', () => {
  return
})
```

Run the unit test command `npm run test:unit`. The sanity test passes, so you know the test system is set up correctly.

Now you can run the test script—`npm run test:unit`—confident that it runs tests as expected. If the test script throws an error, you'll know the problem is with the test files rather than the test setup.

Let's take a step back and think about what *Jest* happened. Sorry. First, you ran the `test:unit` script, which ran Jest. Jest matched Item.spec.js using the default glob pattern, found the `test` function, and ran the second argument (the test), which returned without throwing an error. Jest saved the result and reported back that the test passed.

NOTE   As well as running Jest explicitly, you can also run it in watch mode. Watch mode watches for file changes and reruns tests for files that are updated. You use watch mode by calling Jest with a `--watch` flag. For example, to run the unit test script in watch mode, you would run `npm run test:unit -- --watch`. The first double dash adds the `watch` argument to the npm script. Note that `watch` will rerun all tests if your test script has a `--no-cache` flag.

Great. Now lint the project to make sure the code is formatted correctly. Run the following command to kick off the `lint` script:

```
npm run lint
```

Oh no, errors! The lint errors say that `test` is `undefined`. The problem is the linter does not know you're running test files in Jest, so it doesn't know that the `test` function will be defined globally.

To stop these linting errors, you need to update your ESLint configuration. Open package.json and go to the `eslintConfig` object, and then find the `env` object. This object tells ESLint what environment you are running code in. Add a `jest` property set to `true`. Your `env` object should look like this:

```
"env": {
  "node": true,
  "jest": true
},
```

> **NOTE** ESLint can support multiple environments, like `jest` and `browser`. If you're wondering why the `eslintConfig` in your project doesn't have `env` set to `browser`, it's because it's added under the hood by the eslint-vue plugin.

Run the lint script again: `npm run lint`. Now the linter knows that the test is available globally, so it won't throw any errors. You might have some unrelated errors about formatting issues. Resolve any linting errors before moving on.

> **NOTE** If you have trouble fixing an ESLint error, Google the error's name. You'll find an ESLint page explaining the rule in detail and how to fix it.

Now you have a unit test script with a passing sanity test set up. You can improve the sanity test by using a test assertion.

2.2.2 *Understanding test assertions*

Want to know something interesting? There are exactly 10 billion active Vue users in the world. That's a bold statement I made, and you'd be right to be suspicious. It's completely untrue.

I just made a false assertion. You knew it was false by evaluating what I said—*there are fewer than 10 billion humans on Earth, so unless Vue users aren't human, there's no way there can 10 billion Vue users.*

A *test assertion* works the same way as my false assertion: it's a statement that evaluates to either true or false. You could write my assertion in code as a test assertion using the Jest `expect` function as follows:

```
expect(vueUsers).toEqual(10000000000)
```

If you ran the assertion in a test, the assertion would evaluate to false, and the test would fail with an error.

The `expect` function returns an object of *Jest matchers* that are used to compare values. The `toBe` matcher checks that two values strictly equal (===) each other. you can rewrite your sanity test to use an assertion that always passes.

Replace the test in src/components/__tests__/Item.spec.js with the following code.

Listing 2.2   Using a Jest matcher

```
test('sanity test', () => {
  expect(true).toBe(true)          ◁─┐  Uses the toBe matcher to
})                                   │  assert that true equals true
```

If an assertion fails, it throws an error. The errors thrown by assertions are fancy errors that are formatted by Jest (figure 2.3). We'll call these errors *assertion errors*. Like the nutrition labels on food, assertion errors provide valuable information.

Figure 2.3   A Jest assertion error

Assertion errors are your friends. They give useful information about why the test fails, and importantly they help avoid false positives.

2.2.3   *Avoiding false positives*

In medicine, a false positive is where a test indicates that you have an illness, when you in fact don't. Doctors are careful to avoid false positives, because they cause unnecessary grief to the families of the wrongly diagnosed.

In tests, you also need to avoid false positives. If a test passes, it should pass because the source code works correctly, not because the test was written in a way that it always passes.

A common false positive test is one that uses asynchronous code. Imagine you're testing an object called `runner` that should set `finished` to `true` after 100 ms. In the test, you decide to wait for 100 ms before running the assertion, as shown next.

Listing 2.3   A test that always passes

```
test('sets finished to true after 100ms', () => {
  runner.start()
  setTimeout(() => {
    expect(runner.finished).toBe(true)        ◁──  Asserts that finished
  }, 100)                                            is true after 100 ms
})
```

When you run the test, it fails with a type error: `Uncaught TypeError: runner .start is not a function`. That's fine, you think. You haven't added the `start` method, so it's expected to fail. Next you add the code to make the test pass. When you run the unit test again, the test passes. Great, you think, and move on. Unwittingly, you've added a false positive to your test suite.

The problem is that the test finishes executing before the `setTimeout` callback is invoked—the assertion never runs. You would be surprised at how common this kind of false positive is. I've seen test suites with hundreds of false positives. Like a cautious doctor, you should do everything you can to avoid these painful false positives.

The best way I know to avoid false positives is by using TDD. In chapter 1 I spoke about the red, green, refactor workflow. The red stage is writing a test that fails for the correct reason. The key phrase here is *for the correct reason.*

If you write a test that fails because of a *type error,* such as trying to call a function in a test that doesn't exist, the test fails for the wrong reason. If you make the test pass by fixing the type error, you can't be sure that the test passes because the assertion is evaluating to `true` or because you wrote the test in a way that it always passes, like you did in the example.

A test should fail because the assertion evaluates to `false`. When a test fails with an assertion error, you know that it will fail again if the code changes in a way that the condition becomes false.

Before you add a unit test for a component in the next section, there's one last tip I want to give you on how to keep tests organized.

2.2.4 *Organizing tests with the describe function*

In the old days, people stored sheets of paper in filing cabinets. Searching through a filing cabinet drawer for an important piece of paper could take hours. If you were organized, you would get cardboard dividers to categorize the papers in your filing cabinet; it's a lot easier to find the right sheet of paper when your cabinet is categorized!

Just like this scenario, organized test suites make it easier to find tests. One way to organize unit tests is by using the `describe` function.

The describe function defines a unit test suite as a test suite. When you run tests from the command line, Jest formats the output so that you can see which test suites passed and which test suites failed. The code inside a describe function is known as a *describe block.*

Add a describe function to Item.spec.js, so that the code looks like the next code sample. Copy the code from this sample into src/components/specs/__tests__/ Item.spec.js.

```
describe('Item.vue', () => {
  test('sanity test', () => {
    expect(true).toBe(true
  })
})
```

←⎯⎤ **Defines a test suite**
    ⎥ **called Item.vue**

If you run the tests you'll see the output is nicely formatted into a test suite called Item.vue. This organization makes a test suite much nicer to work in.

The organizational power of the describe function comes with a warning. If you're not careful, you can make test suites more difficult to understand by overusing describe.

Dividers make a filing cabinet drawer easier to navigate. If the filing system is easy to understand, a new colleague can come along, work out the system you're using, and file a piece of paper in the correct category. Great—your system is working.

You might then decide to make it even easier to navigate by using subcategories and subcategories inside subcategories. You could add a color-coded system for optimized organization. Now your system works well for you, but it's too complicated for your colleagues to understand. When they try to file a piece of paper, they spend five minutes deciding where it should fit in your divider structure.

In the same way, it's easy to get carried away with describe blocks. I find that nested describe blocks are a slippery slope. You'll see test files with three or more levels of describe blocks. The more describe blocks, the more brain power it takes to add a new test. You fret over which describe block would be the best place for the new test.

Usually it's unnecessary detail that can be refactored to a single test with a well-written test name. The next two code snippets show you how to flatten nested describe blocks.

```
describe('/api/apis', () => {
  describe('error response',() => {
    describe('with 500', () => {
      test('throws error', () => {
        // test
```

```
      })
    })
  })
})
```

```
describe('/api/apis', () => {
  test('throws error when server responds with 500', () => {
    // test
  })
})
```

Not everybody agrees with me on this, but I'll tell you one thing: I've spent far too much development time trying to decide what `describe` block a new test should go in. You never have that problem with only one `describe` block.

With that warning out of the way, and your sanity test passing using Jest assertions, it's time to write a real unit test for a Vue single-file component.

2.2.5   *Unit testing a component*

Units are the smallest testable parts of an application. In most JavaScript projects functions are the units, but in Vue applications, components are testable units too.

> NOTE   Remember, this book won't teach you Vue basics. If you'd like to learn Vue basics, I recommend *Vue.js in Action,* from Manning: www.manning.com/books/vue-js-in-action.

In this book you're going to write Vue components using the Vue single-file component (SFC) format. SFCs need to be compiled to JavaScript, which means you need to add additional configuration to Jest before you can test them.

2.2.6   *Compiling files with Jest*

Vue single-file components aren't valid JavaScript. You need to compile them before you can use them in a JavaScript application.

To make sure Jest is set up to compile Vue SFCs correctly, you should update your sanity test to import an SFC. Replace the code in src/__tests__/Item.spec.js with the following code.

```
import Item from '../Item.vue'
import Vue from 'vue'

describe('Item.vue', () => {
  test('sanity test', () => {
    console.log(Item)
  })
})
```

Now when you run the unit test script Jest will throw the error telling you that it was unable to parse the Item file.

In your project, you already have a build script that bundles the source code into a JavaScript file that runs in the browser. Under the hood this script uses webpack to do the compilation, including compiling Vue SFCs. Unfortunately, webpack is not compatible with the Jest compilation system, so you can't use webpack to compile your test code.

To compile files that are run by Jest, you need to use programs built specifically for Jest. These programs are known as *Jest transformers*.

> **NOTE** You can read more about transformers on the Jest website at http:// mng.bz/8F85.

You need to use two transformers for your application: babel-jest and vue-jest. babel-jest compiles modern JavaScript into JavaScript that can run in Node, and vue-jest compiles SFCs into JavaScript.

The first thing you need to do is run the following command in the command line to install them both and save them as dependencies:

```
npm install --save-dev babel-jest vue-jest
```

Then you need to tell Jest how to use them. To do this, you create a `jest` field in package.json to configure Jest. Open package.json, and add the field from the next listing.

Listing 2.8 Jest configuration field in package.json

```
"jest": {
  "transform": {
    "^.+\\.js$": "babel-jest",          Uses babel-jest
    "^.+\\.vue$": "vue-jest"            for all .js files
  }                              Transpiles with vue-jest
}                                for all .vue files
```

Now when Jest loads .vue or .js files, it will run them in the correct transformers and convert the files to JavaScript code that can be run by Node (figure 2.4).

When you've copied the code, rerun your unit tests with the following test command:

```
npm run test:unit
```

The test will pass, and you'll see a JavaScript object in the terminal output. Great—Jest is now compiling the Vue SFC into a JavaScript object with a render function.

Render functions are used by Vue as part of the render process to generate the virtual DOM, which is then used to generate DOM nodes. To start the render process, you need to *mount the component*.

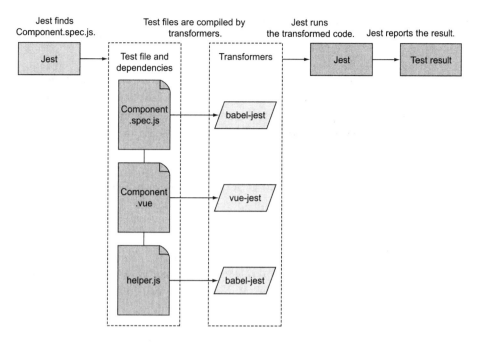

Figure 2.4   Jest compiling a component with vue-jest and babel-jest

2.2.7   *Mounting a component*

When you import a compiled Vue component, it's just an object (or function) with a render function and some properties. To test that the component behaves correctly, you need to switch it on and start the render process. In Vue parlance, you need to *mount the component.*

In chapter 1, you learned that to create a Vue instance you use the new operator with a Vue constructor and an options object. In your test, you'll do the same thing, using the imported component options object.

To create an instance in JavaScript, you use the new operator with a function, also known as a *constructor function.* In Vue, the main Vue function is known as the *base Vue constructor,* because you use it as a constructor to create a Vue instance.

To mount a component, you need to convert the component options into a Vue constructor. Currently in your test, the component options object in your file isn't a valid constructor; it's just a plain old JavaScript object. You can create a Vue constructor from the options using the Vue extend method as follows:

```
const Ctor = Vue.extend(Item)
```

Here, Ctor is a convention that stands for constructor. After you have a constructor, you can create an instance by using the new operator, as follows:

```
const vm = new Ctor()
```

NOTE It's a convention in Vue to refer to an instance as a vm. You can read about the convention in the docs at https://vuejs.org/v2/guide/instance .html.

Normally, Vue uses an el option to find a DOM node in the document to which it should add the rendered DOM nodes. You don't have an el option in your component constructor, so when you create the instance, it won't automatically mount and generate the DOM nodes. You need to call the $mount method explicitly, as follows:

```
const vm = new Ctor().$mount()
```

When you call $mount, Vue will generate the DOM nodes, which you can access in your test using the instance $el property, as shown next:

```
expect(vm.$el.textContent).toContain('item')
```

Now, here comes the hitter. To create a DOM tree, Vue uses DOM methods, like document.createElement. *Vue component unit tests must run in a browser environment.*

This seems like a deal-breaker. Running unit tests in a browser slows them down and introduces a world of complexity.

Fortunately, by default Jest runs tests in a browser environment created with a library called jsdom. Jsdom is a DOM implementation written entirely in JavaScript that runs in Node. Using jsdom instead of a real browser makes the tests run a lot faster.

WARNING Jsdom implements *most* of the DOM API, but some methods are not implemented. If you find that a browser method is throwing an error, it could be an issue with jsdom. We'll look at the limitations of jsdom in more detail in chapter 5.

Let's put all that code together into your first component unit test. Copy the following code into src/components/__tests__/Item.spec.js.

Listing 2.9 Creating a constructor and mounting a component

```
import Item from '../Item.vue'
import Vue from 'vue'

describe('Item.vue', () => {                        Creates a new Vue
  test('renders "item"', () => {                    constructor with        Creates a new Vue
    const Ctor = Vue.extend(Item)                    the Item options        instance, and mounts
    const vm = new Ctor().$mount()                                           the Vue instance
    expect(vm.$el.textContent).toContain('item')
  })                                                 Accesses the DOM element,
})                                                   and checks the text content
```

Run the test with npm run test:unit to get a nice green check mark. Congratulations: you've written your first Vue component unit test!

As you've just seen, mounting a component requires a bit of boilerplate code. Rather than writing this code yourself, you can use a library to mount the component. In the next section, you'll refactor the test to use the Vue testing library—Vue Test Utils.

2.3   Introduction to Vue Test Utils

The Vue Test Utils library makes unit testing Vue components easier. It contains helper methods to mount components, interact with components, and assert the component output. You're going to use this library a lot in your unit tests, so it's important that you understand the API.

2.3.1   Understanding the API

Vue Test Utils exports a `mount` method, which takes a component, mounts it, and returns a *wrapper object* that contains the mounted component instance (a vm). The best way to understand the wrapper object is to interact with it. Install Vue Test Utils as a dev dependency as follows:

```
npm install --save-dev @vue/test-utils
```

Rewrite the sanity test to use the Vue Test Utils `mount` method. Add the next code to src/components/__tests__/Item.spec.js.

Listing 2.10   Using Vue Test Utils to test `textContent`

```
import { mount } from '@vue/test-utils'
import Item from '../Item.vue'

describe('Item.vue', () => {                          Returns a wrapper containing
  test('renders item', () => {                        a mounted Item
    const wrapper = mount(Item)       ◁──┘
    expect(wrapper.vm.$el.textContent).toContain('item')   ◁──┐ Returns the Item
  })                                                           │ text content
})
```

You're probably wondering why `mount` returns a wrapper and not the Vue instance (vm) directly. The wrapper returned by `mount` doesn't just contain the Vue instance; it also includes helper methods that you can use to set props, check instance properties, and perform actions on the instance.

One of the helper methods is `text`, which returns the `textContent` of the instance element, so you can refactor your test to use the `text` method. Replace the test in src/components/__tests__/Item.spec.js with the next code.

Listing 2.11   Using the Vue Test Utils `text` method

```
test('renders item', () => {
  const wrapper = mount(Item)                      Returns the Item
  expect(wrapper.text()).toContain('item')   ◁──┘ text content
})
```

Vue Test Utils helps to write expressive tests that are easy to read. The wrapper API can take a while to get your head around, but by the end of the book you'll be more familiar with the API than you are with your next-door neighbor.

mount works really well on small components, but later in this book you're going to be writing tests on components that render other components. To prepare for the future, you need to learn about the shallowMount method.

2.3.2   *Using shallowMount*

As well as the mount method, Vue Test Utils includes a shallowMount method. Instead of rendering the entire component tree like mount (figure 2.5), shallow-Mount renders the component tree one level deep (figure 2.6).

Just like mount, shallowMount mounts a component and returns a wrapper containing the mounted component. The difference is that shallowMount stubs all the children of a component before it mounts it (figure 2.6).

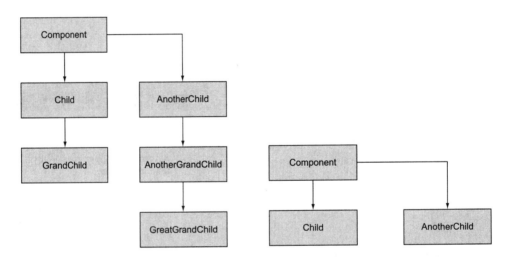

Figure 2.5   **Mounting a component**   Figure 2.6   shallowMount **mounting a component**

shallowMount makes sure that you test a component in isolation. This helps avoid confusing results where a child components rendered output is picked up in your test.

You should refactor the test you wrote earlier with the shallowMount method. Replace the code in src/components/__tests__/Item.spec.js with the code shown next.

Listing 2.12   Using the shallowMount method

```
import { shallowMount } from '@vue/test-utils'          ←  Imports shallowMount
import Item from '../Item.vue'                              from Vue Test Utils

describe('Item.vue', () => {
  test('renders item', () => {
```

```
    const wrapper = shallowMount(Item)
    expect(wrapper.text()).toContain('item')
  })
})
```
◁─── **Stubs any component children and mounts the item**

The test should still pass, as follows: npm run test:unit. In the rest of the book you'll use shallowMount by default instead of mount.

You can write all kinds of tests with Vue Test Utils. For example, you could test that clicking a button opens a pop-up, or that submitting a form sends a POST request to a server. You'll learn how to write tests like these with Vue Test Utils later in this book.

Before the next chapter, I want to show you how to debug tests with Chrome Debugger and take a closer look at the Vue Test Utils wrapper object in the process.

2.4 *Debugging tests with Chrome Debugger*

When a unit test fails, your job is to debug the test, learn why it failed, and fix the code. Debugging is part of the testing process, and you need to get good at it to become a testing master.

A common way to debug tests is to use console.log to see what the values of variables are during the execution of the code. We've all been there—console-logging 10 different values in an attempt to figure out what the heck is going wrong!

console.log works fine, but it's easy to go from console-logging important values, to randomly console-logging in the hope that you find the problem. Programming is not playing with a piñata. When you program, you should not be taking blind swings. You need to understand the code.

One way to help understand code is to use a debugging program. Chrome includes a Debugger that gives you the ability to break code execution at specific points and *step through* the code line by line. When the execution is paused, you can examine variables available to the code at that point during the execution.

In this section, you'll learn how to use Chrome's Debugger when running tests in Jest. You're going to add a breakpoint to the Item test so that you can inspect the wrapper object returned by Vue Test Utils mount function and see what it looks like.

> **IMPORTANT** You need to be running Node 8.4.0 or greater; otherwise, the debugger will not work correctly. To check your node version, enter node --version. If the version is earlier than 8.4.0, install the latest version of Node by following the instructions in appendix A.

To add breakpoints for the node debugger, you add a debugger statement. A debugger statement causes the Node Debugger to break at that point in your code. Add a debugger statement to Item.spec.js, after the wrapper declaration. Your code will look like the following.

Listing 2.13 Using Vue Test Utils to test text

```
import { shallowMount } from '@vue/test-utils'
import Item from '../Item.vue'
```

```
describe('Item.vue', () => {
  test('renders "item"', () => {
    const wrapper = shallowMount(Item)
    debugger                                    ◁———  Chrome Debugger will pause
    expect(wrapper.text()).toContain('item')           on this debugger statement.
  })
})
```

Now you need to run the unit tests in debug mode. This is a common task, so you should add a new `test:unit:debug` script. The script runs Jest without a cache and in one process, in a Node Debugger process. Add the following script to the package.json `script` field:

```
"test:unit:debug": "node --inspect-brk ./node_modules/jest/bin/jest.js --no-
    cache --runInBand"
```

And run the following command:

```
npm run test:unit:debug
```

After running this command, you should see output telling you that the Node Debugger is listening on a WebSocket.

Keep the command line open with the debugger listening. Now open Chrome and navigate to chrome://inspect in the browser. You will see node_modules/jest/bin/jest in the Remote Targets section. This is the Node Debugger process. Click Inspect to open a Chrome Debugger window (figure 2.7).

The Debugger will be paused, so click the Resume Execution button in the top corner to resume execution. You can see the button in figure 2.8.

Figure 2.7 The Chrome Inspect window

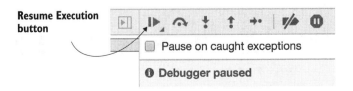

Figure 2.8 The Resume
Execution button

The execution will be stopped on the debugger statement you added to the code earlier. Great—now you have access to all the variables available at this point in the code, including wrapper. Hover over wrapper to see what the object looks like. You can see that it is an instance of a VueWrapper, with element, vm, vnode, and options properties (figure 2.9).

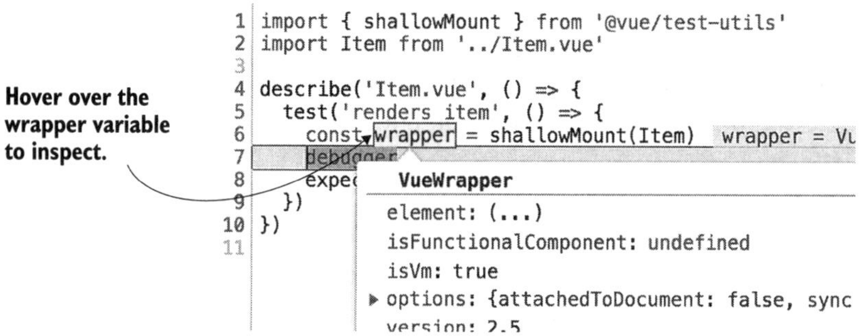

Hover over the wrapper variable to inspect.

```
1  import { shallowMount } from '@vue/test-utils'
2  import Item from '../Item.vue'
3
4  describe('Item.vue', () => {
5    test('renders item', () => {
6      const wrapper = shallowMount(Item)   wrapper = Vu
7      debugger
8      expec          VueWrapper
9    })
10 })             element: (...)
11               isFunctionalComponent: undefined
                 isVm: true
               ▶ options: {attachedToDocument: false, sync
                 version: 2.5
```

Figure 2.9 Inspecting the wrapper

To see the methods, you need to look at the Wrapper prototype. If you click __proto__ and then __proto__ again, you can see the methods available to the wrapper object (figure 2.10).

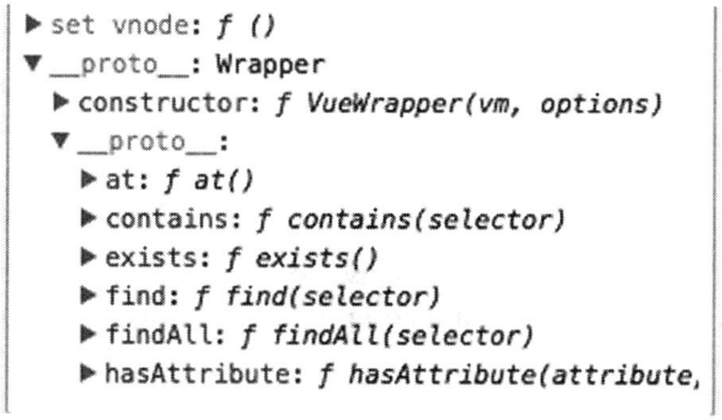

```
▶ set vnode: f ()
▼ __proto__: Wrapper
  ▶ constructor: f VueWrapper(vm, options)
  ▼ __proto__:
    ▶ at: f at()
    ▶ contains: f contains(selector)
    ▶ exists: f exists()
    ▶ find: f find(selector)
    ▶ findAll: f findAll(selector)
    ▶ hasAttribute: f hasAttribute(attribute,
```

Figure 2.10 Inspecting wrapper methods

You'll use a lot of these methods in chapter 3. Right now, click the buttons to the right of the Resume Execution button. If you hover over the buttons, you'll see their names. There's a Step Into Next Function Call button: click it to skip over the next function call and break on the next line. This can be useful if you want to skip over a function without examining what happens inside.

Play around with these buttons to get an idea of how to walk through the execution of the code. This knowledge will come in useful if you need to debug your application later in the book.

> **NOTE**   Some IDEs like WebStorm and VSCode support debugging in the IDE itself. You can see a guide for debugging Jest programs in WebStorm in the docs (http://mng.bz/UMqX), and you can learn how to debug tests running in Jest with VSCode (http://mng.bz/1j7N).

Debugging with Chrome Inspector is like a superpower. You can debug any failing test effectively when you know how to step through the code!

Before you move on to the next chapter, let's go over what you learned.

Summary

- Vue projects follow a common directory structure.
- You can use npm scripts to run project specific scripts, like test scripts.
- Jest finds tests in a project, runs them, and reports on whether they passed or failed.
- You can mount components with the Vue Test Utils `shallowMount` and `mount` methods.
- Vue Test Utils needs to run in a browser environment.
- You can debug Node programs with Chrome.

Exercises

1 Fill in the following template to test that `TestComponent` renders the text "Hello, World!":

```
import { shallowMount } from '@vue/test-utils'
import TestComponent from '../TestComponent.vue'

test('renders Hello, World!', () => {
  // Add test code here
})
```

2 Which Vue Test Utils method would you use to mount a component if you wanted to test the rendered output of a component but not the rendered output of a child component?
   - `mount`
   - `shallowMount`

Testing rendered component output

This chapter covers

- Testing component output
- Writing a static Hacker News feed

If a tree falls in a forest and no one is around to hear it, does it make a sound? More importantly, if a component is mounted and no one writes a test for it, did it generate output?

Testing is about input and output. In a test you supply an input, receive an output, and assert that the output is correct. The most common output of components is the rendered output—the stuff that render functions generate. That's what this chapter is about: testing rendered component output.

To learn how to test component output, you'll write a static Hacker News feed. The news feed is simple, but it gives you the opportunity to test different forms of output and get acquainted with the Vue Test Utils API.

This book is about testing from start to finish, and part of the testing process is converting murky requirements into specifications. The first section of this chapter is about creating specifications from requirements.

After you have the specifications for the static news feed, you'll write tests for the specs. By doing that, you'll learn how to use different Vue Test Utils methods to test the rendered output of Vue components in unit tests. After you've written the news feed, you'll create a progress bar component, a task through which you'll learn how to test styles and classes.

The first thing to do is create the specifications for the static news feed.

3.1 Creating test specifications

A construction company doesn't begin to construct a skyscraper until it has the blue-prints. As a programmer, you shouldn't write tests until you've got the specifications.

Deciding what tests you should write can be difficult at first, but it's a vital skill to learn. To help, you can use the following process for Vue applications:

- Agree on requirements.
- Answer questions on details to get high-level specifications and design.
- Break up design into components.
- Write component-level specifications.

You already know the requirement: you should *write a static Hacker News feed*. There's a lot of room for interpretation there, so you need to hammer down some of the details.

3.1.1 High-level specifications

Requirements are fuzzy descriptions of an application from a user perspective. You need to take requirements and interrogate them until you have technical specifications for how the product should work.

The requirement you've been given is to create a static Hacker News feed. The first question you should have is: what will it look like? Words can mean different things to different people, but it's difficult to misinterpret an image. You can see a design for the Hacker News app in figure 3.1.

The design answers a lot of questions. I have only two more questions:

- How many items should be displayed?
- How do you get the data?

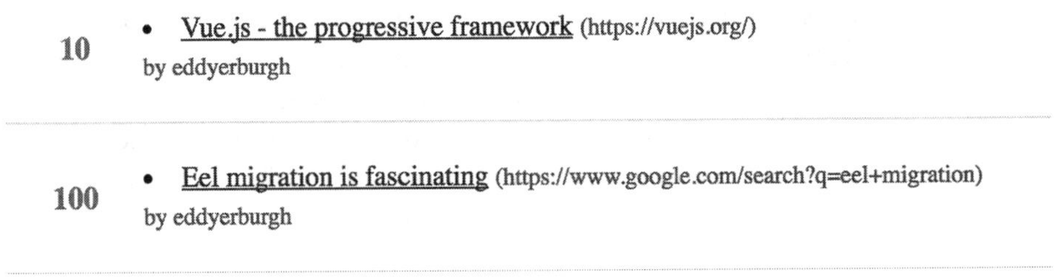

10   • <u>Vue.js - the progressive framework</u> (https://vuejs.org/)
by eddyerburgh

100   • <u>Eel migration is fascinating</u> (https://www.google.com/search?q=eel+migration)
by eddyerburgh

Figure 3.1   Two items from the finished feed

The first question is easy. You're going to display every item that's returned by the data. The next question to answer is *how do you get the data.* For now, you're going to fetch the data before the app is mounted, and then set it as a property on the `window` object. The `window` object is a global variable in a browser environment, so components in the app will be able to access the items.

> **NOTE** If you've been developing for a while, your alarm bell is probably sounding. Adding properties to the `window` object is bad practice. Don't worry—you'll refactor the data fetching in chapter 4.

The code is already written in the src/main.js entry file. It fetches the top news items from the Hacker News API and set them as `items` properties on the `window` object before creating the Vue instance. You can see the data being fetched and added to `window` in listing 3.1.

> **NOTE** This chapter follows on from the app you created in chapter 2. If you don't have the app, you can check out the chapter-3 Git branch by following the instructions in appendix A.

Listing 3.1 Instantiating Vue after fetching data

```
fetchListData('top')                          callback function with the items
  .then((items) => {                          returned from fetchListData
    window.items = items
    new Vue({                                 Sets window.items to items
      el: '#app',                             returned by fetchListData
      render: h => h(App)
    })                          Mounts the application when the
  })                           data is added to window.items
```

> **NOTE** The code in main.js uses a promise to make sure the data is loaded before mounting the app. If you aren't familiar with promises, read about them on the MDN page at https://mzl.la/2j7Nq1C.

The high-level specifications are

- Create a feed using the design in figure 3.1.
- Use the data in `window.items` to render the feed.
- Display all the items in the data.

Congratulations, you've turned a murky requirement into clear high-level specifications for how the feed will work. Now you need to think about component design.

3.1.2 Creating component-level specifications

When you have high-level specifications for an application, you need to think about how you're going to implement them. With Vue applications, that involves deciding how to represent UI elements as components.

At a high level, a feed is simply a list of items. You could represent the Hacker News feed as an `ItemList` component that renders an `Item` component for each item in the data (figure 3.2).

The feed will be made from an `Item-List` component and an `Item` component. Now you need to think about what each of these components should do.

The `ItemList` component is responsible for rendering `Item` components with the correct data. You could write the following specs for `ItemList`:

- Render an `Item` component for each item in `window.items`.
- Pass correct data to each `Item`.

The `Item` component will be responsible for rendering the correct data. In chapter 1, I spoke about the concept of a component contract. A component contract is like a component API. The API for the `Item` component is that it receives an item prop and uses it to render the data. You could write this as specs as follows:

- Render a URL, an author, and a score using the data it receives as an item prop.
- Render a link to the `item.url` with `item.title` as the text.

Now that you've got your specifications, it's time to write tests that implement them. You'll start by writing tests for the `Item` component. To do that, you need to learn how to test rendered text.

The component design for a Hacker News feed

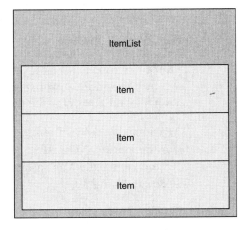

Figure 3.2   `ItemList` containing `Item` components

3.2   *Testing rendered text*

Often you need to test that a component renders some text. I find myself doing it all the time. In this section, you'll learn how to test that components render text and how to test that a specific DOM element renders the correct text.

To learn how to test text, you'll write tests for the `Item` component. The `Item` component has the following specs:

- Render a URL, an author, and a score using the data it receives as an `item` prop.
- Render a link to the `item.url` with `item.title` as the text.

The first spec doesn't specify an element that the URL, author, or score should be rendered in. Therefore, the test should just check that they are rendered *somewhere* in the component output. The second test specifies that the test should be rendered in a link (also known as an `<a>` tag). That test should check that the component renders the text in an `<a>` tag.

To write these tests, you need to provide the `Item` component with props data when you mount it. You can provide props data to components using Vue Test Utils.

3.2.1 *Passing props to a component*

When you write a unit test for a component, you need provide the component with the input it will receive in production. If the component receives a prop in production, you need to provide the prop to the component when you mount it in the test.

You can pass props to components in an options object when you mount a component with Vue Test Utils as shown next.

> **Listing 3.2 Passing props to a component with mounting options**

```
const wrapper = shallowMount(Item, {
  propsData: {
    item: {}
  }
}
```

As well as `propsData`, the options object accepts any options that you normally pass when you create a Vue instance. You'll use the options object a lot throughout this book.

Now that you know how to pass props to a component, you can write a test to check that the `Item` component uses this data to render text.

3.2.2 *Testing the text content of a component*

Sometimes you need to test that a component renders some text. It doesn't matter what element renders the text, just that the text is rendered *somewhere* in the rendered output of a component.

You can test that a component contains text using the Vue Test Utils `text` method:

```
expect(wrapper.text()).toBe('Hello, World!')
```

There's a problem, though. Calling `text` on a component wrapper returns *all* the text rendered by the component. A `toBe` matcher would check that all the text in a component strictly equals the expected value. If you decided to add extra text to the component, the test would break.

A principle of tests is that *a test should not break if the functionality it tests does not change.* It's difficult to write tests that follow this principle, but you should always aim to make your tests future proof. Using a `toBe` matcher to check all rendered text of a component violates this principle.

You can solve this problem by using the `toContain` matcher. The `toContain` matcher checks that a value is contained *somewhere* in the string it is checking. It's a bit like the `string.prototype.includes` method. You could write a test that checks that a component renders some text, such as the following:

```
expect(wrapper.text()).toContain('Hello, World!')
```

Now the assertion will fail only if "Hello, World" isn't rendered at all. You could add as much extra text to the component as you wanted, and the test would still pass. You'll use toContain a lot in this book to check that rendered component output contains a value.

The first spec for the Item component checks that it *renders a URL, an author, and a score using the data it receives as a prop*. These are each independent features of the component, so you should split them into three unit tests.

Each test will mount an Item component with an item object passed down as an item prop and then assert that the rendered output contains the correct text. You'll use the text method and the toContain matcher to write the test.

Add the code shown next to src/components/__tests__/Item.spec.js, replacing the existing code.

Listing 3.3   Passing props to components in a test

```
import { shallowMount } from '@vue/test-utils'
import Item from '../Item.vue'

describe('Item.vue', () => {
  test('renders item.url', () => {
    const item = {
      url: 10
    }
    const wrapper = shallowMount(Item, {        Passes the item object
      propsData: { item }            ◁────      as props to Item
    })
    expect(wrapper.text()).toContain(item.url)   ◁──  Uses toContain to assert
  })                                                  the item.url exists in
})                                                    rendered component text
```

Watch the test fail by running the following test script: npm run test:unit. It should fail with an assertion error telling you that the string did not contain the correct text.

You can make the test pass by updating the component to receive an item prop and render the score. Replace the code in src/components/Item.vue with the following code:

```
<template>
  <li>
      {{ item.url }}
  </li>
</template>

<script>
  export default {
    props: ['item']
  }
</script>
```

You can check the test passes by running npm run test:unit. The other two tests for this component are very similar to the tests you just wrote, so I won't show you how to write them here. In the exercises at the end of this chapter, you can implement them yourself, or you can check out the chapter-4 Git branch to see the finished tests.

For the next spec, you need to check that the `Item` component renders a link to the `item.url` with `item.title` as the text. To test that `Item` renders an `<a>` element with the correct text, you need to access the `<a>` element in a components rendered output.

3.2.3 *Using find*

With Vue applications, it's components all the way down. With Vue Test Utils, it's wrappers all the way down. You interact with the rendered output of components through the wrapper interface.

You can get wrappers for each node in the rendered output using the `find` method. `find` searches the rendered output for the first node that matches a *selector* and returns a wrapper containing the matching node (figure 3.3).

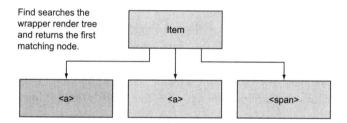

Figure 3.3 `find` **searching the render tree**

For example, you could get the text of an `<a>` element by using an `<a>` selector with `find`, and calling the text on the returned wrapper as follows:

```
wrapper.find('a').text()
```

You'll use this to test that your component renders an `<a>` element with the correct text content.

3.2.4 *Testing the text content of an element*

Sometimes in tests a component must render text somewhere in the component. Other times you need to be more specific and test that a component renders text in a particular element.

The `Item` component should *render a link to the* `item.url` *with* `item.title` *as the text*. This test needs to be more specific than checking that the text is rendered *somewhere* in the component. This text *must* be rendered in an `<a>` element.

> **NOTE** You'll check that the `<a>` element has the correct `href` in the next section—testing DOM attributes.

The test will use `find` to get a wrapper containing an `<a>` element and then call the `text` method to retrieve the text content of the element. Add the following test to the `describe` block in src/components/__tests__/Item.spec.js.

Listing 3.4   Testing component text

```
test('renders a link to the item.url with item.title as text',
➡    () => { const item = {                         ◁── Creates a mock item to
        title: 'some title'                               pass in as prop data
    }
    const wrapper = shallowMount(Item, {    Passes
        propsData: { item }             ◁── prop data      Finds an <a> element
    })                                                     and checks the text
    expect(wrapper.find('a').text()).toBe(item.title)  ◁── rendered is item.title
})
```

Run the unit test script to make sure the test fails for the right reason: `npm run test:unit`. You'll get a Vue Test Utils error that tells you an `<a>` element couldn't be found.

A Vue Test Utils error means the test is *almost* failing for the right reason, but not quite. You can check that the test fails for the right reason after add the `<a>` tag and make the test pass.

To make the test pass, you need to render `item.title` in the `<a>` tag. Open src/components/Item.vue, and replace the `<template>` block with the following code:

```
<template>
    <li>
        <a>{{ item.title }}</a>
        {{ item.url }}
    </li>
</template>
```

Run the unit script again: `npm run test:unit`. It passes, but you never saw it fail for the right reason. If you want to be extra careful (which I always am), you can remove the text from the `<a>` tag to see an assertion error. Be sure to add the text again once you've verified it fails for the correct reason.

In line with TDD, you added the bare minimum source code to pass this test. You're just rendering a title inside an `<a>` element, which is not a full functioning link. The next step is to make it a link by adding a test to check that the `<a>` element has an `href` value!

3.3   *Testing DOM attributes*

I don't always write components that render DOM attributes as part of the component contract, but when I do I write a test for them. Luckily, it's easy to test DOM·attributes with Vue Test Utils.

The specification you're working on is that the Item component *renders a link to the* `item.url` *with* `item.title` *as the text*. You've rendered it with the title text, so now you need to give it an `href` property using the `item.url` value. To do that, you need a way to access the `href` attribute in the test.

A Vue Test Utils wrapper has an `attributes` method that returns an object of the component attributes. You can use the object to test the value of an attribute as follows:

```
expect(wrapper.attributes().href).toBe('http://google.com')
```

You'll use `attributes` in your test to check that the `<a>` element has the correct `href` value. You can `find` a wrapper containing the `<a>` element and then call the `attributes` method to access the `href` value. Replace the *renders a link to the* `item.url` *with* `item.title` *as text* test with the code from the next sample into src/components/__tests__/Item.spec.js.

Listing 3.5   Testing DOM attributes

```
test('renders a link to the item.url with item.title as text', () => {
  const item = {
    url: 'http://some-url.com',
    title: 'some-title'
  }
  const wrapper = shallowMount(Item, {
    propsData: { item }
  })
  const a = wrapper.find('a')
  expect(a.text()).toBe(item.title)
  expect(a.attributes().href === item.url).toBe(true)     ⬅── Asserts that an <a> element
})                                                             has an href attribute with
                                                               value of item.url
```

Run the unit test again: `npm run test:unit`. There isn't an `href` attribute on the `<a>` element, so the test fails.

Take look at the error message: "expected value to be true, received false." This message isn't very useful. Is the test failing because the `href` value is incorrect, or is it failing because the `<a>` element doesn't have an `href` at all?

This kind of assertion error is caused by a *Boolean assertion*. You should avoid Boolean assertions like I avoided long-distance running at school.

3.3.1   *Avoiding Boolean assertions*

Boolean assertions are assertions that compare Boolean values. When they fail, the assertion error isn't clear about why the test failed: "expected false to equal true."

With a Boolean assertion, you're left wondering: *Did the element contain an incorrect attribute value? Was the attribute even rendered?* The Boolean assertion error refuses to tell you.

The alternative to Boolean assertions are expressive *value assertions*. Like the name suggests, a value assertion is an assertion that compares one value against another value.

When a test fails with a value assertion, you get a descriptive error message—"expected 'some value' to equal 'somevalue'." Aha! You look at the test code and see that a component was expecting a prop of `some value`, but someone accidentally deleted a space in the code. When a unit test throws a value assertion error, you get a useful clue to start you on your debugging trail.

You can rewrite the test from earlier to use a value assertion. In src/components/ __tests__/Item.spec.js, replace the Boolean assertion in the *renders a link to the* item.url *with* item.title *as text* test with the with the following line:

```
expect(a.attributes().href).toBe(item.url)
```

Run the tests again: npm run test:unit. The assertion error is much clearer now. You can see that the test is failing because the <a> element href attribute is undefined.

Armed with useful information, you can make the test pass. In src/components/ Item.vue, add an href prop that takes item.url. You need to *bind* the href to the <a> tag using with the v-bind directive colon (:) shorthand, because you're using a dynamic value. Edit the <a> tag to look like this:

```
<a :href="item.url">{{ item.title }}</a>
```

> **NOTE** You need to use the v-bind directive to pass dynamic data as an HTML attribute. To learn more about the v-bind directive, see the Vue documentation at https://vuejs.org/v2/api/#v-bind.

Now run the test script: npm run test:unit. If you added the href correctly, the test will pass. Great, you've got the functionality for the Item component written and tested—the component fulfills its contract.

The next component to test is the ItemList component. The first test that you write will check that it renders an Item component for each item in the window .items array. To write this test, you need to learn how to test how many components are rendered by a parent component.

3.4   *Testing how many components are rendered*

In this book, you've been using the shallowMount method to mount components. shallowMount doesn't render child components, so the unit tests you write are testing only the root-level component. Doing so makes unit tests more focused and easier to understand. But what if you need to check that a root component renders child components?

This is a common scenario. I find myself writing lots of tests that check that components are rendered. Previously, you used the find method to access an element, but find returns the first matching node, so it's no good if you want to check the total number of nodes rendered. To do that, you can use the findAll method.

3.4.1   *Using findAll*

The findAll method is to document.querySelectorAll as find is to document .querySelector. findAll searches the rendered output for nodes that match a selector and returns an arraylike object containing wrappers of matching nodes.

The arraylike object is known as a *wrapper array*. Like a JavaScript array, a wrapper array has a length property. You can use the wrapper array length property to check how many elements exist in the component tree, as shown next.

Listing 3.6 Using the wrapper array `length` property

```
const wrapper = mount(ItemList)
wrapper.findAll('div').length
```
Length equals the number of `<div>`
elements rendered by TestComponent.

findAll uses a selector to match nodes in the rendered output. If you use a Vue component as a selector, findAll matches instances of the component, as shown in the next code sample.

Listing 3.7 Using a component as a selector

```
import Item from '../src/Item.vue'

const wrapper = mount(ItemList)
wrapper.findAll(Item).length
```
Length equals the number
of Item instances.

You'll use this technique to write your test. Remember the specification: ItemList *should render an* Item *component for each item in* window.items.

In the test, you'll set the window.items property to be an array with some objects in it. Then you'll mount the component and check that ItemList renders the same number of Item components as the objects in the items array.

Remember that a good unit test has an expressive assertion error. Assertion errors are more expressive when you use matchers suitable for the assertion. When you test that an array, or an arraylike object, has a length property, you can use the toHave-Length matcher.

Create a new test file src/views/__tests__/ItemList.spec.js. Copy the following code into src/views/__tests__/ItemList.spec.js.

Listing 3.8 Testing child components

```
import { shallowMount } from '@vue/test-utils'
import ItemList from '../ItemList.vue'
import Item from '../../components/Item.vue'

describe('ItemList.vue', () => {
  test('renders an Item for each item in window.items', () => {
    window.items = [{},{},{}]
    const wrapper = shallowMount(ItemList)
    expect(wrapper.findAll(Item))
      .toHaveLength(window.items.length)
  })
})
```
Sets items data for
the component to use

Mounts
ItemList

Uses a WrapperArray length property to check that
an Item is rendered for each item in window.items

Now run the unit tests with the command npm run test:unit. This will give you a useful assertion error—"Expected value to equal: 3 Received: 1."

The principle of the smallest possible mocks

Often, in tests, you need to pass mocked data to a component or function. In production, this data might be large objects with tons of properties.

Large objects makes tests more complicated to read. You should always pass the least amount of data that's required for the test to work.

To make the test pass, add the next code to src/views/ItemList.vue.

Listing 3.9   Using v-for to render items based on an array

```
<template>
    <div class="item-list">
        <item v-for="item in displayItems" :key="item.id"></item>        ◁─┐
    </div>                                                                  │
</template>                                                                 │
                                              Renders an Item for each object│
                                                 in the displayItems array  │
<script>
import Item from '../components/Item.vue'

export default {
  components: {
    Item
  },
  data () {                          Makes the items from the data/
    return {                         items array available to the
      displayItems: window.items  ◁─┘component as displayItems
    }
  }
}
</script>
```

Run the tests again: npm run test:unit. The test should pass. Great—that's the first ItemList spec done.

Now you need to write a test for the second spec: *each* Item *should receive the correct data to render.* You need to test that ItemList passes the correct data to each Item. To do that, you need to learn how to test component props.

3.5   *Testing props*

For components that take props, it's vital that they receive the correct prop to behave correctly. You can write tests that check that a component instance has received the correct props using Vue Test Utils.

The second spec for ItemList is that *each* Item *should receive the correct data to render.* It's important that each Item component receives the correct data as a prop. Part of the `Item` component contract is that it receives the correct data. You can't expect an employee to work if you don't supply a salary, and you can't expect an `Item` to render correctly if you don't supply an `item` prop.

To test that a component receives a prop, you can use the Vue Test Utils `props` method.

3.5.1 Using the Vue Test Utils props method

`props` is a Vue Test Utils wrapper method. It returns an object containing the props of a wrappr component instance and their values, shown in the following listing.

Listing 3.10 Testing props

```
const wrapper = shallowMount(TestComponent)
expect(wrapper.find(ChildComponent).props()          <──── Calls the props method to get an
 ➥ .propA).toBe('example prop')                              object of ChildComponent props
```

You can use the `props` method to assert that each `Item` component receives the correct `item` prop. Instead of adding a new test, you should update the previous test description and assertion.

In src/views/__tests__/ItemList.spec.js, replace the *renders an* `Item` *for each item in* `window.items` with the following code.

Listing 3.11 Testing props using the `props` method

```
test('renders an Item with data for each item in window.items', () => {
  window.items = [{}, {}, {}]
  const wrapper = shallowMount(ItemList)        ┐ Creates a WrapperArray
  const items = wrapper.findAll(Item)       <───┘ of Item components
  expect(items).toHaveLength(window.items.length)        ┐ Loops through
  items.wrappers.forEach((wrapper, i) => {          <────┘ each Item
    expect(wrapper.props().item).toBe(window.items[i])          <────┐
  })
})                        Asserts that the Item at index i has a prop item
                          with a value matching the item at index i
```

If you run the tests with `npm run test:unit` you'll see that `item` is `undefined`. This is expected, because you aren't passing any data to the `Item` components yet. To make the test pass, you need to pass an `item` prop to each `Item` component that you render.

Open src/views/ItemList.vue, and replace the `<template>` block with the next code.

Listing 3.12 Passing props to a child component

```
<template>
  <div class="item-list">
  <item
    v-for="item in displayItems"
    :key="item.id"
```

Loops through each item object in the displayItems array

Gives each Item component a unique key; notice you have access to an item object in the loop

```
        :item="item"
    />
    </div>
</template>
```
◁——— Passes the item as an item
        prop to the Item component

Now run the test script again: npm run test:unit. You'll see the code pass.
Congratulations—you've written tests and code for the news feed.

Before you move on to the next component, I want to take a moment to talk about
a common gotcha when testing props. If you're not careful, this one will trip you up.

3.5.2 *Avoiding gotchas when testing props*

One big gotcha can catch you out when you test component props. If a component
does not declare that it will receive a prop, the prop will not be picked up and added
to the Vue instance.

For a component to receive a prop, *the component must declare that it will receive the
prop*. This can catch you off guard if you're following TDD and you write tests for the
parent before you finish the child component.

Listing 3.13   Declaring a prop in a single-file component

```
<script>
export default {
  props: ['my-prop']
}
</script>
```
◁——— Declaring that the component
        receives a prop named my-prop

> **NOTE** You can read in detail how to declare received component props in
> the Vue docs at http://mng.bz/ZZwP.

For demonstration purposes, open src/components/Item.vue, and remove the
props property. If you run the test again, the ItemList test will fail. Make sure to
add props back in to pass the test before moving on.

Now you've completed the specs for the Item and ItemList components. But if
you run the dev server (npm run serve), you'll see that the components are far from
finished. It would be embarrassing to show this to your boss and say, "There you go,
I've finished all the specs!" The application is missing the style and pizzazz that it
deserves.

To style the components, you need to add some static HTML and CSS. The thing is,
HTML and CSS don't work well with unit tests. Adding presentational HTML is an iter-
ative process, and unit tests can really slow this process down. Another key part of styling
is manual testing. Unless you're a CSS superstar, you need to manually test that the
HTML and CSS style your application correctly. Unit tests get in the way of this process.

Later in this book, you'll learn how to capture manual testing for static HTML with
snapshot tests. For now, you can add style to your components without any tests. The
big takeaway here is that *you don't need to unit test presentational HTML.*

You've finished writing the news feed. There are no more unit tests to write. Before you move on to the next chapter, you'll learn how to test classes and styles by writing tests for a progress bar component.

3.6 Testing classes

One of the questions that developers new to frontend testing have is whether they should test element classes. Frustratingly, the answer is that it depends. Let's look at an example where you should test element classes.

Your Hacker News application is going to render a progress bar. The `ProgressBar` component will indicate that a page is loading. You can see an example in figure 3.4.

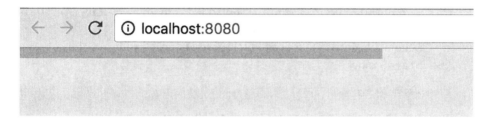

Figure 3.4 The progress bar in progress

I've done the hard work of getting the following specs and requirements for you:

- The ProgressBar should be hidden by default.
- The ProgressBar should initialize with 0% width.

The root element in the `ProgressBar` component should be hidden by default. You can hide the `ProgressBar` with a `hidden` class, which will apply a CSS rule to hide the element.

So to check that the element is hidden, you will test that the component root element has a class of `show`. You can do that with the wrapper `classes` method.

3.6.1 Using the classes method

The Vue Test Utils `classes` wrapper method returns an array of classes on the wrapper root element. You can assert against the array to see whether an element has a class. The test will shallow-mount the ProgressBar and check that the array returned by the `classes` method contains `hidden`.

The `classes` method returns an array. Earlier, you used the `toContain` matcher to check that one string contained another. That `toContain` matcher is more versatile than Leonardo DiCaprio. Not only can it compare string values, it can also compare values in an array. Add the code from the next listing to src/components/__tests__/ProgressBar.spec.js.

Listing 3.14 Testing a class with the `classes` method

```
import { shallowMount } from '@vue/test-utils'
import ProgressBar from '../ProgressBar.vue'

describe('ProgressBar.vue', () => {
  test('is hidden on initial render', () => {
    const wrapper = shallowMount(ProgressBar)
    expect(wrapper.classes()).toContain('hidden')
  })
})
```

> Checks that the root element has a class name including hidden

Before you run the test for the `ProgressBar` component, you should add the component file and a simple `<template>` block. That way, you can mount the component in the test and get an assertion error. If a file doesn't exist, then the test will fail when it tries to import the file. You want the test to fail with an assertion error, so you should always create a minimal file before running a unit test.

Create a file in src/components/ProgressBar.vue, and add the following empty `<template>` block:

```
<template></template>
```

Now run the tests: `npm run test:unit`. The test will fail with a friendly assertion error. To make it pass, you need to update the component template. Add the following code to src/components/ProgressBar.vue:

```
<template> <div class="hidden" /> </template>
```

Check that the test passes before moving on: `npm run test:unit`. You have only one spec for the `ProgressBar` left—the `ProgressBar` *should initialize with 0% width*. The width will be added as an inline style, so you need to learn how to test inline styles to write this spec.

3.7   *Testing style*

Sometimes you don't need to test style—not Italian suit kind of style, but inline CSS styles. Normally testing style isn't valuable, but you *should* write tests for some cases of inline styles: for example, if you add an inline style dynamically.

The `ProgressBar` component you're going to write needs to have 0% width when it initializes; it will increase over time, which makes it appear to load. In the next chapter, you'll add methods to control the component, like `start` and `finish`. For now, you'll just test that it's initialized with a width style of 0%.

To test an inline style, you need to access the wrapper element directly and get the style value.

3.7.1   *Accessing a wrapper element*

The DOM has a notoriously ugly API. Often you will use libraries to abstract over it and make code more expressive—that's one of the benefits of Vue Test Utils—but sometimes you should use the DOM API directly.

To use the DOM API with Vue Test Utils, you need to access a DOM node. Every wrapper contains an `element` property, which is a reference to the root DOM node that the wrapper contains. You can use the `element` property to access the element's inline styles as follows:

```
wrapper.element.style.color
```

The test you write will check that the wrapper root element has a `width` style value of 0%. To test that, you'll shallow-mount the component and access the element's `style` property. Open src/components/__tests__/ProgressBar.spec.js, and add the test from the following listing to the `describe` block.

> **Listing 3.15 Testing style by accessing wrapper element**

```
test('initializes with 0% width', () => {
  const wrapper = shallowMount(ProgressBar)
  expect(wrapper.element.style.width).toBe('0%')   ⟵─┐  Checks the wrapper element's
})                                                      inline width property
```

Now run the test script – `npm run test:unit`. It will fail because the root element has no `width` value. To make the test pass, copy the following code into the `<template>` block:

```
<template>
  <div
    class="hidden"
    :style="{
    'width': '0%'
  }" />
</template>
```

If you run the tests again, they'll pass. Great—those are all the tests that you'll write in this chapter. Now is a good time to talk about styling an application.

3.7.2 Adding style to an application

Style is an important part of frontend development. You could write the greatest HTML in the world, but without some CSS your application is going to look bad.

The process of adding style involves manual testing. After you've written CSS, you need to check in a browser that the styles have been applied correctly. If you're a great developer, then you'll probably test it on multiple devices and browsers.

Because styling applications involves manual testing, unit tests that check only static presentational elements are not valuable. One benefit of unit tests is that they save you time, because you can run them without checking the code manually. Unit tests for static elements often take longer to write than the time they save. Save yourself time, and don't write unit tests when you're styling!

This book is about automated testing, so styling that should be manually tested won't be included here. That said, style is important for the Hacker News application, so the chapter Git branches contain fully styled components. At the beginning of each chapter, you can switch to the chapter branch to see the styles for the code from the previous chapter.

Now you have all the specs written for this chapter. You've learned *how* to test component output. Before you move on to the next chapter, I want to take a minute to talk about *when* you should write tests for rendered component output.

3.8 *When to test rendered component output*

In testing, less is more. Every extra unit test you write *couples* your test code to your source code. When you write unit tests, you need to be more miserly than Scrooge McDuck.

> **DEFINITION** Coupling is the interdependence between modules of code. If test code is coupled to source code, it means the test code is dependent on the details of your source code, rather than the functionality of the code.

Tightly coupled code makes it difficult to refactor, because you can break tens of tests in a file when you decide to change the implementation. To avoid this, remember the following principles when testing component output:

- Test only output that is dynamically generated.
- Test only output that is part of the component contract.

Generally, you should test only output that's *dynamically generated*. Dynamically generated sounds very formal, but what it means is that a value is generated in the component using JavaScript. For example, an `Item` component at index 2 might have the class `item-2`, generated using the component index. You should write a test for this, because you're adding logic to generate the prop, and logic is prone to errors.

You should also test output that's part of the component contract. If it's part of the contract, then it's important enough to sacrifice the coupling of code.

> ### The unit testing Goldilocks rule
>
> Writing unit tests is a constant struggle between writing enough tests and not writing too many. I call this the unit testing Goldilocks rule—not too many, not too few, but just enough. Thousands of tests for a small application can be as damaging to development time as no tests.
>
> In this book, I'll give you examples when you should write a test and when you shouldn't. The rules I lay out in this book aren't set in stone—they're general principles. You should decide on a test-by-test basis whether you should write a test for your component.

If you follow these rules, you will never write tests for presentational elements and static CSS classes. You should add presentational style without writing unit tests.

If you want to see what you built, you can run the dev server: npm run serve. Go to http://localhost:8080 in your browser. You should see a great Hacker News application, using your static data. In the next chapter, you'll flesh out the application by learning to test methods.

Summary

- You can test DOM attributes, component props, text, and classes using Vue Test Utils Wrapper methods.
- find and findAll return wrappers of nodes in the rendered output of a component mounted with Vue Test Utils.
- You should only test component output if the output is generated dynamically or the output is part of the component contract

Exercises

1 Write a test in src/components/__tests__/Item.spec.js to test that Item renders the item.score and item.author values. When you have written the tests, make them pass by adding code to src/components/Item.vue.

2 Write a test to check that the following component renders the Child component with the correct test-prop value of some-value:

```
// TestComponent.vue
<template>
  <div>
    <child testProp="some-value" />
  </div>
</template>

<script>
  import Child from './Child.vue'

  export default {
    components: { Child }
  }
</script>
// Child.vue
<script>
  export default {
    props: ['testProp']
  }
</script>
```

3 Write a test to check that the <a> tag has an href with the value of https://google.com:

```
// TestComponent.vue
<template>
  <div>
    <a href="https://google.com">Link</a>
  </div>
</template>
```

4 Write a test to check that the <p> tag has a color style with the value of red:

```
// TestComponent.vue
<template>
  <div>
    <p style="color: red">Paragraph</p>
  </div>
</template>
```

Testing component methods

This chapter covers

- Testing component methods
- Testing code that uses timer functions
- Using mocks to test code
- Mocking module dependencies

A Vue application without methods is like a smoothie without fruit. Methods contain juicy logic that adds functionality to Vue components, and that logic needs to be tested.

Testing self-contained methods isn't complicated. But real-world methods often have *dependencies*, and testing methods with dependencies introduces a world of complexity.

A *dependency* is any piece of code outside the control of the unit of code that's under test. Dependencies come in many forms. Browser methods, imported modules, and injected Vue instance properties are common dependencies that you'll learn to test in this chapter.

To learn how to test methods and their dependencies, you're going to add start and stop methods to the ProgressBar component in the Hacker News

63

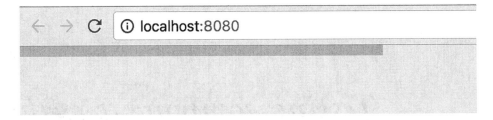

Figure 4.1   The finished progress bar at 80% complete

application (figure 4.1). These methods will start and stop the progress bar running. To make the progress bar increase in width over time, the component will use timer functions, so you'll need to learn how to test code that uses timer functions.

After you've added methods to the `ProgressBar` component, you'll refactor the application to fetch data in the `ItemList` component and use the progress bar to indicate that the data is being fetched. These tasks will introduce challenges like testing that a function was called, testing asynchronous code, and controlling the behavior of module dependencies—code that's imported into one module from another.

You'll start by writing tests for the `ProgressBar` methods.

4.1 *Testing public and private component methods*

In Vue, you can add functionality to components by creating component methods. Component methods are useful places to write logic that is too complex for the component template.

Often, components use methods internally, like logging a message to the console when a button is clicked, as shown in the next listing.

Listing 4.1   Calling a method on click

```
<template>
  <button @click="logClicked" /> //
</template>

<script>
export default {
  methods: {
    logClicked() { //
      console.log("clicked");
    }
  }
};
</script>
```

Calls logClicked when the button is clicked

Defines the logClicked method

You can think of these as *private methods*—they aren't intended to be used outside of the component. Private methods are implementation details, so you don't write tests for them directly.

Alternatively, you can create methods, such as that shown in the next listing, that are intended to be used by other components. You can think of these as *public methods*.

> **Listing 4.2 Creating a public method**

```
const vm = new Vue({              ◁───┐  Creates a Vue instance
  methods: {                          │  with the logHello method
    logHello() {
      console.log("hello");
    }
  }
});
                                      │  Calls logHello from outside
vm.logHello()                    ◁────┘  the component
```

Public methods are a less common pattern in Vue, but they can be powerful. You should always write tests for public methods, because public methods are part of the component contract.

> **NOTE** You're following on from the app you made in chapter 3. If you don't have the app, you can check out the chapter-4 Git branch following the instructions in appendix A.

In the previous chapter you created a `ProgressBar` component. Right now it's just a static component, but in this chapter you'll add public methods so that you can control it from other components in the application.

   The `ProgressBar` component will have three methods: `start`, `finish`, and `fail`. The `start` method will set the progress bar running, the `finish` method will hide the bar, and the `fail` method will put the bar into an error state.

> **NOTE** To avoid repetition, in this chapter you'll implement only the `ProgressBar` `start` and `finish` methods. I'll leave it to you to implement the `fail` method in the exercises at the end of the chapter. You can see the fully implemented `fail` method in the chapter-7 Git branch.

To write tests for the progress bar you need to learn how to test public methods and how to write tests for code that use timer functions.

4.1.1 Testing public component methods

The process of testing public methods is simple: you call the component method and assert that the method call affected the component output correctly.

   Imagine you have a pop-up component that exposes a `hide` method. When the `hide` method is called, the component should have its `style.display` property set to none. To test that the `hide` method worked correctly, you would mount the component, call the `hide` method, and check that the component has a `style.display` value of none, as shown in the following code.

Listing 4.3   Testing a public method

```
test('is hidden when hide is called', () => {
  const wrapper = shallowMount(Popup)
  wrapper.vm.hide()
  expect(wrapper.element.style.display).toBe('none')
})
```

Mounts the component

Calls the public hide method on the component instance

Asserts that the wrapper root element has a display none style

This is how you test public methods: you call the method and assert that the component output is correct. The tests you write for the `ProgressBar` component will follow this pattern.

The specs for `ProgressBar` follow:

- `ProgressBar` should display the bar when `start` is called.
- `ProgressBar` should set the bar to 100% width when `finish` is called.
- `ProgressBar` should hide the bar when `finish` is called.
- `ProgressBar` should reset the width when `start` is called.

These tests will be pretty simple, because they are self-contained methods without any dependencies. The first test will check that the root element removes a `hidden` class when `start` is called. You can check that it doesn't have a class by using the Vue Test Utils `classes` method and the Jest `not` modifier. The `not` modifier negates an assertion as follows:

```
expect(true).not.toBe(false)
```

You have an existing test that checks that the bar initializes with a `hidden` class. You can replace that with the new test that checks that it initializes with a `hidden` class and removes it when `start` is called. Add the code from the next listing to src/components/__tests__/ProgressBar.spec.js.

Listing 4.4   Testing component state

```
test('displays the bar when start is called', () => {
  const wrapper = shallowMount(ProgressBar)
  expect(wrapper.classes()).toContain('hidden')
  wrapper.vm.start()
  expect(wrapper.classes()).not.toContain('hidden')
})
```

Asserts that the hidden class exists

Triggers the test input by calling the start method on the component instance

Asserts that the hidden class was removed

When you run the test with `npm run test:unit`, the test will display an error because `start` is not a function. This isn't one of those friendly assertion errors that you know and love; it's a useless type error.

Type errors don't aid you in the quest for a failing assertion. You should stop type errors like this by adding boilerplate code to the unit you're testing. In src/

components/ProgressBar.vue add a `<script>` block with a `methods` object of empty methods in the component options, as follows:

```
<script>
export default {
  methods: {
    start() {},
    finish() {}
  }
}
</script>
```

Now run the test again with `npm run test:unit` to check that it fails with a descriptive assertion error. When you've seen an assertion error, you can make the test pass by adding the code from the next listing to src/components/ProgressBar.vue.

Listing 4.5 ProgressBar.vue

```
<template>
  <div
    :class="{
      hidden: hidden
    }"
    :style="{
      'width': '0%'
    }"/>
</template>

<script>
export default {
  data() {
    return {
      hidden: true
    }
  },
  methods: {
    start () {
      this.hidden = false
    },
    finish() {}
  }
}
</script>
```

Defines a dynamic hidden class that is added to element if hidden is true

Defines the component methods

Sets the instance state inside the start method

Check that the test passes: `npm run test:unit`. Great—now the `ProgressBar` root element removes the `hidden` class when `start` is called. Next you want to test that calling `finish` sets the progress bar width to 100% and hides the bar. This will make the progress bar appear to finish loading and then disappear.

You'll write two tests—one to check that the width is set to 100% and one to check that the `hidden` class is added. You can use the same approach that you did in the earlier test—call the method and then assert against the rendered output. Add the following code to src/components/__tests__/ProgressBar.spec.js.

Listing 4.6   Testing public methods

```
test('sets the bar to 100% width when finish is called', () => {
  const wrapper = shallowMount(ProgressBar)
  wrapper.vm.start()
  wrapper.vm.finish()
  expect(wrapper.element.style.width).toBe('100%')
})

test('hides the bar when finish is called', () => {
  const wrapper = shallowMount(ProgressBar)
  wrapper.vm.start()
  wrapper.vm.finish()
  expect(wrapper.classes()).toContain('hidden')
})
```

Puts the component in a dirty state by calling start

Triggers the test input by calling the finish method on the component instance

Asserts that the element has a width of 100%

Check that the tests fail with an assertion error. To make the tests pass, you need render the width using a `percent` value and reset the state in the `finish` method.

To do that, you can add a `percent` property to the component and use it to render the width. In src/components/ProgresBar.vue, update the `data` method to return an object with `percent` set to 0 using the following code:

```
data() {
    return {
      hidden: true,
      percent: 0
    }
  },
```

In the same file, update the `width` style in the `<template>` block to use the `percent` value as follows:

```
'width': `${percent}%`
```

Finally, replace the `finish` method in src/components/ProgressBar.vue with the following code:

```
finish() {
  this.hidden = true
  this.percent = 100
}
```

Make sure the tests pass: `npm run test:unit`.

Now you have a `finish` method that sets the width to 100% and a `start` method that will start the component running from 0%. The component is going to start and finish multiple times during the application lifecycle, so `start` should reset the ProgressBar to 0% when it's called.

You can check this by calling the `finish` method to set the width to 100%, and then calling the `start` method and asserting that the width is reset to 0%.

Add the following code to the `describe` block in src/components/__tests__/ProgressBar.spec.js:

```
test('resets to 0% width when start is called', () => {
  const wrapper = shallowMount(ProgressBar)
  wrapper.vm.finish()
  wrapper.vm.start()
  expect(wrapper.element.style.width).toBe('0%') //
})
```

The test will fail because `finish` sets the width to 100 and `start` doesn't reset it. To make the test pass, you need to update the `ProgressBar start` method. Add the following code to the `start` method in src/components/ProgressBar.vue:

```
this.percent = 0
```

Run the test again: `npm run test:unit`. The test will pass—nice.

These are the kind of tests I love—small, self-contained, and easy to understand. With tests like these, you're free to refactor the implementation of the methods however you like, as long as the component maintains its contract and generates the correct output.

As you can see, these kinds of tests are nice and simple: provide an input, call a method, and then assert the rendered output. The real complexity of testing methods is when methods have dependencies, like timer functions. To test that the progress bar increases in width over time you need to learn how to test timer functions.

4.2 *Testing timer functions*

Timer functions are JavaScript asynchronous functions and their counterparts, like `setTimeout` and `clearTimeout`. Timer functions are a common feature in JavaScript applications, so you need to be able to test code that uses them. But timer functions run in real time, which is bad news for speed-sensitive unit tests.

> **NOTE** If you're not familiar with timer functions like `setTimeout`, I recommend reading this great introduction in the Node docs—https://nodejs.org/en/docs/guides/timers-in-node.

Unit tests should run faster than Usain Bolt sprints 100 meters. Every extra second a unit test takes to run makes the test suite worse, so testing code that uses timer functions can be problematic. Think about it. If you want to test that a component does something after 500 ms using `setTimeout`, then you would need to wait for 500 ms in the test. This delay would hammer the performance of a test suite, which usually runs hundreds of tests in a few seconds.

The only way to test timer functions without slowing down tests is by *replacing* the timer functions with custom functions that can be controlled to run synchronously. One of the great features of JavaScript (or worst, depending who you ask!) is how malleable it is. You can easily reassign global variables, as follows:

```
setTimeout = () =>{ console.log('replaced') }
```

You could replace timer functions with functions that behave like timer functions but that use a method to control the time and run the timer functions synchronously. Functions like this that are created to replace existing functions in tests are known as *mock functions.*

It would be complicated to replace the timer functions with mock functions yourself, but you can use a library to replace them for you. The Jest testing framework that you're using is a kitchen sink framework. It has almost all the features you need to test JavaScript, without the need to reach for other libraries. One useful Jest feature is fake timers.

4.2.1   *Using fake timers*

Fake timers are mock functions that replace global timer functions. Without fake timers, testing code that uses timer functions would be horrendous.

In the Hacker News app, the `ProgressBar` component will use the `setInterval` timer function to increment its width over time, so you need to use fake timers to test it.

> **NOTE** `setInterval` is a timer function that executes a callback function at a regular interval.

You can use lots of libraries to mock fake timers, but in this book I'll show you how to use Jest fake timers. Jest fake timers work by replacing the global timer functions when you call the `jest.useFakeTimers` method. After you've replaced the timers, you can move the fake time forward using a `runTimersToTime`, as shown in the next listing.

> **NOTE** The `jest` object is a global object added by Jest when it runs the tests. The `jest` object includes lots of test utility methods, like fake timers, that you'll use in this chapter.

Listing 4.7   Using fake timers

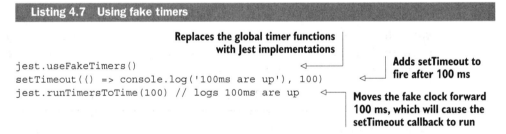

```
                          Replaces the global timer functions
                             with Jest implementations
                                                                    Adds setTimeout to
jest.useFakeTimers()                                     ◁─────     fire after 100 ms
setTimeout(() => console.log('100ms are up'), 100)  ◁─┘
jest.runTimersToTime(100) // logs 100ms are up     ◁─┐
                                                     Moves the fake clock forward
                                                     100 ms, which will cause the
                                                     setTimeout callback to run
```

The safest way to use fake timers in a test suite is to call `useFakeTimers` before each test runs. That way, the timer functions will reset before every test.

You can run functions before each test by using the `beforeEach` hook. This hook is useful for performing setup for tests.

Because you're going to write tests for code that uses a timer function, you should add a `beforeEach` hook to enable fake timers in the `ProgressBar` test file. Add the code in the following listing to the top of the `describe` block in src/components/__tests__/ProgressBar.spec.js.

Listing 4.8 Calling `useFakeTimers` before each test

```
beforeEach(() => {
  jest.useFakeTimers()
})
```

→ **Function to run before each test**

→ **Replaces global timer functions**

The progress bar will appear to load by increasing its width 1% every 100 ms after the `start` method is called. You can test this by calling the `ProgressBar` `start` method, and then moving the fake time forward and asserting that the width has increased by the expected amount. You should add a few assertions to make sure the time increments correctly.

Add the code from the next listing to the `describe` block in src/components/ __tests__/ProgresBar.spec.js.

Listing 4.9 Moving the time forward with fake timers

Moves the global time forward 100 ms, and fires any timer callback that is scheduled to run after 100 ms

```
test('increases width by 1% every 100ms after start call', () => {
  const wrapper = shallowMount(ProgressBar)
  wrapper.vm.start()
  jest.runTimersToTime(100)
  expect(wrapper.element.style.width).toBe('1%')
  jest.runTimersToTime(900)
  expect(wrapper.element.style.width).toBe('10%')
  jest.runTimersToTime(4000)
  expect(wrapper.element.style.width).toBe('50%')
})
```

→ **Asserts that the wrapper element has the correct style**

Moves the time forward again by 900 ms; note that the total time now elapsed is 1,000 ms

Now, run the test and watch it fail: `npm run test:unit`. To make the test pass, you need to use `setInterval` in the `ProgressBar` `start` method.

You already have code that uses the `percent` property to set the width of the root element. So you just need to update the `start` method to change the `percent` value every 100 ms. You'll also save the timer ID returned by `setInterval`, so that you can clear the interval in a later test. Open src/components/ProgressBar.vue and edit the `start` method to include the following code.

Listing 4.10 Using a timer function in a component

```
start () {
  this.hidden = false
  this.percent = 0
  this.timer = setInterval(() => {
    this.percent++
  }, 100)
}
```

→ **Creates an interval, and saves it as a property of the vm, so you can use a reference in the future**

→ **Increments the percent**

Now the progress bar will increment over time! There's still a final test to add to make sure the timer is removed when the progress bar stops running.

You might be wondering why you saved a reference to the `setInterval` call in the component. This is so that you can stop the interval running when the `finish` method is called, by calling its counter method `clearInterval`. To test that `clear-Interval` is called, you'll learn how to use spies.

4.2.2 Testing using spies

When a government wants to find secret information, it sends in its spies. When developers want to find secret information about functions, we use our own spies!

Often when you test code that uses an API that you don't control, you need to check that a function in the API has been called. For example, suppose you were running code in a browser and wanted to test that `window.clearInterval` was called. How would you do that?

One way is to use *spies*. Lots of libraries implement spies, but because you're using kitchen-sink Jest, you can create a spy with the `jest.spyOn` function. The `spyOn` function gives you the ability to check that a function was called using the `toHave-BeenCalled` matcher, as shown in the next listing.

> **Listing 4.11 Using a spy to test `someMethod` was called**

```
jest.spyOn(window, 'someMethod')          ◁──── Creates a spy
window.someMethod ()
expect(window.someMethod).toHaveBeenCalled()          ◁┐
```

**Uses a toHaveBeenCalled matcher
to test whether a spy was called**

In your `ProgressBar` component, when the `finish` method is called, you should call `clearInterval` with the timer ID returned from the original `setInterval` call. This will clear the timer and stop potential memory leaks.

This presents two problems. First, how do you test that a function was called with an argument? Here, spies have your back. You can test that a spy was called with a specific argument by using the `toHaveBeenCalledWith` matcher as follows:

```
expect(window.someMethod).toHaveBeenCalledWith(123)
```

The next question is, how do you know what value `clearInterval` should be called with? To do that, you need to control the return value of `setInterval`. The fake timer functions can be configured to return a value using a `mockReturnValue` function, so you can configure `setInterval` to return any value you want, as follows:

```
setInterval.mockReturnValue(123)
```

In your test, you'll configure `setInterval` to return a value. Then you'll spy on `clearInterval`, call the `finish` method, and check that `clearInterval` was called with the value returned by `setInterval`. Copy the code from the next listing into src/components/__tests__/ProgressBar.spec.js.

Listing 4.12 Using jest.spyOn to test `clearInterval`

```
test('clears timer when finish is called', () => {        Spies on the
  jest.spyOn(window, 'clearInterval')                     clearInterval function
  setInterval.mockReturnValue(123)                Configures setInterval
  const wrapper = shallowMount(ProgressBar)       to return 123
  wrapper.vm.start()                                       Calls start to
  wrapper.vm.finish()                                      start the timer
  expect(window.clearInterval).toHaveBeenCalledWith(123)
})
```
Asserts that the clearInterval mock was called
with the value returned from setInterval

This kind of test makes me uncomfortable. You had to use methods to control how functions behave—which means you've made assumptions about how a function works. The more assumptions in a test, the more chance there is of one being wrong and the test passing even though the production code is failing. Sometimes there's no other way to test an external method except by making assumptions, but you should feel slightly guilty each time you do it. In your tests, keep assumptions to a minimum.

Now make sure the test fails with an assertion error: npm run test:unit. You can make the test pass by calling `clearInterval` with the timer ID in the `finish` method. Open src/components/ProgressBar.vue, and add the code from the next listing to the `finish` method in `ProgressBar`.

Listing 4.13 ProgressBar.vue

```
finish () {
  this.percent = 100
  this.hidden = true                       Clears the setInterval timeout with
  clearInterval(this.timer)                the timer ID saved to this.timer
}
```

Run the tests: npm run test:unit. Great—the `ProgressBar` component is finished. Now you can set it up so that other components in your applications can run the progress bar by calling the `start` and `finish` methods. You can do that by adding a mounted `ProgressBar` as a Vue instance property.

4.3   *Adding properties to the Vue instance*

A common pattern in Vue is to add properties to the Vue base constructor. When a property is added to the Vue constructor, every child instance has access to those properties. You can add Vue instance properties by adding a property to the Vue constructor *prototype* as shown in the next listing.

> **DEFINITIONS** An object's `prototype` property is used to implement inheritance in JavaScript. Prototypal inheritance is a big topic—too big for me to

teach in this book. If you want to learn about prototype-based inheritance, you can read the following guide on MDN—http://mng.bz/1daY.

Listing 4.14 Adding an instance property to the Vue prototype

```
Vue.prototype.$instanceProperty = 'hello'          ◁─┐  Adds a property to the Vue
                                                       constructor prototype
const ChildComponent = {                    ◁─
  template: '<p>{{$instanceProperty}}</p>'       A ChildComponent that will have
}                                                access to $instanceProperty

new Vue({
  el: '#app',
  render: h => ChildComponent
})
```

You're going to use a clever technique and add a mounted `ProgressBar` component instance as a $bar instance property. That way, each component in the app can start the `ProgressBar` by calling $bar.start and stop the `ProgressBar` by calling $bar.finish.

> **TIP** In Vue, it's a convention to give methods added to the prototype a dollar sign ($) prefix. This is to avoid possible naming collisions with local instance state values.

While you're in main.js you should remove the data-fetching logic, which you'll reimplement in the `ItemList` component. Replace the code in src/main.js with the following code.

Listing 4.15 Adding a Vue instance to the prototype

```
import Vue from 'vue'
import App from './App'                                         Adds the mounted
import ProgressBar from './components/ProgressBar'              progress bar to the
                                                               base Vue constructor
Vue.config.productionTip = false          Creates a mounted    prototype, which will
                                          ProgressBar instance  be available to child
const bar = new Vue(ProgressBar).$mount()        ◁─            component instances
Vue.prototype.$bar = bar                              ◁─
document.body.appendChild(bar.$el)        ◁─   Adds the ProgressBar root element
                                               to the Document <body>
new Vue({               ◁─┐  Creates a new Vue
  el: '#app',              instance using #app
  render: h => h(App)     as the root element
})
```

With the new code in main.js, you're creating a separate Vue instance of the `ProgressBar` component and adding it to the Vue base constructor prototype. Now you can write the code and tests for other components in the app that will call the `ProgressBar` methods.

This is a good time to demonstrate the downside of unit tests. Run the unit tests in the command line with `npm run test:unit`. They all pass. The thing is, your app is now completely broken!

If you run the dev server, you'll see that the app doesn't render any items. This is a problem with unit tests. Although unit tests tell you that units work in isolation, you don't know that they work when they are connected in production. By the end of the book you'll have a test suite that doesn't suffer from this problem by supplementing the unit tests with end-to-end tests, but for now just know that you can't rely on unit tests alone!

Let's move on. The plan is to rewrite the `ItemList` component to fetch data and set the progress bar running while the data is fetched. To write tests for this functionality, you need to learn how to test with mocks.

4.4 Mocking code

Production code can be messy. It can make HTTP calls, open database connections, and have complex dependency trees. In unit tests, you can ignore all of that nonsense by mocking code.

In simple terms, mocking code is *replacing code you don't control with code you do control.* Three benefits to mocking code follow:

1 You can stop side effects like HTTP calls in tests.
2 You can control how a function behaves, and what it returns.
3 You can test that a function was called.

Earlier, you wrote tests for code that used timer functions. Instead of using the native timer functions, you used Jest to replace them with *mock functions* you could control. In other words, you used Jest to mock the timer functions.

In this section you'll learn how to mock code in tests by refactoring the `ItemList` component to fetch the Hacker News data and run the progress bar. The first test that you'll write will check that ItemList calls the instance property $bar `start` method. To write that test, you need to learn how to mock Vue instance properties.

4.4.1 Mocking Vue instance properties in components

It's a common pattern in Vue to add properties to the Vue prototype. If a component uses an instance property, the instance property becomes a dependency of the component.

In your application, you have a mounted `ProgressBar` as a $bar instance property that will be available to all component instances. This works because under the hood all your component instances are created using the Vue base constructor.

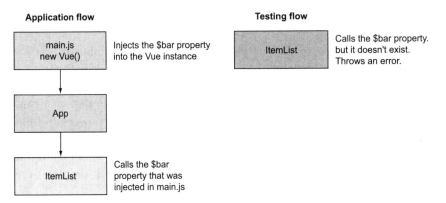

Figure 4.2   Injecting a property into the Vue instance tree

In your tests, however, you mount components directly. The main.js entry file isn't run, so $bar is never added as an instance property (figure 4.2). I call this the *leaky bucket* problem. When your component uses Vue instance properties, it's like a bucket with holes in it. If you mount the component in your tests without patching the holes by adding the required properties, the bucket will leak, and you'll get errors.

To solve the leaky bucket problem, you need to add properties to the Vue instance before you mount the component in a test. You can do that with the Vue Test Utils mocks option shown next.

Listing 4.16   Injecting an instance property with the `mocks` option

```
shallowMount(ItemList, {
  mocks: {
    $bar: {
      start: () => {}
    }
  }
})
```

The `mocks` option makes it easy to control instance properties. You just need to make sure you use it to patch the holes before you run the test.

Now that you know how to mock $bar in your tests, the next thing to do is figure out how to test that the $bar.start function was called. One way to do that is with a Jest mock function.

4.4.2   Understanding Jest mock functions

Sometimes in tests you need to check that a function was called. You can do that by replacing the function with a mock function that records information about itself.

Let's look at a simple implementation of a mock function. The mock function has a `calls` array to store details on the function calls. Each time the function is called, it pushes the arguments it was called with to the `calls` array, as shown in the next listing.

Listing 4.17 Storing function calls

```
const mock = function(...args) {
  mock.calls.push(args)                    ◁─┐ Pushes arguments
}                                            └ to the calls array
mock.calls = []          ◁─┐ Initializes the
mock(1)                    └ calls array
mock(2,3)                              ┌ Calls are stored
mock.calls // [[1], [1,2]]    ◁─────────┘ in an array
```

You can add lots of cool features to mock functions, but it doesn't make sense to write your own mock functions when other solutions exist. Kitchen-sink Jest includes a mock function implementation. You can create a mock function by calling `jest.fn`, shown in the next code sample.

Listing 4.18 Using a Jest mock function

```
const mockFunction = jest.fn()      ◁─┐ Creates a
mockFunction(1)                       └ mock function
mock(2,3)                                      ┌ Accesses the
mockFunction.mock.calls // [[1], [1,2]]  ◁─────┘ function calls
```

You can combine Jest mock functions with Jest matchers to write expressive tests as follows:

```
expect(mockFunction).toHaveBeenCalled()
```

You probably recognize that matcher. You used it before to test that the spied `clear-Interval` function was called. Under the hood, `jest.spyOn` and `jest.useFake-Timers` use Jest mock functions. `jest.fn` is just another interface for creating a Jest mock function.

Armed with Jest mock functions, you're ready to write some tests. You can check that the `ItemList` component sets the progress bar running when it mounts by mounting `ItemList` with a `$bar` object using a mock function, as follows:

```
const $bar = {
  start: jest.fn()
}
```

Then you can use the Jest `toHaveBeenCalledTimes` matcher to assert that `start` was called. Add the code from the next listing to the `describe` block in src/views/ __tests__/ItemList.spec.js.

Listing 4.19 Stubbing a function with a Jest mock

```
test('calls $bar start on load', () => {    ┌ Creates a fake
  const $bar = {                        ◁───┘ $bar object
    start: jest.fn(),      ◁─┐ Creates a jest mock
    finish: () => {}         └ using the jest.fn method
  }
```

```
shallowMount(ItemList, {mocks: { $bar }})
expect($bar.start).toHaveBeenCalledTimes(1)
})
```

Makes $bar available
as this.$bar in ItemList

**Uses the toHaveBeenCalledTimes matcher
to check that $bar.start was called**

The test will fail with a nice assertion error when you run npm run test:unit. To call start when the component is mounted and pass the test, you need to learn about Vue lifecycle hooks.

4.4.3   *Using Vue lifecycle hooks*

Vue lifecycle hooks are built-in, optional functions that run at points during a component's lifecycle. Lifecycle hooks are like instructions. When a component runs, it looks for the instructions for what to do at certain stages; if they exist, it executes them.

> **NOTE**   You can see a detailed diagram of all the lifecycle hooks on the Vue website at http://mng.bz/wE2P.

To make sure the ItemList component starts the progress bar when it's mounted, you'll use the beforeMount hook. This hook runs—you guessed it—before the component mounts.

In your app, you have a failing test that you added in the previous section. It tests that ItemList calls $bar.start when the component is mounted. You can make that pass by adding a beforeMount hook.

Open src/views/ItemList.vue and add a beforeMount function that calls $bar.start in the component options object. You can see an example in the following listing.

Listing 4.20   Using the beforeMount lifecycle event

```
beforeMount () {
  this.$bar.start()
}
```

Run the tests with npm run test:unit. Hmm, the test now passes, but a previous test is failing! It's the leaky bucket problem—the previous test is trying to call $bar.start when it doesn't exist. The solution is to pass in a $bar object with a start method in the broken test. In the next section you'll update this broken test to change how it receives data, so you can fix the broken test then.

Now when your app starts, the progress bar will start. The purpose of this is to make it visible to the users that the application is loading data. The next step is to actually load the Hacker News data. You'll do this in the ItemList component. Remember that you get the Hacker News data by calling functions in an API file. To test that you're calling API functions in the ItemList component, you need to learn how to mock imported module dependencies.

4.5 *Mocking module dependencies*

Trying to isolate a unit to test can be like removing a plant from the ground. You pull the plant out, only to discover the roots are tangled around other plants. Before you know it, you have pulled up half the garden.

When a JavaScript file imports another module, the imported module becomes a module dependency. Most of the time, it's fine to have module dependencies in a unit test; but if the module dependency has side effects, like making a HTTP request, it can cause problems.

Mocking module dependencies is the process of replacing an imported module with another object. It's a useful tool to have in your testing tool belt.

In your code, you're going to fetch data in the `ItemList` component. `ItemList` will make a call to the `fetchListData` function exported by src/api/api.js. The `fetch-ListData` function makes a request to an external Hacker News API (figure 4.3).

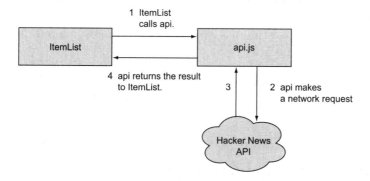

Figure 4.3 Importing a function from another file

HTTP requests don't belong in unit tests. They slow down your unit tests, and they stop unit tests from being reliable (HTTP requests are never 100% reliable). You need to mock the api.js file in your unit test so that `fetchListData` never makes an HTTP request (figure 4.4).

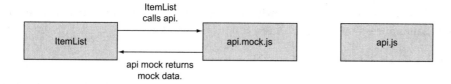

Figure 4.4 Stubbing a file import

You can stub a file in a couple of ways. One way is to use Jest spies, as shown in the next listing.

Listing 4.21 Mocking a module dependency

```
import * as api from '../../api/api'          ◁────
                                                        Imports the exports from api on an api
                                                        object. You need to import the functions
                                                        as an object in order to use jest.spyOn.

jest.spyOn(api, 'fetchListData')             ◁────
                                                        Replaces fetchListData
                                                        in the Jest mock function

api.fetchListData.mockImplementation(() => Promise.resolve([])) //    ◁────

                                                        Changes the implementation
                                                        of fetchListData
```

This works fine, but according to the JavaScript spec, the code in listing 4.21 is not valid. With ES modules, *you cannot reassign imported module values.* Because of this, you need to find another way.

Luckily, there's an alternative. Jest has its own *module resolver*, which you can configure to return files that you want.

NOTE A module resolver is a function that finds a file and makes it available to another file. Usually in JavaScript you use the node module resolver. You can read about the node module system in the node docs—http://mng.bz/qB1r.

Let's use the Jest mock system to mock module dependencies and help write tests.

4.5.1 *Using Jest mocks to mock module dependencies*

Jest provides an API to choose which files or functions are returned when one module imports another module. To use this feature, you need to create a *mock file* that Jest should resolve with, instead of the requested file. The mock file will contain functions that you want the test to use instead of the real file functions.

Imagine you wanted to mock a file called http-service.js that exports a `fetchData` function, as follows:

```
export function fetchData() {
  return fetch('https://example.com/data')
}
```

`fetch` makes an HTTP request, which you don't want. Instead, you can create a mock file that exports a mock `fetchData` function, as follows:

```
export const fetchData = jest.fn()
```

You create a mock file by adding a file to a __mocks__ directory with the same name as the file you want to mock. For example, to mock the api.js file you would create a src/api/__mocks__/api.js file that exports a `fetchListData` mock function.

You tell Jest to mock a file by calling the `jest.mock` function as follows:

```
jest.mock('./src/api.js')
```

After this function is called, when a module imports src/api/api.js, Jest will resolve using the mock file you created instead of the original file.

It's time to create your own mock file. Add a __mocks__ directory in the src/api directory, and create a file named api.js (full path: src/api/__mocks__/api.js). In the file, you'll export a `fetchListData` mock function. The mock function should return a promise that resolves with an array, because the real `fetchListData` function returns a promise with an array of items.

By default, Jest mock functions created with `jest.fn` are no-operation functions—they don't do anything. You can set the implementation of a mock function by calling `jest.fn` with the intended function implementation. For example, you could create a mock function that always returned `true` as follows:

```
jest.fn(() => true)
```

Add the mock `fetchListData` function from the next listing into src/api/__mocks__/api.js.

Listing 4.22   Creating a mock file

```
export const fetchListData = jest.fn(() => Promise.resolve([]))
```
⟵

Sets fetchListData as the Jest mock function that returns a resolved promise

Now you have a mock file that you can use to write tests for code that calls the `fetchListData` function from the api file. These tests are going to be asynchronous, because even when they are mocked, promises still run asynchronously, so you need to learn to test asynchronous code.

4.5.2   *Testing asynchronous code*

Asynchronous code requires some careful testing. I've seen it bite people before, and it will bite people again. Luckily, though, if you're working with promises or `async/await` functions, writing asynchronous tests is easy!

> **DEFINITION**   `async/await` functions can be used to write asynchronous code in a way that looks synchronous. If you're unfamiliar with `async/await`, you can read about them at this blog post—https://javascript.info/async-await.

Imagine you're testing a `fetchData` function that returns a promise. In the test, you need to test the resolved data returned by `fetchData`. If you use `async/await`, you can just set the test function to be an asynchronous function, tell Jest to expect one assertion, and use `await` in the test, as shown in listing 4.23.

> **NOTE**   The reason you should set the number of assertions in an asynchronous test is to make sure all the assertions execute before the test finishes.

Listing 4.23   Writing an asynchronous test

```
test('fetches data', async () => {
  expect.assertions(1)
  const data = await fetchListData()
  expect(data).toBe('some data')
})
```

Uses async as a test function

Sets the number of assertions the test should run, so that the test fails if a promise is rejected

Waits until the async function finishes executing

NOTE   If the function you are testing uses callbacks, you will need to use the done callback. You can read how to do this in the Jest docs—http://mng.bz/7eYv.

But when you're testing components that call asynchronous code, you don't always have access to the asynchronous function you need to wait for. That means you can't use await in the test to wait until the asynchronous function has finished. This is a problem, because even when a function returns a resolved promise, the then callback does not run synchronously, as shown in the next listing.

Listing 4.24   Testing a promise

```
test('awaits promise', async () => {
  expect.assertions(1)
  let hasResolved = false
  Promise.resolve().then(() => {
    hasResolved = true
  })

  expect(hasResolved).toBe(true)
})
```

Resolved promise that sets hasResolved to true in the then callback

hasResolved is still false, because the then callback has not run, so the assertion fails.

But fear not, you can wait for fulfilled then callbacks to run by using the flush-promises library, shown next.

Listing 4.25   Flushing promises

```
test('awaits promises', async () => {
  expect.assertions(1)
  let hasResolved = false
  Promise.resolve().then(() => {
    hasResolved = true
  })
  await flushPromises()

  expect(hasResolved).toBe(true)
})
```

Resolved promise that sets hasResolved to true in the then callback

Waits until all pending promise callbacks have run. If you remove this line the test will fail, because the code inside hasResolved will not run before the test finishes.

NOTE   If you want to know how flush-promises works, you need to understand the difference between the microtask queue and the task queue. It's quite technical stuff and definitely not required for this book. If you're interested you can read this excellent post by Jake Archibald to get you started—https://jakearchibald.com/2015/tasks-microtasks-queues-and-schedules.

You'll use flush-promises throughout this book to wait for promises in asynchronous tests, so you need to install it as a development dependency. Enter the following command in the command line:

```
npm install --save-dev flush-promises
```

After that overview of asynchronous testing and module dependency mocking, you're ready to use the skills to write asynchronous tests. In case you've forgotten, you're going to move the data-fetching logic into the `ItemList` component. Before you add new tests, you will refactor the existing tests to use `fetchListData`, instead of setting data on `window.items`.

The first thing you need to do is tell Jest to use the mock api file you created. Add the following code to the top of the file in src/views/__tests__ /ItemList.spec.js.

Listing 4.26 Mocking a module dependency with Jest

```
jest.mock('../../api/api.js')
```

You need to import flush-promises to wait for pending promises. You also need to import the mock `fetchListData` function to configure what it returns. Add the following code below the existing import declarations in src/views/__tests__/ItemList .spec.js:

```
import flushPromises from 'flush-promises'
import { fetchListData } from '../../api/api'
```

Now you can refactor the existing test to use `fetchListData`. Replace the existing *renders an* `Item` *with data for each item in* `window.items` test with the code in the following listing.

Listing 4.27 Stubbing a module dependency in tests

```
                                              Defines four assertions so that the
                                              test fails if a promise is rejected
test('renders an Item with data for each item', async () => {
  expect.assertions(4)                     ◄─────────────────────
  const $bar = {                 ◄───┐  Adds a $bar mock with finish and start
    start: () => {},                 │  functions, so that this test does not error when
    finish: () => {}                 │  you use the finish function in a future test
  }
  const items = [{ id: 1 }, { id: 2 }, { id: 3 }]
  fetchListData.mockResolvedValueOnce(items)    ◄───┐  Configures
  const wrapper = shallowMount(ItemList, {mocks: {$bar}})  │  fetchListData to resolve
  await flushPromises()                              │  with the items array
  const Items = wrapper.findAll(Item)
```

```
expect(Items).toHaveLength(items.length)          ◁──┐  Waits for promise
Items.wrappers.forEach((wrapper, i) => {              │  callbacks to run
  expect(wrapper.vm.item).toBe(items[i])
})
})
})
```

Now the test will fail with an assertion error. Before you make the test pass, you'll add new tests to make sure the correct progress bar methods are called when the data is loaded successfully and when the data loading fails.

The first test will check that `$bar.finish` is called when the data resolves, using the same flush-promises technique. You don't need to mock the implementation of `fetchListData`, because you set it resolve with an empty array in the mock file.

Add the test from the next listing to the `describe` block in src/views/__tests__/ItemList.spec.js.

Listing 4.28 Using flush-promises in a test

```
test('calls $bar.finish when load is successful', async () => {
  expect.assertions(1)
  const $bar = {
    start: () => {},
    finish: jest.fn()
  }
  shallowMount(ItemList, {mocks: {$bar}})        Waits for pending
  await flushPromises()          ◁──┘             promise callbacks

                                                          ┌─  Asserts that the
  expect($bar.finish).toHaveBeenCalled()   ◁──────────────┘   mock was called
})
```

Run the tests with npm run test:unit. *Make sure you see an assertion error.* Asynchronous tests are the biggest cause of false positives. Without the Jest expect.assertions call, if an assertion is inside an asynchronous action but the test doesn't know that it's asynchronous, the test will pass because it never executes the assertion.

After you've seen an assertion error, you can update ItemList to make the tests pass. Open src/views/ItemList.vue, and replace the <script> block with the code in the next listing.

Listing 4.29 ItemList.vue

```
<script>
import Item from '../components/Item.vue'
  import { fetchListData } from '../api/api'        ◁──┐  Imports methods
                                                        │  from the api file
export default {
components: {
  Item
},
beforeMount () {                               ┌─  Calls the loadItems method before
  this.loadItems()          ◁──────────────────┘   the component is mounted
},
```

```
    data () {
      return {
        displayItems: []        ←─┐  Sets the default displayItems
      }                             to an empty array
    },
    methods: {                 ┌─ Declares the
      loadItems () {        ←──┘  loadItems function        ┌─ Calls the ProgressBar start
        this.$bar.start()                               ←──┘  method to start the bar running
        fetchListData('top')                          ←──┐
        .then(items => {                                  └─ Fetches items for the
          this.displayItems = items    ←──┐                 Hacker News top list
          this.$bar.finish()              │
        })                      ┌─ Sets the component
      }                            displayItems to the
    }                            returned Items
  }
}
</script>
```

Phew, that was some heavy refactoring. Make sure the tests pass with npm run test :unit.

The final test of this chapter will check that $bar.fail is called when the fetchListData function is unsuccessful (even though it's not yet implemented in the ProgressBar component!). You can test this by mocking fetchListData to return a rejected promise. Add the code from the following listing to the describe block in src/views/__tests__/ItemList.spec.js.

Listing 4.30   Listing 4.30 Mocking function to reject

```
test('calls $bar.fail when load unsuccessful', async () => {
  expect.assertions(1)
  const $bar = {
    start: () => {},
    fail: jest.fn()
  }                                                       ┌─ Rejects when fetchListData is called,
  fetchListData. mockRejectedValueOnce()        ←──────┘  so you can test an error case
  shallowMount(ItemList, {mocks: {$bar}})
  await flushPromises()
                                              ┌─ Asserts that the
  expect($bar.fail).toHaveBeenCalled()  ←──┘  mock was called
})
```

If you run the tests, you'll see that the test fails with an error message that no assertions were called. This is because you used expect.assertions(1) to tell Jest that there should be one assertion. When the fetchListData returned a promise, it caused the test to throw an error, and the assertion was never called. This is why *you should always define how many assertions you expect in asynchronous tests*.

You can make the test pass by adding a catch handler to the fetchListData call in ItemList. Open src/views/ItemList.vue, and add update the loadItems method to include a catch handler as follows:

```
loadItems () {
  this.$bar.start()
```

```
fetchListData ('top')
.then(items => {
  this.displayItems = items
  this.$bar.finish()
})
.catch(() => this.$bar.fail())
}
```

Congratulations, you've moved the data-fetching logic to the ItemList component! Before you go off into the world with your new mocking knowledge like a driver who has just gotten their license, I need to talk to you about using mocks responsibly.

4.5.3   *Using mocks in moderation*

With great power, comes great responsibility. Mocking is a testing superpower, but you need to use mocks carefully.

You've learned how to use mocks in different ways: to control the return of a function, to check that a function was called, and to stop side effects like HTTP requests. These are all great use cases for mocking, because they are difficult to test without mocks. But mocking should always be a last resort.

Mocking increases the coupling between a test and production code, and it increases the assumptions your test makes. Each extra mock in a test is new opportunity for your test code and production code to go out of sync.

Mocking module dependencies is the most heavy-handed form of mocking. You should mock only files with side effects that will slow down tests. Some common side effects that slow down tests follow:

- HTTP calls
- Connecting to a database
- Using the filesystem

I'm not telling you not to use mocks. I just want to warn you that they are potentially dangerous and cover my back so you can't get angry at me if you use too many mocks in your future tests!

In the next chapter you'll learn how to test events in Vue. You'll build on the techniques you learned in this chapter, including using mocks, to test an interactive email sign-up form.

Summary

- Public methods without dependencies are simple to test, by calling the component and asserting the component output.
- You can test code that uses timer functions by mocking the timer functions with Jest fake timers.
- You can test that dependencies are called by using Jest spies and Jest mock functions.
- You can use mock functions to control the return value of a dependency.

- You can mock Vue instance properties using the Vue Test Utils `mocks` option.
- You can use Jest mock methods to change how a Jest mock function behaves.
- You can mock module dependencies with `jest.mock`.

Exercises

1 In this chapter you tested `finish` and `start` methods in the `ProgressBar` component, but you didn't write a `fail` method. Can you write a test to check that the `ProgressBar` root element has an error class added to it after `fail` is called? Add the test code to src/components/__tests__/ProgressBar.spec.js.

2 Can you write a test to check that the `ProgressBar` root element has a `width` style property of 100% after `fail` is called? Add the test code to src/components/__tests__/ProgressBar.spec.js.

Testing events

If money makes the world go around, then events make web apps go around. Without events, websites would be static HTML pages; with events, websites can become powerful applications that respond to user interactions.

In Vue applications, you will encounter two types of events: native DOM events and Vue custom events. In this chapter you'll learn about both types of events and how to test them.

So far in this book, you've written unit tests for components in a Hacker News application. The Hacker News application is a great example of a real-world app. But there's one problem—it doesn't use any events!

Events are an important part of most Vue applications, and before you can call yourself a testing master, you should know how to test them. In this chapter, you'll take a break from the Hacker News app. Instead, you'll write a pop-up email

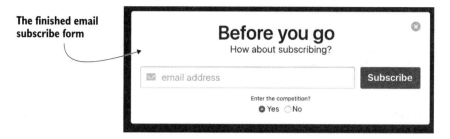

The finished email subscribe form

Figure 5.1   The finished pop-up email subscribe form that you'll create in this chapter

subscribe form—you know, the kind of form that appears when your mouse leaves a page and asks you to *subscribe for more content* (figure 5.1).

The sign-up form will be made from three components—a `Modal` component, a `Form` component, and an `App` component. There's already some code for each of these components added in the starter branch of the project.

> **NOTE**   To follow this chapter, you need to clone the chapter-5 project and check out the starter branch. You can find instructions to do this in appendix A.

The first section of this chapter is about testing native DOM events. To learn how to test DOM events, you'll write tests for the `Modal` component. In the second section, you'll refactor the `Modal` component to use Vue custom events.

The third section of this chapter focuses on testing input forms. Input forms have some nuances that can be tricky when you first encounter them. You'll write tests for the `Form` component to see how to test text-input elements and radio buttons.

The final section of this chapter is about the limitations of jsdom. So far, jsdom has been working great, but you're going to find that there are some issues with using a pure JavaScript DOM for unit tests.

After you have cloned the project and run `npm install`, you can begin. The first topic you'll learn is how to test native DOM events.

5.1   *Testing native DOM events*

Native DOM events are how the browser alerts JavaScript code that something interesting has happened. Lots of DOM events are available. For example, clicking an element triggers a `click` event, hovering the cursor over an element triggers a `mouseenter` event, and submitting a form triggers a `submit` event.

> **NOTE**   If you aren't familiar with native DOM events, MDN has a great primer you can read at http://mng.bz/mmEa.

In Vue apps you can use event listeners to respond to events with handler functions. Each time an event is triggered on the element, the handler function is called.

For example, to increment a count value when a button is clicked, you would use a v-on directive with a click argument as follows:

```
<button v-on:click="count++">Add 1</button>
```

Vue provides a shorthand notation for the v-on directive, which I'll use in this chapter. The following is the same example using the @ shorthand:

```
<button @click="count++">Add 1</button>
```

Native DOM events are often the input for a component unit test. For example, imagine you wanted to test that clicking a button hides an element. In the test, you would trigger a click event on the button element and then assert that the element is removed from the DOM.

In this section you're going to add a test to check that the Modal component calls an onClose prop when a close button is clicked. To test that a prop is called when a <button> element is clicked, you need a way to dispatch a click event on the <button> element. You can do that with the Vue Test Utils trigger method.

5.1.1   *Using the Vue Test Utils trigger method*

In Vue Test Utils, every wrapper has a trigger method that dispatches a *synthetic event* on the wrapped element.

> **DEFINITION**   A synthetic event is an event created in JavaScript. In practice, a synthetic event is processed the same way as an event dispatched by a browser. The difference is that native events invoke event handlers asynchronously via the JavaScript event loop; synthetic events invoke event handlers synchronously.

trigger takes an eventType argument to create the event that is dispatched on the wrapper element. For example, you could simulate a mouseenter event on a <div> by calling trigger on the wrapper of a <div> element, as shown in the next listing.

> #### Listing 5.1   **Triggering a** mouseenter **event**

```
const wrapper = shallowMount(TestComponent)
wrapper.find('div').trigger('mouseenter')
```

> **NOTE**   The trigger method can be used to simulate any DOM event. For example, it could simulate an input event, a keydown event, or a mouseup event.

The test that you'll write checks that an onClose prop is called when a button is clicked. To test this, you need to create a mock function, pass it in as an onClose prop, and then dispatch a click event on a button using trigger. Then you can assert that the mock function was called correctly.

Add the code from the following listing into the describe block in src/compo-nents/__tests__/Modal.spec.js.

Listing 5.2   Triggering a test by dispatching a DOM event

```
test('calls onClose when button is clicked', () => {      Creates a mock to pass to
  const onClose = jest.fn()                                the modal component
  const wrapper = shallowMount(Modal,
    propsData: {                         Shallow-mounts the modal
      onClose                            component with an onClose prop
    }
  })                                     Dispatches a DOM click
  wrapper.find('button').trigger('click')    event on a button element
  expect(onClose).toHaveBeenCalled()
})                                       Asserts that the
                                         mock was called
```

You'll notice there's an existing test in the file, which checks that the modal renders the default slot content. This is part of the Modal component's contract: it renders a default slot. You don't need to change this test.

NOTE   You might be concerned about using a generic <button> tag selector to find a rendered node. Theoretically, you might add an extra <button> element to the Modal before the close button in the DOM structure, which would cause the test to break. Unfortunately, this is an unavoidable aspect of unit testing Vue components. Some developers add IDs to elements to avoid this coupling, but I find that adding attributes for testing is often unnecessary. In my experience, it's rare that you need to update a test because you decide to change the DOM structure of a component.

To make both tests pass, you need to update the Modal component to call the onClose prop when the close button is clicked. Add the code from the next listing to src/components/Modal.vue.

Listing 5.3   Calling a prop when button is clicked

```
<template>
  <div>
    <button                    Adds onClose as a click handler using
      @click="onClose"         v-on directive @ shorthand
    />
    <slot />
  </div>
</template>

<script>
export default {
  props: ['onClose']
}
</script>
```

Run the tests to make sure they pass: npm run test:unit. Congratulations—you've learned how to trigger native DOM events in tests.

Most of the time when you test native DOM events, you call trigger with the correct event name. Sometimes, though, your code will use values from the event target. You'll learn how to write tests that use the event target later in section 5.3.

Before you learn how to test forms, you'll learn how to test Vue custom events. If you open src/App.vue, you'll see that you're passing a closeModal method as the onClose prop to the Modal component. The closeModal method sets display Modal to false, so the App component won't render the Modal component. This implementation is fine, but to teach you how to test Vue custom events, I'm going to have you refactor the App to listen to a Vue custom event instead.

5.2   *Testing custom Vue events*

What's better than native DOM events? Vue custom events! Vue has its own custom event system, which is useful for communicating to a parent component.

Custom events are emitted by Vue instances. Just like DOM events, components can listen for Vue events on child components with the v-on directive as follows:

```
<my-custom-component @custom-event="logHello" />
```

> **NOTE**   if you want to read more about Vue custom events, check out the Vue docs at http://mng.bz/5N4O.

Custom events are useful for communicating from a child component to a parent component. A child component can emit a custom event, and a parent component can decide how to respond to the event.

There are two parts to the Vue custom event system—the parent component that listens to a custom event and the component that emits the event. That means there are two different testing techniques to learn:

- For components that emit events, the emitted event is the component *output.*
- For parent components that listen to custom events, an emitted event is the component *input.*

To learn how to test Vue custom events, you'll refactor the app to use Vue custom events instead of native DOM events in the Modal and App components. You'll start by rewriting the Modal component to emit a custom Vue event.

5.2.1   *Testing that components emit custom events*

Vue custom events are emitted by a component instance with the Vue instance $emit method. For example, to emit a close-modal event, make a call like this from the component:

```
this.$emit('close-modal')
```

Emitting a custom event is part of a component's contract. Other components will rely on a child component emitting an event, which means it's important to test that a component emits an event when it's provided the correct input.

You can test that a component emits an event with the Vue Test Utils `emitted` method. Calling `emitted` with an event name returns an array that includes the payload sent in each emitted event.

> **NOTE** You can use `emitted` to test that an event was called in the correct order or with the correct data. Check out the Vue docs to see other examples of testing with emitted—http://mng.bz/6jOe.

You're going to write a new test for the `Modal` component to check that a `close-modal` event is emitted when the close button is clicked. You can do this by dispatching a click on the button and then asserting that a `close-modal` event was emitted by the component instance using the `emitted` method. Open src/components/__tests__/Modal.spec.js. Delete the *calls* `onClose` *when button is clicked* test, and add the test from the following listing.

> **Listing 5.4 Testing that a component emits an event**

```
test('emits on-close when button is clicked', () => {      Dispatches a DOM click
  const wrapper = shallowMount(Modal)                       event on a button element
  wrapper.find('button').trigger('click')       ◄──┘
  expect(wrapper.emitted('close-modal')).toHaveLength(1)    ◄──┐  Asserts that
})                                                              close-modal was
                                                               emitted once
```

Run the tests to make sure the new test fails: npm run `test:unit`. You can make the test pass by refactoring the `Modal` component to emit an event when the button is clicked. The `$emit` call will be inline in the template, so you can omit `this`. Open src/components/Modal.vue, and update the `<button>` to emit a `close-modal` event on click as follows:

```
<button @click="$emit('close-modal')" />
```

The component doesn't receive any props now, so you can delete the entire `<script>` block in src/components/Modal.vue. The tests will pass when you run the command npm run `test:unit`. Good, you've converted the `Modal` component to emit a custom event.

How about one more test to check an emitted custom event? In the project, you'll see you have a `Form` component in src/component/Form.vue. This is going to be the form for users to submit their email. You'll add a test to check that the form emits a `form-submitted` event when the `<form>` element is submitted. Create a test file—src/components/__tests__/Form.spec.js—and add the code from the next listing.

Listing 5.5   Testing a Vue custom event is emitted

```
import Form from '../Form.vue'
import { shallowMount } from '@vue/test-utils'            Dispatches a submit event
                                                              on a button element
describe('Form.vue', () => {
  test('emits form-submitted when form is submitted', () => {
    const wrapper = shallowMount(Form)
    wrapper.find('button').trigger('submit')            ◁────────────────
    expect(wrapper.emitted('form-submitted')).toHaveLength(1)      ◁──────
  })                                                    Asserts that the form-submitted
})                                                       custom event was emitted
```

To make the test pass, you'll add a submit event listener to the form element. In the event handler, you can emit `form-submitted`. Copy the code from the next listing into src/components/Form.vue.

Listing 5.6   Emitting a custom event on form submit

```
<template>
    <form @submit="onSubmit">            ◁───┐  Adds an onSubmit submit
        <button />                           │  listener with v-bind
    </form>
</template>

<script>

export default {
  methods: {
    onSubmit () {
      this.$emit('form-submitted')       ◁───┐  Emits a form-submitted event
    }                                        │  in the onSubmit method
  }
}
</script>
```

Run the tests to watch them pass: `npm run test:unit`. The application is already listening for the `form-submitted` event in the App (src/App.vue) component. When the `Form` component emits a `form-submitted` event, the App `closeModal` method will fire and remove the `Modal` component from the page (you can check this by running the dev server: `npm run serve`).

You've written tests for the first part of the custom event system, where an emitted event is the output of a component. Now you need to learn how to write tests for components where an emitted event is the input for the component.

5.2.2   *Testing components that listen to Vue custom events*

If a Vue component emits an event and no component is listening, does it make a sound? I'm not sure, but you could write a test to see!

Like you saw earlier, components can listen to custom events emitted by their child components and run some code in response, as follows:

```
<modal @close-modal="closeModal" />
```

You just refactored the `Modal` component to emit a `close-modal` event. That changed the component's existing contract—to call an `onClose` prop when the modal is closed—which broke the app. You need to update the `App` component to listen to the `close-modal` event and hide the `Modal` when the `close-modal` event is emitted. Of course, you'll write a test to make sure that it does.

To test that a component responds correctly to an emitted event. you can emit the event from the `Modal` component by getting the `Modal` instance wrapper and accessing the vm property as follows:

```
wrapper.find(Modal).vm.$emit('close-modal')
```

In the `App` component test, you'll emit a `close-modal` event from the `Modal` and check that the `Modal` component is removed from the rendered output in response.

Create a test file for `App` in src/__tests__/App.spec.js. Add the code from the following listing to the src/__tests__/App.spec.js file.

Listing 5.7 Testing that the component responds to Vue custom event

```
import App from '../App.vue'
import { shallowMount } from '@vue/test-utils'
import Modal from '../components/Modal.vue'

describe('App.vue', () => {                              Shallow-mounts the
  test('hides Modal when Modal emits close-modal', () => {   App component
    const wrapper = shallowMount(App)          <-
    wrapper.find(Modal).vm.$emit('close-modal')      <-  Emits a close-modal
    expect(wrapper.find(Modal).exists()).toBeFalsy()  <-  event from the
  })                                                        Modal instance
})                        Asserts that the Modal isn't
                          rendered anymore using
                          the toBeFalsy matcher
```

You can pass the test by updating the `App` component to listen to the `close-modal` event on the `Modal` component. Open src/App.vue, and replace the `Modal` start tag with the following code:

```
<modal
  v-if="displayModal"
  @close-modal="closeModal"
>
```

And just like that, the tests will pass: npm run test:unit.

You've seen how to write unit tests for components that use DOM events and Vue custom events. You'll write tests like these often; triggering an event is a common input for components. The principle is simple: you need to trigger or emit an event in the test, and then assert that the tested component responds correctly.

Another common element that uses events is an input form. Input forms often use the value of form elements in an event handler to do something interesting with, like validating a password. Because input forms are so common, they deserve their own section.

5.3   *Testing input forms*

From contact forms, to sign-up forms, to login forms, input forms are everywhere! Input forms can contain a lot of logic to handle validation and perform actions with input values, and that logic needs to be tested.

In this section you'll learn how to test forms by writing tests for a `Form` component. The form will have an email input for users to enter their email address, two radio buttons for users to select whether they want to enter a competition, and a Subscribe button (figure 5.2).

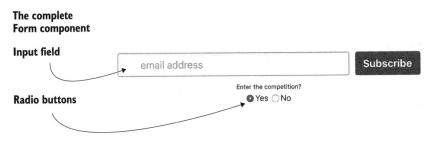

Figure 5.2   The finished form

When a user submits the form, the component should send a POST request to an API with the email address the user entered and the value of the radio buttons. To keep things simple, it won't include any validation logic.

So the specs for the form are

- It should POST the value of email input on submit.
- It should POST the value of the *enter competition* radio buttons on submit.

The first test to write will check that you send a POST request with the email entered by the user. To do this, you need to learn how to test text-input values.

5.3.1   *Testing text control inputs*

Input elements are used to collect data entered by the user. Often, applications use this data to perform an action, like sending the data to an external API.

An interesting thing to note about input elements is that they have their own state. Different element types store their state in different properties. Text control inputs, like `text`, `email`, and `address`, store their state in a `value` property.

To test that event handlers use a `value` correctly, you need to be able to control the `value` property of an input in your tests. A lot of people get confused about how to set the value of an input form. A common misconception is that simulating a `keydown` event with a `key` property changes the element value. This is incorrect. To change the `value` property of an input in JavaScript, you need to set the `value` property on the element directly, as follows:

```
document.querySelector('input[type="text"]').value = 'some value'
```

When you write a test that uses an input `value`, you must set the `value` manually before triggering the test input, like so:

```
wrapper.find('input[type="text"]').value = 'Edd'
wrapper.find('input[type="text"]').trigger('change')
expect(wrapper.text()).toContain('Edd')
```

In Vue, it's common to use the `v-model` directive to create a two-way binding between an input `value` and component instance data. For a bound value, any changes a user makes to the form value will update the component instance data value, and any changes to the instance property value is applied to the input `value` property, as shown in the next listing.

> **NOTE** If you aren't familiar with the `v-model` directive, you can read about it in the Vue docs—https://vuejs.org/v2/api/#v-model.

Listing 5.8 Using `v-model` to bind data

```
new Vue({
  el: '#app',                          The initial
  data: {                              value of message        Binds the input element to message
    message: 'initial message'   <──┘                          data. The initial value of the input
  },                                                            element will be the initial message.
  template: '<input type="text" v-model="message" />',    <──┘
  mounted() {
    setTimeout(() => this.message = '2 seconds', 2000)  <──┐  Causes the input element
  }                                                          value to be updated to
})                                                           2 seconds, after 2,000 ms
```

Unfortunately, setting the input `value` property directly won't update the bound value. To update the `v-model` of a text input, you need to set the `value` on the element and then trigger a `change` event on the element to force the bound value to update. This is due to the implementation of `v-model` in Vue core and is liable to change in the future. Rather than relying on the internal implementation of `v-model`, you can use the wrapper `setValue` method, which sets a value on an input and updates the bound data to use the new value, shown in the next listing.

> **Listing 5.9   Updating the value and `v-model` value of an input in a test**

```
const wrapper = shallowMount(Form)
const input = wrapper.find('input[type="email"]')        ◁──── Gets a wrapper of
input.setValue('email@gmail.com')              ◁───             an input element
```
Sets the value of the input element
and updates the bound data

In the test that you're writing, you need to set the value of an input element with `setValue`, trigger a form submit, and check that the input element value is sent as part of a POST request. You know how to set the value and dispatch an event, but to assert that a POST request is sent, you need to decide how the POST request will be made by your component.

A common way to make HTTP requests is to use a library, like the axios library. With axios you can send a POST request using the axios `post` method, which takes a URL and an optional data object as arguments, as follows:

```
axios.post('https://google.com', { data: 'some data' })
```

> **NOTE** axios is a library for making HTTP requests, similar to the native `fetch` method. There's no special reason to use this library over another HTTP library; I'm just using it as an example.

The application you're working on is already set up to use axios. It uses the vue-axios library to add an `axios` Vue instance property (you can see this in src/main.js). That means you can call axios from a component as follows:

```
this.axios.post('https://google.com', { data: 'some data' })
```

Now that you know how you'll make a POST request, you can write an assertion that will check that you call the `axios.post` method. You do that by creating a mock axios object as an instance property and checking that it was called with the correct arguments using the Jest `toHaveBeenCalledWith` matcher.

The `toHaveBeenCalledWith` matcher asserts that a mock was called with the arguments that it's passed. In the following test, you're checking that the `axios.post` was called with the correct URL and an object containing the `email` property:

```
expect(axios.post).toHaveBeenCalledWith(url, {
  email: 'email@gmail.com'
})
```

The problem is, if you add extra properties to the axios data in later tests, the test will fail, because the argument objects do not equal each other. You can future-proof this test by using the Jest `expect.objectContaining` function. This helper, shown in the next listing, is used to match *some* properties in the data object, rather than testing that an object matches exactly.

Listing 5.10 Using `objectContaining`

```
const data = expect.objectContaining({
  email: 'email@gmail.com'
})
expect(axios.post).toHaveBeenCalledWith(url, data)
```

Now the test will always pass as long as the `email` property is sent with the correct value.

It's time to add the test. It looks quite big, but if you break it down it's really a lot of setup before you trigger the `submit` event. Add the code from the next listing to src/components/__tests__/Form.spec.js.

Listing 5.11 Testing a mock was called with a `v-model` bound input form value

```
test('sends post request with email on submit', () => {
  const axios =                              ◁─┐  Creates a mock axios object
    post: jest.fn()                             │  with a post property
  }
  const wrapper = shallowMount(Form, {       ◁─┐  Shallow-mounts the form with the
    mocks: {                                     │  axios mock as an instance property
      axios
    }
  })
  const input = wrapper.find('input[type="email"]')      ┐  Sets the value
  input.setValue('email@gmail.com')             ◁────────┘  of the input
  wrapper.find('button').trigger('submit')   ◁─┐  Submits
  const url = 'http://demo7437963.mockable.io/validate'  │  the form
  const expectedData = expect.objectContaining({
    email: 'email@gmail.com'
  })
  expect(axios.post).toHaveBeenCalledWith(url, expectedData)   ◁──┐
})
                                                Asserts that axios.post was
                                                called with the correct URL
                                                value as the first argument
```

Before you run the tests, you need to update the previous test. Currently the previous test will error because the form component will try to call `axios.post`, which is `undefined`—the leaky bucket problem in practice. The instance property dependency doesn't exist, so you need to mock the instance property to avoid errors in the test.

In src/components/__tests__/Form.spec.js, replace the code to create the wrapper in the *emits form-submitted when form is submitted* test with the following code snippets:

```
const wrapper = shallowMount(Form, {
  mocks: { axios: { post: jest.fn() } }
})
```

Now update the component with the code from the next listing.

> **Listing 5.12   Form component**

```
<template>
  <form name="email-form" @submit="onSubmit">
    <input type="email" v-model="email" />
    <button type="submit">Submit</button>
  </form>
</template>

<script>
export default {
  data: () => ({
    email: null
  }),
  methods: {
    onSubmit (event) {
      this.axios.post('http://demo7437963.mockable.io/validate', {
        email: this.email
      })
      this.$emit('form-submitted')
    }
  }
}
</script>
```

◁─── **Binds the input to the component email property with the v-model directive**

◁─── **Calls the axios.post method**

You've just seen how to write a test for components that use an input element's value in the assertion. You can use `setValue` for all input elements that use a text control, like `text`, `textarea`, and `email`. But you need to use a different method for other input types, like radio buttons.

5.3.2   *Testing radio buttons*

Radio buttons are buttons you can select. You can select only one button from a radio group at a time. Testing radio buttons is slightly different from testing a text-input element.

Your website is having a competition! Everybody who sees the sign-up modal will have the chance to enter the competition. When the form is submitted, you'll send the user's selection (using the radio button's value) in the POST request to the API. I sense another test to write!

Testing radio buttons is similar to testing input forms. Instead of the internal state being `value`, the internal state of radio buttons is `checked`. To change the selected radio button, you need to set the `checked` property of a radio button input directly, as shown in listing 5.13.

> **NOTE**   The `checked` property is like the `value` property. It's the state of a radio button that's changed by a user interacting with the radio input.

Listing 5.13 Updating the value and `v-model` value of a radio button input in a test

```
const wrapper = shallowMount(Form)
const radioInput = wrapper.find('input[type="radio"]')          ◁──┐  Gets a wrapper of a
radioInput.element.checked = true                    ◁───┐         │  radioInput element
                                                         │
                        Sets the checked property of the │
                        radioInput element directly ─────┘
```

Setting the `checked` value directly suffers the same problem as setting a text-control value directly: the `v-model` isn't updated. Instead, you should use the `setChecked` method as follows:

```
wrapper.find('input[type="radio"]').setChecked()
```

You should really write two tests. The first test will check that the form sends `enter-Competition` as `true` by default, because the Yes check box is selected by default. For brevity, I won't show you how to write that test. The test that you'll write instead will select the No radio button, submit the form, and assert that `enterCompetition` is false.

This is a big old test, but once again, it's mainly setup. You can see the same technique of putting an input element into the correct state using `setSelected` before dispatching an event to trigger the submit event handler. Add the code from the next listing to the `describe` block in src/components/__tests__/Form.spec.js.

Listing 5.14 Testing a component is called with the correct values

```
test('sends post request with enterCompetition checkbox value on submit', ()
    => {
  const axios = {
    post: jest.fn()
  }
  const wrapper = shallowMount(Form, {          ◁──┐  Shallow-mounts the Form
    mocks: {                                         │  component with an axios mock object
      axios
    }
  })
  const url = 'http://demo7437963.mockable.io/validate'
                                                        ┌─ Sets the No radio
  wrapper.find('input[value="no"]').setChecked()   ◁───┘   button as checked
  wrapper.find('button').trigger('submit')

  expect(axios.post).toHaveBeenCalledWith(url, expect.objectContaining({ // ◁─┐
    enterCompetition: false                                                   │
  }))                                              Asserts that axios.post was called with │
})                                                  the correct enterCompetition value ───┘
```

Submits the form (label pointing to `wrapper.find('button').trigger('submit')`)

To make the tests pass, you need to add the radio inputs and update the `onSubmit` method to add the `enterCompetition` value to the data object sent with `axios.post`.

Add the following radio inputs to the `<template>` block in src/components/Form .vue:

```
<input
  v-model="enterCompetition"
  value="yes"
  type="radio"
  name="enterCompetition"
/>
<input
  v-model="enterCompetition"
  value="no"
  type="radio"
  name="enterCompetition"
/>
Add enterCompetition to the default object:
data: () => ({
  email: null,
  enterCompetition: 'yes'
}),
```

Finally, update the axios call to send an `enterCompetition` property. The test expects a Boolean value, but the values of the radio buttons are strings, so you can use the strict equals operator to set `enterCompetition` as a Boolean value as follows:

```
this.axios.post('http://demo7437963.mockable.io/validate', {
  email: this.email,
  enterCompetition: this.enterCompetition === 'yes'
})
```

Run the unit tests to watch them pass: `npm run test:unit`. You've added all the tests that you can to test the form functionality.

Ideally you would add one more test to check that submitting the form doesn't cause a reload, but using jsdom it's not possible to write. Every parent dreads the inevitable birds-and-the-bees conversation; I always dread the inevitable limitations-of-jsdom conversation.

5.4   *Understanding the limitations of jsdom*

To run Vue unit tests in Node, you need to use jsdom to simulate a DOM environment. Most of the time this works great, but sometimes you will run into issues with unimplemented features.

In jsdom, the two large unimplemented parts of the web platform are

- Layout
- Navigation

Layout is about calculating element positions. DOM methods like `Element.get-BoundingClientRects` won't behave as expected. You don't encounter any problems with this in this book, but you can run into it if you're using the position of elements to calculate style in your components.

The other unimplemented part is navigation. jsdom doesn't have the concept of pages, so you can't make requests and navigate to other pages. This means `submit` events don't behave like they do in a browser. In a browser, by default a `submit` event makes a GET request, which causes the page to reload. This behavior is almost never desired, so you need to write code to prevent the event from making a GET request to reload the page.

Ideally, you would write a unit test to check that you prevent a page reload. With jsdom, you can't do that without extreme mocking, which isn't worth the time investment.

So instead of writing a unit test, you would need to write an end-to-end test to check that a form submission doesn't reload the page. You'll learn how to write end-to-end tests in chapter 14. For now, you'll add the code without a test.

To stop the page from reloading, you can add an event modifier to the v-bind directive. Open src/components/Form.vue and add a `.prevent` event modifier to the submit v-bind as follows:

```
<form name="email-form" @submit.prevent="onSubmit">
```

The modifier calls `event.preventDefault`, which will stop the page from reloading on submit.

As I said earlier, the two parts of jsdom that aren't implemented are navigation and layout. It's important to understand these limitations, so you can guard against them. When you encounter the limitations, instead of mocking, you should supplement your unit tests with end-to-end tests that check functionality that relies on unimplemented jsdom features.

Now that you're preventing default, you have a fully functioning form. You can open the dev server and have a look: `npm run serve`. Obviously this form is nowhere near ready for public consumption. It has no styling and is incredibly ugly. The point is, you now have a suite of unit tests that check the core functionality and can freely add style without being slowed down by unit tests.

> **NOTE** To see what the finished application looks like, you can go to http:// mng.bz/oN4Z.

In the next chapter, you're going to learn about Vuex. The chapter is intended for readers who don't have experience with Vuex; if you have used it before, then you can skip ahead to chapter 7 to learn how to test Vuex.

Summary

- You can trigger native DOM events with the wrapper `trigger` method.
- You can test that a component responds to emitted events by calling `$emit` on a child component instance.
- You can test that a component emitted a Vue custom event with the wrapper `emitted` method.
- jsdom doesn't implement navigation or layout.

Exercises

1 How do you simulate a native DOM event in tests?

2 How would you test that a parent component responds to a child component emitting an event?

Understanding Vuex

This chapter covers

- What Vuex is
- What *state* means
- How to use Vuex in a project

Vuex is a large topic. Before you learn how to test Vuex in an application in chapter 7, you need to understand the fundamentals of it. In this chapter, you'll learn what Vuex is and how it makes it easier to manage data in an app.

> **NOTE** If you're already familiar with Vuex, you can skip ahead to the next chapter.

As an app grows in size, so does the data that the app uses. Making sure data stored in different components stays in sync is challenging and can lead to difficult-to-track bugs. Vuex is the solution to that problem.

Vuex is described as a *state management library*. That description isn't useful if you don't know what *state* means, so the first section of this chapter is about understanding state in the context of a Vue application.

> **NOTE**   If you've used Redux before, a lot of the Vuex concepts will be familiar to you. The main difference between Vuex and Redux is that Vuex *mutates* the store state, whereas Redux creates a new store state on every update.

After you understand what state is, I'll explain to you the problem Vuex solves. Finally I'll teach you the technical details of Vuex—what a Vuex store is and what parts make up a Vuex store.

First, you need to understand state.

6.1   *Understanding state*

People use the term *state* to refer to lots of different concepts, and if you Google what state is, you can end up confused. I had a hard time understanding what it was when I was learning to program.

In the context of Vue applications, *state* is the data that is currently stored in a running application. Imagine a Gmail inbox. If you want to delete some email messages from your inbox, you would click the check box next to the messages you wish to delete. You wouldn't refresh the page when all the emails were checked, because you know you would lose the data about which check boxes were selected. These selected check boxes are part of the *state* of the page, and refreshing the page would lose that state.

To look at a more technical example, imagine a `Counter` Vue component that renders a `count` value. It has a button that increments the counter value when it's clicked. When the component is mounted, clicking the button increments the `count` value rendered in the DOM, as shown in the next listing.

Listing 6.1   Counter component

```
<template>
  <div>
    <h1>{{count}}</h1>
    <button @click="count++">increment</button>        ◁─┐ Renders the
  </div>                                                   count value
</template>

<script>
  export default {
    data: () => ({          ◁─┐ The initial
      count: 0                 state of the app
    })
  }
</script>
```

The current value of `count` is the state of the component instance. You might have 10 different counter components in your application, and each of them could have a different `count` value. Each of those counter instances has a different state.

In Vue, the state of an application describes how an application should be rendered. In fact, state is the main reason that JavaScript frameworks like Vue exist. JavaScript frameworks make it easy to keep the view layer of an application in sync with the application state.

A good definition is that state is the current value of data inside a running application. It could be data returned from an API call, data triggered by user interactions, or data generated by the application.

Now that you understand state, you'll be able to understand what Vuex does for you and the problem it solves.

6.2 The problem Vuex solves

Coordinating state between components can be tricky. If components rely on the same data but don't communicate with each other when that data changes, you can end up with bugs.

Let's use a real-world example. Imagine an outdoor store with two employees, Nick and Anna. At the beginning of the day, they each count how many tents they have in stock and find there are three tents to sell.

Nick and Anna spend the day on the shop floor, Nick sells one tent, and Anna sells two. Nick thinks two tents are left—he sold one and there were three this morning. Anna thinks there's one left, because she sold two. In fact, no tents are left.

When a customer comes in and asks to buy a tent from Nick, he makes the sale, because he thinks there are still two in stock. The customer wants the tent mailed to him, so Nick takes payment from the customer without checking whether any tents remain in stock. When he goes out back, he finds out there are no tents left, and he has to make an embarrassing call to the customer.

The issue here is that Nick and Anna both had a different value for the number of tents in stock. They both had their own state. The problem was, their states became out of sync.

This can happen in a Vuex application when two components have their own state for the same data. State changes in one component might not change the value of a related state in another component—either because there is a bug or because someone forgot to write the code to keep the data in sync.

One solution for Nick and Anna is to use a computer to track how many tents are in stock. When one of them makes a sale, they enter it into the computer, and the computer deducts one from the total number of tents remaining. Now when a customer asks Nick if she can buy a tent, Nick can check the computer system and be sure there is a tent left to sell before he takes a payment.

In an application, Vuex is like the computer. It's a central source of truth that stores the state the application uses to render.

In a Vuex application, components get data from a *Vuex store*. When the components need to update the state, they make changes to the store state, which will cause all components that depend on the data to rerender with the new data. By using a Vuex store, you avoid the problem of data getting out of sync between components.

DEFINITION   The Vuex store is the Vuex container that includes the state and the methods to interact with the state.

Now that you've seen the problem Vuex solves in the abstract, you can learn how to implement Vuex.

6.3   *Understanding the Vuex store*

At the heart of every Vuex app is the store.

NOTE   In this book, when I talk about *the store*, I'm talking about *the Vuex store*.

To understand the store, you need to understand a core concept that Vuex follows—one-way data flow. One-way data flow means that data can flow in only one direction. The benefit of one-way data flow is that it's easier to track where the data in an app is coming from. It simplifies the application lifecycle and avoids complicated relationships between components and the state.

NOTE   There's a great talk from Facebook about the benefits of one-way data flow on: http://mng.bz/y12E.

I'll show you how to refactor a `Counter` component to use Vuex. There's no need to copy the code. The purpose of the `Counter` component is to demonstrate how Vuex fits into an app.

You can see the `Counter` component in listing 6.2. All the state it uses is local, if you update the `count` value; it's updated only inside the scope of the component. You can refactor it to use a `count` value from a store state. That way, any other component that wants to use the `count` value can access the `count` value from the store.

Listing 6.2   `Counter` **component**

```
<template>
  <div>
    {{count}}
    <button @click="count++">Increment</button>
  </div>
</template>

<script>
  export default {
    data: () => ({
      count: 3
    })
  }
</script>
```

To use Vuex, you need to create a Vue store with some initial state.

6.3.1 Creating a store

To use Vuex, you need to install Vuex with npm, create a store, and pass it to the root Vue instance. The code would look like the following listing.

> **Listing 6.3 Creating a Vuex store**

```
// ..
Vue.use(Vuex)                         ◁─── Installs Vuex on Vue

const store = new Vuex.Store({        ◁─── Creates a store
  state: {                                  instance
    count: 0         ◁─── Sets the
  }                        initial state
})

new Vue({
  store,             ◁─── Passes the store instance
  // ..                   to the Vue instance
})
```

After you've created a store and passed it to the Vue instance, you can access it from inside a component. If you refactored the Counter component to read the count value from the store, it would look like the next code sample.

> **Listing 6.4 Using Vuex in a component**

```
<template>
  <div>
    {{$store.state.count}}                          ◁─── Uses the count value
    <button @click="$store.state.count++">Increment</button>   ◁───
  </div>                                                  Increments the count
</template>                                               value in the store
```

The refactored component is implementing the same functionality as the original Counter component, but it commits a Vuex faux pas. The component mutates the state directly in the button-click handler.

As well as being a library, Vuex is also a pattern to follow. In the Vuex pattern you should never directly mutate the state; instead, you should change the state with Vuex mutations.

6.3.2 Understanding Vuex mutations

Although components can read directly from the store state, in the Vuex pattern, components should never write to the state directly. To update the store state, you should *commit mutations*.

commit is a Vuex function that you call with a mutation name and optional value; the commit function then calls the mutation with the state. For example, you could commit an increment mutation to increment the count value in the store as follows:

```
$store.commit('increment')
```

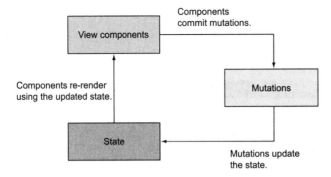

Figure 6.1   One-way data flow

Figure 6.1 shows the Vuex pattern. The main benefit of this pattern is that it makes it possible to track state changes in the application using the Vue dev tools plugin.

In the `Counter` component example, you need to create a mutation to update the `state.count` value. You add mutations inside the object used to create the store. The new store with an increment mutation would look like the next listing.

Listing 6.5   Adding a mutation

```
const store = new Vuex.Store({
  state: {
    count: 0
  },
  mutations: {
    increment(state) {          ◁─── Defines an
      state.count++                   increment mutation
    }
  }
})
```

After you've defined a mutation on the store, you can `commit` the increment mutation from the `Counter` component. The `commit` function calls the mutation that matches the string it was called with and calls the mutation with the `state` object. You never call a mutation directly. In the next listing, you can see the `Counter` component committing an increment mutation.

Listing 6.6   Committing a mutation

```
<template>
  <div>
    {{$store.state.count}}
    <button @click="$store.commit('increment')">Increment</button>      ◁───┐
  </div>                                                                     │
</template>                                              Commits an ─────────┘
                                                        increment mutation
```

You use mutations to update the store state. A few features to note about mutations follow:

- Mutations edit the `state` object directly.
- Mutations must be called with the `commit` function.
- In the Vuex pattern, mutations are the only way to make changes to a store state.
- Mutations must be synchronous—they can't contain actions like API calls or database connections.

Picture the Vuex store as a bank. In a bank, the tellers are the only people who can withdraw or deposit money to an account. Bank tellers are like mutations—they can edit the state directly. When you want to change the amount of money in an account by withdrawing or depositing, you need to ask the teller to change the value for you.

To keep mutations trackable in the Vue dev tools, mutations must be synchronous. If you want to edit the state asynchronously, you can use actions.

6.3.3 *Understanding Vuex actions*

You can think of Vuex actions as asynchronous mutations, although there is a bit more to them than that. Suppose you need to make an AJAX call to fetch data to `commit` to the Vuex store. You could do this inside a component method, as shown in the following code sample.

Listing 6.7 Committing mutations asynchronously

```
// ..
methods: {                              Makes a get request
  fetchItems () {                         to an endpoint      Commits data if the
    this.$store.commit('fetchItems')                          request is successful
    fetch('https://endpoint.com/items')           <─┘
      .then(data => this.$store.commit('fetchItemsSuccess', data.json()))  <─┐
      .catch(() => this.$store.commit('fetchItemsFailure'))       <──────┐
  }
}                                                          Commits a failure
// ..                                                      if the request fails
```

What if you wanted to call this action inside another component? You'd have to copy the code, which isn't ideal. Instead, you could create a Vuex action that performs the same functionality. You could refactor `fetchItems` and add it as an action in a store, as shown in the next listing. Note that actions receive a context object. This context object exposes the same set of methods/properties on the store instance.

NOTE You can read more about the context object in the Vuex docs—https://vuex.vuejs.org/guide/actions.html.

Listing 6.8 Committing mutations inside a Vuex action

```
const store = new Vuex.Store({
  state: {
```

```
   // ..
 },
 mutations: {
   // ..
 },
 actions: {
   fetchItems (context) {
     context.commit('fetchItems')
     fetch('https://endpoint.com/items')
       .then(data => context.commit('fetchItemsSuccess'), data.json
       .catch(() => context.commit('fetchItemsFailure'))
   }
 }
})
```

Defines a fetchItems action, which receives a context object

Commits a fetchItemsSuccess mutation if the fetch call is successful

Commits a fetchItemsFailure mutation if the fetch call fails

Then you could *dispatch the action* inside a component with the store `dispatch` method, shown next. `dispatch` is similar to the `commit` method, but you use it for actions.

Listing 6.9   Dispatching an action

```
methods: {
  fetchItems () {
    this.$store.dispatch('fetchItems')
  }
}
```

To continue with the bank metaphor, sending a check to your bank is like an action. After you've posted the check, you can carry on with your day, safe in the knowledge that after the bank teller receives the check in the mail, they will deposit the check into your account, which will update the amount of money you have.

The key features of actions follow:

- Actions are asynchronous.
- Actions can commit mutations.
- Actions have access to the store instance.
- Actions must be called with the `dispatch` function.

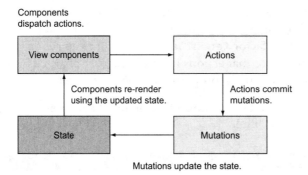

Figure 6.2   Dispatching actions in the Vuex lifecycle

Vuex actions are like mutations, except they can be asynchronous. Instead of editing the store directly, they can commit mutations (figure 6.2). Actions are useful for when you want to perform an asynchronous task, like an API call.

The final part of a store for you to learn is Vuex getters.

6.3.4 Understanding Vuex getters

Vuex getters are like computed properties for stores. They reevaluate their value only when the data they depend on has changed.

> **NOTE** Computed properties are properties of Vue components that update only when the data they depend on has changed. You can read about computed properties in the Vue docs—https://vuejs.org/v2/guide/computed .html.

Imagine you have an array of `product` objects in a store state. Some of those `product` objects have a `show` property set to `false`. You could create a getter function to return all the products with a `show` property set to `true`, as shown in the next listing.

Listing 6.10   A getter

```
const store = new Vuex.Store({
  state: {
    // ..
  },
  mutations: {
    // ..
  },
  getters: {
    filteredProducts (state) {        ◁
      return state.products.filter(product => product.show)
    }
  }
})
```

Defines a filteredProducts getter that returns all items in the state.products array with a truthy show value

Getters are called only when the data they depend on changes. If the data hasn't changed, they return their previous calculations. You can think of them as cached functions. Remember the bank example from earlier? Imagine you wanted to know how much you have in your combined bank accounts. The total amount in all accounts isn't saved as a value in the computer system, so the teller gets all the account totals, adds them together to get the overall total, and writes the total down on a piece of paper. Now you know how much you have, but it took the teller a few minutes to calculate it.

Later that day, you come back to the bank and want to know the total again. The teller knows you haven't withdrawn or deposited any money, so they pick up the piece of paper and show it to you. This time, they didn't need to spend five minutes calculating the total balance. This is how getters work. They perform logic on your data and then save (or cache) the value so that the value doesn't need to be recomputed if the data it relies on hasn't changed.

If you've withdrawn from your account since the time the teller wrote down your account total, the teller will need recalculate to make sure the value is up to date. In the same way, if a dependency of a getter updates, the getter will reevaluate the value (figure 6.3).

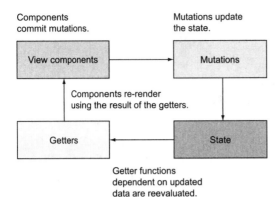

Figure 6.3   **Computing data with getters**

You can access getters inside components on the $store instance. You can see an example in the next listing of what this might look like.

Listing 6.11   Using a getter inside a component

```
<template>
  <div>
    <div v-for="product in $store.getters.filteredProducts">       ◁─┐
    {{product.id}}
    </div>                                              Loops through items in the
  </div>                                                filteredProducts getter │
</template>
```

NOTE You can read a more in-depth explanation of the Vuex store architecture in the Vuex docs—https://vuex.vuejs.org/en/intro.html.

Now you've seen all the parts of a Vuex store. In the next chapter, you'll learn how to write tests for a Vuex store, and components that use Vuex. You'll write tests for getters, actions, and mutations and learn how to test against a running store instance.

Summary

- Vuex is a state-management library that solves the problem of coordinating state between components.
- Vuex uses a one-way data flow pattern to make the flow of data easy to reason about.
- The Vuex store is built from state, mutations, actions, and getters.
- The state contains the data used to render the application
- Mutations are used to change the store state.
- Actions can be asynchronous. Actions are usually used to commit mutations after an API call has finished
- Getters are functions used to compute values using data from the store.

Testing Vuex

7

Vuex (a state-management library for Vue) is essential for large Vue apps. To become a Vue testing master, you should learn how to test Vuex effectively.

In this chapter, you'll learn how to test a Vuex store and Vuex-connected components. To learn how to test Vuex, you'll refactor the Hacker News application you've been working on to use Vuex.

> **NOTE** This chapter doesn't go into detail about Vuex basics. If you don't already understand how getters, actions, and mutations are used to create a store, you should read chapter 6, "Understanding Vuex."

Currently the Hacker News app fetches and stores data locally inside a view component by calling an API method. You're going to move this logic out into a Vuex store, so that other parts of the application can use the data.

In the first section of this chapter, I'll give you a high-level overview of the store design. It's important to think about the design of the store before you write any tests. After I've shown you the store design, you'll create a bare-bones Vuex store and add it to the application.

After you've added the store, you can start writing tests. You can use two approaches to unit testing a store. You can either test each part of the store separately, or combine the parts together to create a store instance and test the store instance directly. Both testing approaches have benefits and drawbacks, so I'll teach you both techniques in this chapter.

Vuex isn't much good if your components don't use the stored data. In the final section of this chapter, you'll learn how to test Vuex-connected components by updating the `ItemList` component to get its data from the Vuex store.

Before you write the tests, you need to understand the store design.

7.1 *Understanding the store design*

You can't write tests for a feature without a design, and you can't write tests for Vuex store without a store design! Let's take a high-level look at what the store should do.

The store will fetch and store items from the Hacker News API. Inside your application, you'll dispatch a Vuex action that will call the Hacker News API and add the returned items to the store. Then the `ItemList` component will use the store data to render the items.

Hacker News is made up of different feeds, or *lists*, of items, with different list types, like jobs, new, and show. So far, you've implemented the top list, which is a list of the trending items on Hacker News, but in the next chapter you'll add support for the other list types.

The action that fetches items will be called `fetchListData`—because it fetches all the data for a list type. The `fetchListData` method will take the type as a string in the payload object, as follows:

```
dispatch('fetchListData', { type: 'top' })
```

A list contains hundreds of items. You're not going to render hundreds of items on each page, so you'll use a Vuex getter to returns the first 20 of the current items in the store. You'll call the getter `displayItems`. You can see an illustration of how the store works in figure 7.1.

Now that you know what you're going to write, you can start writing the store. Before you write any tests, you'll add Vuex to the application.

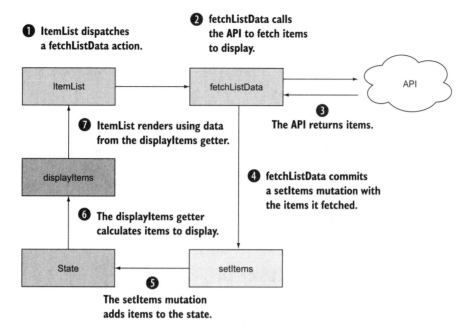

Figure 7.1 Calling `fetchListData` in the application

7.2 Adding Vuex to the project

To use Vuex in an app, you need to add some boilerplate code. In this section, you'll build a bare-bones store before you start to write tests.

Unit tests work really well for some code, but they don't work at all for other parts of a code base. Configuration, like creating a Vuex store, doesn't benefit from unit tests. Remember, the primary benefit of tests is that they let you know you haven't broken existing functionality. Configuration is often the least-edited part of a code base. It's very rare that you rewrite configuration code often enough for unit tests to save you more time than they take to write and maintain.

If you do make changes to the store configuration code, you will find out very quickly from a manual test, or an end-to-end test, that the store is broken. For this reason, you shouldn't waste time writing unit tests for Vuex store configuration explicitly.

To create a store, you need to instantiate a new `Vuex.Store` with a configuration object that contains the initial state, mutations, actions, and getters. You can see an example in the following listing.

Listing 7.1 Instantiating a Vuex store

```
const store = new Vuex.Store({
  state: {
```
The initial state
of the store

```
    count: 0
  },
  mutations: {                          ◁────┐   The store
    increment (state) {                       │   mutations
      state.count++
    }
  }
})
```

Instead of creating the configuration object when you instantiate a store, you should separate the store configuration object into a separate file, as shown in the next listing. This will make it easier to write tests against a running store instance later in this chapter.

Listing 7.2   Instantiating a Vuex store with a configuration object

```
import storeConfig from './store/store-config'

const store = new Vuex.Store(storeConfig)
```

You should also create separate files for the mutations, getters, and actions to keep the code modular and easy to reason about. You'll create the files with empty methods now, before you write tests for the files.

The benefit of adding empty methods is that you avoid type errors. Remember, when a unit test tries to call a method that doesn't exit, the test fails with an unhelpful type error. Type errors are terrible in unit tests—they don't prove that the test fails for the correct reason. You should create empty methods and functions in files that you plan to write tests for, to make sure you don't get type errors.

The mutations file will contain a `setItems` mutation, which will add items to the store state. Remember, in the Vuex pattern, mutations are the only way to update the state. Create a src/store/mutations.js file, and add the following code:

```
export default {
  setItems () {
  }
}
```

The actions file contains the store actions. You're going to have only one action—`fetchListData`. This action will call the API, fetch the items you need asynchronously, and commit a mutation to update the store state with the items. Create a src/store/actions.js file, and add the following code to the file:

```
export default {
  fetchListData () {
  }
}
```

The application will use a `displayItems` getter to calculate the items to render. You should also add a `maxPage` getter to calculate how many pages of items there are (you'll use that getter in chapter 10 when you add pages to the feed). Create a src/ store/getters.js file, and add the following code to the file:

```
export default {
  displayItems () {
  },
  maxPage () {
  }
}
```

Now that you have separate mutations, actions, and getters files, you can combine them into a store config object. Create a store config file at src/store/store-config.js, and add the following code.

Listing 7.3 A store configuration object

```
import actions from './actions'
import mutations from './mutations'
import getters from './getters'

const state = {                    ⟵——┐ The initial
  items: []                             │ state
}

export default {                   ⟵——┐ Exports the store configuration
  state,                                │ used to create the store
  getters,
  actions,
  mutations
}
```

The next step is to use the store config object to create the store instance. You'll do that in the app entry file.

   To use Vuex, you need to add it as a dependency. Add Vuex as a dependency with the following command:

```
npm install --save vuex
```

Vuex is a plugin, so you need to install it with `Vue.use` before you create the store.

> **NOTE** You can read about the plugin system in detail in the Vue docs— https://vuejs.org/v2/guide/plugins.html#Using-a-Plugin.

After Vuex is installed on Vue, you can create the store instance and pass it to the Vue instance. Replace the code in the src/main.js entry file with the following code.

Listing 7.4 Installing Vuex

```
import Vue from 'vue'
import Vuex from 'vuex'
import App from './App'
```

```
import ProgressBar from './components/ProgressBar'
import storeConfig from './store/store-config'

Vue.use(Vuex)                              ◁——┐ Installs Vuex

const store = new Vuex.Store(storeConfig)    ◁——┐ Creates a
                                                  Vuex store
Vue.config.productionTip = false

const bar = new Vue(ProgressBar).$mount()
Vue.prototype.$bar = bar
document.body.appendChild(bar.$el)

new Vue({
  el: '#app',
  store,                                   ◁——┐ Adds the store instance
  render: h => h(App)                          to the Vue instance
})
```

Now you have a bare-bones store created and passed to the root Vue instance. It's time to write some unit tests for each of the Vuex store parts.

7.3   Testing Vuex store parts separately

One approach to testing a Vuex store is to test the store parts separately. The benefit of testing parts separately is that the unit tests are small and focused. When a unit tests fails, you'll know exactly what part of the store is causing the problem.

All the store parts are JavaScript functions, so the tests are relatively simple. You'll begin by writing tests for Vuex mutations.

7.3.1   Testing mutations

Mutations *mutate* the state of a Vuex application (hence the name *mutation*). Compared to components, mutations are simple to unit test because they're just plain old JavaScript functions.

As you saw in chapter 5, a mutation function takes the store state as the first argument and an optional payload object as the second argument. Inside the function, you mutate the state with a new value, as shown in the next listing.

Listing 7.5   A mutation

```
setName: (state, { name }) => {          ◁——┐ Destructures
  state.name = name              ◁——┐ Mutates    the payload
}                                       the state
```

Mutations are never called directly. To call a mutation in an app, you must call a `commit` function with the name of the mutation. For example, if you wanted to run the `set-Name` mutation with a name property in the payload, you would call `commit` like this:

```
store.commit('setName', { name: 'Edd' })
```

Under the hood, `commit` calls a mutation with the store state and an optional payload object. To write a unit test for a mutation, you call the mutation with the same arguments. You create a fake state object and payload object, call the mutation with the fake state and payload, and assert that the state object was mutated with the correct value.

The test that you write will check that `setItems` sets `state.items` to the `items` value in the payload object. To test this, create a `state` object, call the mutation with the state and a payload object, and assert that the state `items` property is set to the items sent in the payload.

Create a test file in src/store/__tests__/mutations.spec.js, and add the code from the next listing.

Listing 7.6   Testing a mutation

```
import mutations from '../mutations'

describe('mutations', () => {
  test('setItems sets state.items to items', () => {
    const items = [{id: 1}, {id: 2}]          ⟵ Creates an items array that
    const state = {              ⟵ Creates a fake   you'll add to the payload object
      items: []                    state object
    }
    mutations.setItems(state, { items })      ⟵ Calls the setItems mutation
    expect(state.items).toBe(items)      ⟵       with the fake state object
  })                                                and a payload object
})          Asserts that state.items has been set to
            the items passed in the payload object
```

Run the tests with `npm run test:unit`, and make sure the test fails for the correct reason. Now you need to make it pass. To do that, you'll reassign `state.items` to the items in the payload object.

Add a line in src/store/mutations.js that reassigns the parameter, so your file looks like the following code.

Listing 7.7   A simple mutation

```
setItems (state, { items }) {          ⟵ Destructures
  state.items = items      ⟵ Sets the items store   the payload
}                             state value to the items
                             from the payload
```

Check that the tests are running with `npm run test:unit`. Great—you've got a mutation written and tested. Mutations are usually simple functions like this, so tests for them are often small and self-contained—my favorite kind of unit test!

The final assertion of a mutation test should always check that a `state` object was mutated correctly, because that's the purpose of a mutation. You can think of the mutated `state` object as the output of a mutation. If your mutations don't mutate the `state` object, then you're using them incorrectly.

Now you've got a mutation that updates the store state. Next you'll write a getter that uses the state to return the items that should be rendered.

7.3.2   *Testing Vuex getters*

Like mutations, Vuex getters are plain old JavaScript functions. Getters always return a value, which makes deciding what to test easy—you will always assert the return value of the getter function. To test getters, you call the getter function with a fake `state` object that includes the values the getter will use and then assert that the getter returns the result you expect.

Imagine you had a store with a `state.products` array of product objects. You could create an `inStockProducts` getter to return all products with a `stock` value greater than 0, as follows:

```
export const getters = {
  inStockProducts: (state) => {
    return state.products.filter(p => p.stock > 0)
  }
}
```

You can test this getter by passing in a fake `state` object with a `products` array and testing that the `inStockProducts` getter returns the correct number of products, like so:

```
test('inStockProducts returns products in stock', () => {
  const state = {
    products: [{stock: 2}, {stock: 0}, {stock: 3}]
  }
  const result = getters.inStockProducts()
  expect(result).toHaveLength(2)
})
```

In the Hacker News app, the `displayItems` getter will compute the items to display. For now, the app will display the first 20 items from the `state.items` array.

The test should check that the `displayItems` getter returns the first 20 items from the `state.items` array. In the test, you'll create a fake `state` object with an `items` array of 21 items. Then you'll call the `displayItems` getter with the `state` object. Finally, you'll assert that the getter returns an array of 20 items matching the first 20 items of the mock `items` array.

Create a file in src/store/__tests__/getters.spec.js, and add the code from the following listing to the file.

Listing 7.8   Testing that an array is returned

```
import getters from '../getters'

describe('getters', () => {
  test('displayItems returns the first 20 items from state.items', () => {
    const items = Array(21).fill().map((v, i) => i)
```

Creates an array with 21 items using fill and map to set each item to a number

```
    const state = {
      items
    }
    const result = getters.displayItems(state)
    const expectedResult = items.slice(0, 20)
    expect(result).toEqual(expectedResult)
  })
})
```

Creates a fake state object to pass in to the displayItems getter

Gets the return value of the getter

Asserts that the returned array is first 20 items of the original array

Now you can update the getter to return the first 20 items from `state.items`. Open src/store/getters.js, and update `displayItems` with the following code.

Listing 7.9 A getter

```
displayItems (state) {
    return state.items.slice(0, 20)
}
```

Returns the first 20 items

After you've checked that the test passes—`npm run test:unit`—you need to add another test for the `maxPage` getter. This getter will calculate how many *pages* of items you have. For example, if there were 60 items, and you display 20 items per page, then `maxPage` is 3.

The test will call the getter with a state that has 49 items. The number should be rounded up to the nearest integer, so you should expect the result to equal 3 (because the app displays 20 items per page). Add the test from the next listing to the `describe` block in src/store/__tests__/getters.spec.js.

Listing 7.10 Testing a getter

```
test('maxPage returns a rounded number using the current items', () => {
  const items = Array(49).fill().map((v, i) => i)
  const result = getters.maxPage({
    items
  })
  expect(result).toBe(3)
})
```

Creates an array of 49 items

Check that the test fails for the right reason. Now update the `maxPage` getter in src/store/getters.js to calculate the max page value as follows:

```
maxPage(state) {
  return Math.ceil(state.items.length / 20)
}
```

Testing chained getters
As well as using the state to calculate data, getters can use other getters to calculate data. Using the result of previous getters is known as *chaining* getters (because you chain their return values to get a new value).

> **(continued)**
> The Hacker News application doesn't use chained getters, but the technique to test
> them is similar to testing normal getters. The difference is that chained getters
> receive an object with the result of other getters as their second argument. You can
> write unit tests for chained getters by following the same technique of calling the get-
> ters with a fake `state` object and a fake `getters` object.

Now you've seen how to test mutations and getters. The final part of a Vuex store to
test is actions.

7.3.3 *Testing Vuex actions*

Actions give you the ability to `commit` mutations asynchronously. Often, actions
make API calls and `commit` the result. Because they can be asynchronous and make
HTTP requests, actions are often more complex to write unit tests for than mutations
or getters.

Like mutations, you never call an action function directly in your app. Instead, you
dispatch an action with the store `dispatch` method. Like the `commit` method,
`dispatch` takes two arguments. The first argument is a type; this is the identifier used
to call the action. The second argument is a payload. To call `fetchListData` with a
type of `top`, you'd call dispatch as follows:

```
dispatch('fetchListData', { type: 'top' }).
```

Like `commit`, `dispatch` calls the action for you. The first parameter of an action is a
`context` object. The `context` object contains the store state and store methods, like
`commit`. The second parameter of an action is the payload object—this is the data
that the action was dispatched with.

To test actions, you call the function in the same way Vuex calls it and assert that
the action does what you expect it to. Often, this means mocking to avoid making an
HTTP call.

> **NOTE** Remember, you should never make HTTP calls in your unit tests.
> HTTP calls make unit tests take longer to run and can make the tests flaky.

In the Hacker News application, you have one action—`fetchListData`. `fetchList-
Data` will call the API `fetchListData` method to get all the items of a certain list
type. You'll then commit `setItems` with the items returned by the `fetchListData`
API method to save the items to the store, which will cause the `displayItems` getter
to reevaluate and any components that rely on the data to rerender.

To test that the `fetchListData` action behaves correctly, you need to use extreme
mocking. In other words, you're going to add lots of mock functionality to test that
the action function calls the correct methods with the correct values. At the end of
this chapter, I'll show you an alternative way to test actions with less mocking; but to
test actions separately, mocking is your only option.

Extreme mocking is dangerous

Extreme mocking is where you mock complex functionality in tests. Extreme mocking can be dangerous.

The more mocks you use, the less accurate your tests are. Mocks don't test real functionality; they're testing assumed functionality.

The more you mock, the more assumptions you make. When your mock assumptions are incorrect, bugs can be introduced. There's nothing more frustrating than debugging a failing unit test, only to find the problem was with the mock itself!

Mocks also make a test more difficult to understand and maintain. Tests become more expensive to write. You need to be sure that the extra time it takes to write and maintain mocks is paid off by the time you save by running the unit tests.

In the `fetchListData` action test, you will assert that `context.commit` is called with the result of the `fetchListData` API call. You'll create a fake `context` object with a `commit` method. In the action, you will use only `commit` from the `context` object, so you don't need to add any other properties to the fake `context` object. See the next listing.

Listing 7.11 Calling an action with a fake `context` object

```
const context = {
  commit: jest.fn()
}
actions.fetchListData(context, { type: 'top' })
```

Now you know how to call the action in the test. Next you need to determine how to check that the action calls `commit` with `setItems` as well as the result of the `fetchListData` API method. You can check that `commit` was called with the correct values with the Jest `toHaveBeenCalledWith` matcher. But to know what values `commit` should be called with, you need to control the data that `fetchListData` returns.

You can use the `jest.mock` function to control what `fetchListData` returns. Remember, in the src/api directory there's a __mocks__ directory with a mock api.js file. Calling `jest.mock` with the relative path of the src/api/api.js file sets Jest to intercept imports of the file and return the mock file instead.

In the mock api.js file, `fetchListData` is a `jest` mock function, so you can call the `mockImplementation` method to change how `fetchListData` behaves. You can add logic inside the mock implementation function to check that it was called with the correct type value. If the function is called with the correct type, the function will return a resolved promise with an array of items. You can then check that `commit` was called with the items returned by the `fetchListData` mock.

In the test, you'll mock the `fetchListData` API method to return a resolved promise containing an array. For the `fetchListData` API method to return the correct items, it must be called with the type passed to the `fetchListData` action in the payload object. You can make sure it's called with the correct argument by adding custom functionality to resolve with items only if `fetchListData` is called with the correct type, as shown next:

```
fetchListData.mockImplementationOnce(calledWith => {
  return calledWith === type
    ? Promise.resolve(items)
    : Promise.resolve()
})
```

When `fetchListData` is mocked, you can call the `fetchListData` action with a fake `context` object. The API `fetchListData` method returns a promise, so you need to write an asynchronous test that will `await flushPromises`, to clear the promise queue. Then you can assert that the `commit` mock function was called with the correct arguments.

It's a big test with a lot going on. Add the code from the following listing to src/store/__tests__/actions.spec.js.

Listing 7.12   Testing that `commit` was called in an action

```
import actions from '../actions'
import { fetchListData } from '../../api/api'
import flushPromises from 'flush-promises'

jest.mock('../../api/api')

describe('actions', () => {
  test('fetchListData calls commit with the result of fetchListData',
    async () => {
      expect.assertions(1)
      const items = [{}, {}]                    // Creates the data you need to pass in the tests
      const type = 'top'
      fetchListData.mockImplementationOnce(calledWith => {    // Returns a resolved promise with the items if fetchListData is called with the correct type; otherwise, returns an empty resolved promise
        return calledWith === type
          ? Promise.resolve(items)
          : Promise.resolve()
      })
      const context = {                         // Creates a mock context object
        commit: jest.fn()
      }
      actions.fetchListData(context, { type })
      await flushPromises()                     // Waits for pending promise handlers
      expect(context.commit).toHaveBeenCalledWith('setItems', { items })    // Asserts that commit was called with the correct value
    })
})
```

Now you need to update the `fetchListData` action to commit `setItems` with the result of the `fetchListData` API method. To do that, you need to import `fetchListData` in the actions file. Add the following `import` statement to the top of src/store/actions.js:

```
import { fetchListData } from '../api/api'
```

Now add the code from the next listing to the `fetchListData` action in src/store/actions.js.

Listing 7.13   Calling `commit` inside a promise chain

```
fetchListData({ commit }, { type }) {
  return fetchListData(type)
    .then(items => commit('setItems', { items }))
}
```

Returns a promise, so that the action can be used in a promise chain

Calls commit with the result of fetchListData

Check that the test passes with `npm run test:unit`. For such a small amount of code, that test was big because it included lots of mocking. It was a large mock implementation for a relatively simple action. Imagine if the action were more complex!

With that action test, you've now written separate tests for each the actions, mutations, and getters in the store. The benefit of writing tests for each part of the store is that tests are specific. If the code breaks and a test fails, you will know exactly which part of the store isn't working.

But there are some big downsides to testing a Vuex store granularly. The biggest problem is that you often need to mock Vuex functionality. Like you saw earlier, extreme mocking makes tests difficult to write and can lead to bugs.

There's an alternative. Instead of testing actions, mutations, and getters separately, you can combine them into a store instance and test against that!

7.4   Testing a Vuex store instance

The alternative to testing mutations, getters, and actions separately is to combine them into a store instance and test the running instance. That way, you avoid mocking Vuex functions.

Earlier in the book, I talked about how a good unit test provides input and asserts an output. You can apply the same principles when you test a Vuex store.

Mutations and actions are the inputs for a store. You trigger changes in a Vuex store by committing a mutation or dispatching an action. The output of a store is the store state or the result of getters.

Let's look at an example. Imagine you want to test an `increment` mutation that updates a `count` state value by 1. To test it, install Vuex on the Vue constructor, create a store, and commit a mutation. Then you can assert that the state changes after committing a mutation, as shown next.

Listing 7.14   Testing a Vuex store instance

```
test(increment updates state.count by 1', () => {
  Vue.use(Vuex)
  const store = new Vuex.Store(storeConfig)
  expect(store.state.count).toBe(0)
```

Installs Vuex on a Vue constructor

Creates a store with a storeConfig object

Asserts the initial state

```
  store.commit('increment')
  expect(store.state.count).toBe(1)
})
```

Commits an increment mutation on a store instance

Asserts that the count value was incremented by 1

See, testing a store is easy! But don't get too excited—a big old gotcha can bite when you test a store like this. Like many problems in JavaScript, it's a problem with object references.

NOTE If you don't know what an object reference is, or how object references work in JavaScript, you can read about them in the blog post "Explaining Value vs. Reference in Javascript," by Arnav Aggarwal: http://mng.bz/MxWm.

The `state` object in a Vuex store is a reference to the `state` object defined in the store config object. Any changes to a Vuex store state will mutate the store config state. If you wrote another test that checked `count`, the initial `count` state would be 1, because the store config `state` object was mutated by the previous test.

The last thing you want in unit tests is mutations leaking between tests. The solution is to clone the store config object to remove any object references. That way you can keep using the base store config object, and you'll have a fresh store in each test.

In listing 7.15, you can see what the counter test would look like if you rewrote it with a cloned store config object using a `cloneDeep` method. `cloneDeep` does what you expect—it clones an object. Mutations to the state will affect only the `clonedStoreConfig` object, not the original store config object.

> **Listing 7.15 Cloning a store config object in a store instance test**

Clones the storeConfig object, so that Vuex doesn't reference the storeConfig.state object

```
test('increment updates state.count by 1', () => {
  Vue.use(Vuex)
  const clonedStoreConfig = cloneDeep(storeConfig)
  const store = new Vuex.Store(clonedStoreConfig)
  expect(store.state.count).toBe(0)
  store.commit('increment')
  expect(store.state.count).toBe(1)
})
```

Creates a store with the cloned store config

Like a leaky faucet, leaky tests can be a real nuisance. Now you know to avoid a leaky store object by cloning it before you use it to create a store instance, but there's another possibility for leaky tests that you need be aware of.

In these example tests, Vuex was installed on the Vue base constructor. Installing plugins on the base constructor can cause leaky tests because future tests use the polluted Vue constructor. To avoid them, you need to learn how to use a `localVue` constructor.

7.4.1   Understanding the localVue constructor

A `localVue` constructor would be a cool name for a Vue contracting company, but
that's a musing for another time. Here the `localVue` constructor is a way to keep unit
tests isolated and clean.

To understand the `localVue` constructor, you need to understand how the *Vue
base constructor* is used in Vue. You learned this in chapter 1, but as a reminder, every
Vue instance is created using a Vue constructor. By default, you use the base Vue constructor that's exported by the Vue library, shown in the next listing.

> **Listing 7.16   Creating a Vue instance with the base Vue constructor**

```
import Vue from 'vue'

new Vue({
  el: '    #app',
  template: '<div />'
})
```

Under the hood, Vue Test Utils uses the base Vue constructor to mount components.
The problem with the base Vue constructor is that any *changes to the Vue base constructor
affect all future instances created with the constructor.* This can cause leaky tests, where
changes to the constructor from a previous test affect future tests (figure 7.2).

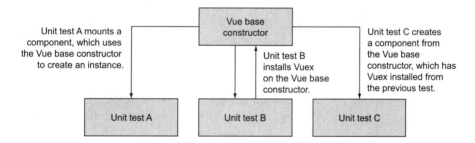

Figure 7.2   Polluting the Vue base class

Leaky tests are more frustrating than a mosquito in your ear, and after they've been
added to a test suite, they're difficult to track down and fix. For this reason, you
should avoid changes to the Vue constructor at all costs.

This works fine in principle, but often in tests you need to install Vue plugins, and
those plugins can make changes to the Vue base constructor. To install plugins and
avoid polluting the Vue base constructor, you can use a `localVue` constructor created
with Vue Test Utils. A `localVue` constructor is a Vue constructor that has been
extended from the Vue base constructor. You can install plugins on a `localVue` constructor without affecting the Vue base constructor.

> ## Vue—the master copy
>
> In school, the teacher doesn't give you the master copy of a workbook to write on. The teacher photocopies it so that you can use it without affecting the original workbook.
>
> Think of the Vue base constructor as the master copy. If you change the Vue base constructor, you change every copy that's made from Vue in the future. A `localVue` constructor is like a photocopy of the master copy. It's the same as the original and can be used in the same way, but you can make changes to it without affecting the original.

You create a `localVue` constructor with the `createLocalVue` function. Be careful—a `localVue` constructor extends from the Vue base constructor, so any previous changes to the Vue base constructor will be included in the `localVue`.

By default, Vue Test Utils uses the Vue base constructor when it mounts a component. To use a `localVue` constructor instead, you need to tell Vue Test Utils to mount using the `localVue` constructor with the `localVue` option, as shown in the next listing.

Listing 7.17   Using a `localVue` constructor with Vue Test Utils

```
import { createLocalVue, shallowMount } from '@vue/test-utils'

// ..

const localVue = createLocalVue()          Creates a localVue
localVue.use(Vuex)                          constructor

                                            Installs Vuex on
                                            the constructor
shallowMount(TestComponent, {
  localVue               Uses localVue to mount
})                       the component
```

> **NOTE** It's worth noting that not all plugins need to use `localVue`. I recommend you use `localVue` for all plugin installs, however, to be on the safe side.

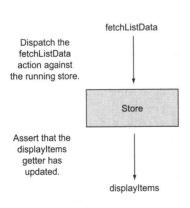

Figure 7.3   Testing a store instance

Now that you're clued in to the localVue constructor, it's time to write a test that uses it. Remember, the Hacker News application contains one action for the store—`fetchListData`. `fetchListData` calls the `fetchListData` API method and updates the store with the items. The output for the app is the `displayItems` getter.

Your test should make sure that dispatching `fetchListData` updates the value of the `displayItems` getter. This test will treat the store as a black box and will be completely unaware of the `setItems` mutation that's used to add the items to the store state (figure 7.3).

Note that you do still need to mock the `fetchListData` API call. If you don't, the unit test will make an API call and slow down your tests. You do, however, avoid mocking any Vuex functions.

You're also going to use the `cloneDeep` method you saw earlier. `cloneDeep` is exported by a helper library called `lodash`. Run the following command to add `lodash.clonedeep` as a development dependency:

```
npm install --save-dev lodash.clonedeep
```

Now you can write the test. Create a new file, src/store/__tests__/store-config.spec.js, and add the code from the next listing to it. This test will pass without any changes, because you've already added the store functionality.

Listing 7.18 Testing a Vuex store instance

```
import Vuex from 'vuex'
import { createLocalVue } from '@vue/test-utils'
import cloneDeep from 'lodash.clonedeep'
import flushPromises from 'flush-promises'
import storeConfig from '../store-config'
import { fetchListData } from '../../api/api'        ◁─── Mocks the API

jest.mock('../../api/api')

const localVue = createLocalVue()                     ◁─── Installs Vuex on the
localVue.use(Vuex)                                         localVue constructor

                               Helper function to create
                               an array of 22 objects
function createItems () {      ◁───
  const arr = new Array(22)
  return arr.fill().map((item, i) => ({id: `a${i}`, name: 'item'}))
}

describe('store-config', () => {
  test('dispatching fetchListData updates displayItems getter', async () => {
    expect.assertions(1)
    const items = createItems()                       ◁─── Creates mock items for the test
    const clonedStoreConfig = cloneDeep(storeConfig)
    const store = new Vuex.Store(clonedStoreConfig)   ◁─── Creates a store from a
    const type = 'top'                                     cloned config object
    fetchListData.mockImplementation((calledType) => { ◁
      return calledType === type                          Returns items if
        ? Promise.resolve(items)                          fetchListData is called
        : Promise.resolve()                               with the correct type
    })
    store.dispatch('fetchListData', { type })         ◁─── Dispatches the action

    await flushPromises()

    expect(store.getters.displayItems).toEqual(items.
slice(0, 20))                                         ◁─── Asserts that displayItems
  })                                                       returns the first 20 items
})
```

Run the test to watch it pass—`npm run test:unit`. If you want, you can change a value and check that the test fails for the right reason.

The benefit of testing a store instance is that you avoid mocking Vuex and tests are less implementation-specific. You could refactor the internals of the store, and the store-config test would still pass as long as the store maintains its contract.

The downside to testing the entire store is that tests are less specific. If a test for the store instance fails, it can be difficult to find out what part of the code caused the failure. You lose one of the benefits of unit tests—unit tests for a store instance aren't fine-grained.

There isn't a correct way to write tests for a Vuex store. Some people prefer testing everything individually because the tests are more specific and easier to debug. Some people prefer testing the entire store, because you write fewer tests and the tests are less brittle. Personally, I prefer testing a store instance because I don't like mocking, but I recommend using the technique you find easiest to write and reason about.

Now that you have the store built and tested, it's time to use it in the application. In the next section, you'll learn how to test Vuex-connected components.

7.5   *Testing Vuex in components*

Vuex isn't much use if you don't use it in your components. In this section, you'll learn how to test Vuex-connected components. When a component connects to a Vuex store, the store becomes a dependency of the component. If the component isn't passed a store with the correct actions, getters, mutations, or state, it won't behave correctly.

You can use one of two ways to provide a Vue store to a component in a test. The first is to create a mock `store` object and add it to the Vue instance with the `mocks` options shown in the next listing. This approach works fine if the store is simple, but a complex store will lead to mocking Vuex functionality, and you know my opinions on mocking!

Listing 7.19   Mocking a store in a test

```
const $store = {                                  Creates a fake
    actions: {                                    store object
        fetchListData: jest.fn()
    }
}
shallowMount(TestComponent, {
    mocks: {                          Mocks a store with the
        $store                        mocks mounting option
    }
})
```

The alternative is to create a real store instance with Vuex and mock data. This approach is more robust, because you don't need to rewrite Vuex functionality. I'll teach you this technique when you write tests for the `ItemList` component.

You're going to refactor the `ItemList` view component to use a Vuex store. It will dispatch the `fetchListData` action to fetch the items when the component mounts and get the items to display from the `displayItems` getter.

The `ItemList` source code changes are small, but you need to radically alter the test code to pass a store to the component when it's mounted. Every test needs to be rewritten.

Before you add a test to the file, you'll add some boilerplate code to create a store before each test. Each needs a store instance, so instead of repeating the code in each test you'll create a store in a `beforeEach` test setup function. This is a common test pattern people use to reset variables before each test.

You'll create `store` and `storeOptions` variables at the top of the `describe` block. Then, before each test in the `beforeEach` function, you'll create a store and assign it to the `store` variable so that each test has a fresh store.

Replace the existing code in src/views/__tests__/ItemList.spec.js with the code in the following listing.

Listing 7.20 Using `beforeEach` to reassign values

```
import { shallowMount, createLocalVue } from '@vue/test-utils'
import Vuex from 'vuex'
import flushPromises from 'flush-promises'
import ItemList from '../ItemList.vue'
import Item from '../../components/Item.vue'

const localVue = createLocalVue()          ⟵ Creates a localVue constructor
localVue.use(Vuex)                          ⟵ Installs Vuex on the constructor

describe('ItemList.vue', () => {
  let storeOptions                          ⟵ Defines the variables that will be reassigned before each test
  let store

  beforeEach(() => {
    storeOptions = {                        ⟵ Reassigns storeOptions before each test
      getters: {
        displayItems: jest.fn()             ⟵ Sets the getter as a mock. Getters must be functions, because you're creating a store.
      },
      actions: {
        fetchListData: jest.fn(() => Promise.resolve())   ⟵ Sets the mock action
      }
    }
    store = new Vuex.Store(storeOptions)    ⟵ Reassigns the store as a new store before each test is run, so you have a fresh store for each test
  })
})
```

Now you can add tests that use the store created by the `beforeEach` method. The benefit of this approach is that you avoid repeating code; the downside is that it can make tests more difficult to understand at first glance.

Add the test code from the next listing to the `describe` block in src/views/Item List.vue, below the `beforeEach` function.

Listing 7.21 Controlling a getter in a fake store

```
test('renders an Item with data for each item in displayItems', () => {
  const $bar = {
```

```
    start: () => {},
    finish: () => {}
  }
  const items = [{}, {}, {}]
  storeOptions.getters.displayItems.mockReturnValue(items)   ⟵───┐  Mocks the return
  const wrapper = shallowMount(ItemList, {          ⟵──┐           │  result of displayItems
    mocks: {$bar},                                      │
    localVue,                                           │  Mounts an instance
    store                                               │  with an injected store
  })
  const Items = wrapper.findAll(Item)
  expect(Items).toHaveLength(items.length)
  Items.wrappers.forEach((wrapper, i) => {
    expect(wrapper.vm.item).toBe(items[i])
  })
})
```

Make sure the test is failing correctly: npm run test:unit. To make the test pass, you need to update ItemList to use data from the displayItems getter to render the items. In the ItemList template, update the item loop to use the displayItems getter as follows:

```
<item
 v-for="item in $store.getters.displayItems"
 :key="item.id"
 :item="item"
/>
```

Now you can delete some unused code. Remove the data function, and delete the fetchListData call in the loadItems method. You can also delete the fetchList-Data import at the top of the <script> block.

Check that the tests pass: npm run test:unit. The component is now reading from a store getter, but you aren't dispatching the action to add items to the store.

The next step is to make sure the component dispatches the correct action when it mounts. Before you write a test to check for the action, you'll add the tests to check that the $bar methods are called. Copy the code from the next listing into the describe block in src/views/__tests__/ItemList.spec.js.

Listing 7.22   Providing a store to a component in tests

```
test('calls $bar start on load', () => {
  const $bar = {
    start: jest.fn(),
    finish: () => {}
  }
  shallowMount(ItemList, {mocks: {$bar}, localVue, store})
  expect($bar.start).toHaveBeenCalled()
})

test('calls $bar finish when load successful', async () => {
  expect.assertions(1)
```

```
  const $bar = {
    start: () => {},
    finish: jest.fn()
  }
  shallowMount(ItemList, {mocks: {$bar}, localVue, store})
  await flushPromises()
  expect($bar.finish).toHaveBeenCalled()
})
```

Now you can add the test to check that the `fetchListData` action was dispatched. Replace the store `dispatch` function with a mock, and then assert that the mock was called with the correct arguments. Add the following code to the `describe` block in src/views/__tests__/ItemList.spec.js.

Listing 7.23   Testing that `dispatch` was called in a component

```
test('dispatches fetchListData with top', async () => {
  expect.assertions(1)
  const $bar = {
    start: () => {},
    finish: () => {}
  }
  store.dispatch = jest.fn(() => Promise.resolve())          ◁——  Sets dispatch to a
  shallowMount(ItemList, {mocks: {$bar}, localVue, store})         mock function so you
  expect(store.dispatch).toHaveBeenCalledWith('fetchListData', {   can check whether it
    type: 'top'                                              ◁——   was called correctly
  })
})                                                    Asserts that dispatch was
})                                                    called with the correct arguments
```

Make sure the tests fail for the correct reason. Now you can replace the `loadItems` method in src/views/ItemList.vue with the following code:

```
loadItems () {
this.$bar.start()
this.$store.dispatch('fetchListData', {
  type: 'top'
})
  .then(items => {
    this.displayItems = items
    this.$bar.finish()
  })
}
```

Check that the unit tests pass—npm run test:unit. Congratulations—you've updated the application to use Vuex! You can open the dev server to see it in action by running npm run serve. You haven't added any new functionality to the app, but you've moved to Vuex. You can do lots of great things in chapter 9 with Vue Router. It's going to be easy to transform the static application into a complex, multipage app.

There's one more test to write. You should test that the component calls `$bar.fail` when `fetchListData` fails. You can change the implementation of `fetchListData` to fail by editing the `storeOptions` object in the test. Add the code from the following listing to the `describe` block in src/views/__tests__/Item List.spec.js.

> **Listing 7.24   Mocking an action to throw an error**

```
test('calls $bar fail when fetchListData throws', async () => {
  expect.assertions(1)
  const $bar = {
    start: jest.fn(),
    fail: jest.fn()
  }
  storeOptions.actions.fetchListData.mockRejectedValue()
  shallowMount(ItemList, {mocks: {$bar}, localVue,
  ➥ store})
  await flushPromises()
  expect($bar.fail).toHaveBeenCalled()
})
```

mockRejectedValue is syntactic sugar around mockImplementation(() => Promise.reject()). It means fetchListItem will return a rejected promise.

Mounts a component

Asserts that $bar.fail was called

To make this test pass, you need to add a catch inside the `loadItems` method. Open src/views/ItemList.vue, and add the following catch statement below the promise chain:

```
.catch(() => this.$bar.fail())
```

Check that the tests pass with `npm run test:unit`.

With that test, you've reached the end of this chapter. You've learned how to test Vuex store getters, mutations, and actions in isolation and how to test them when they're combined as a store instance. You also learned how to test a component that uses a Vuex store.

At the moment, the `ItemList` tests contain a lot of repetition. In the next chapter, you'll refactor the `ItemList` tests to use factory functions to make the file more manageable.

Summary

- Vuex mutations, getters, and actions can be tested without Vue Test Utils.
- You can test components that use Vuex by creating a Vuex store with mock data.
- Any test that installs a plugin should use a localVue constructor.

Exercises

1. What are the downsides to testing actions, getters, and mutation functions individually?
2. What are the downsides to creating a full store and testing it?
3. Write the code to shallow-mount a component with a Vuex store installed on a localVue constructor. The store config object will be imported from another file:

```
import storeConfig from './store-config'
```

Organizing tests
with factory functions

As a test suite grows in size, you start to see repeated code. One way to avoid this is to use *factory functions* to organize tests.

Factory functions are functions that return new objects or instances (you might know them as *builders*). You can add factory functions to tests that require repetitive setup to remove code duplication.

Using factory functions is a pattern that helps keep test code easy to read and understand. In this chapter, you'll learn what factory functions are, how they can reduce repetition in tests, and how they improve your test code structure.

After you've learned what factory functions are and the benefits that they bring, you'll refactor the test code in ItemList.vue to use factory functions.

8.1   *Understanding factory functions*

Factory functions make it easier to create objects by extracting the logic used to create the objects into a function. The best way to explain factory functions is with an example. Imagine you were writing tests for a component that used a Vue instance $t property. Each time you created a wrapper with Vue Test Utils, you would need to mock the $t function, as shown in the next listing.

Listing 8.1   Creating a wrapper object

```
const wrapper = shallowMount(TestComponent, {
  mocks: {
    $t: () => {}
  }
}
```

Instead of adding the same mocks option to each shallowMount call, you could write a createWrapper function that creates and returns a wrapper with the mocks option, as shown next.

Listing 8.2   Using a createWrapper function

```
function createWrapper() {
  return shallowMountMount(TestComponent, {
    mocks: {
      $t: () => {}
    }
  })
}

const wrapper = createWrapper()
const wrapper2 = createWrapper()
const wrapper3 = createWrapper()
```

Using factory functions in tests offers two benefits:

- You avoid repeating code.
- Factory functions give you a pattern to follow.

In this section, I'll talk you through both of these benefits in detail, as well as the trade-offs of factory functions. First, let's take a look at why you should avoid repetition by discussing the DRY principle and how factory functions keep code DRY.

8.1.1   *Keeping code DRY*

Don't repeat yourself (DRY) is a well-known programming principle. The DRY principle states that if you find yourself writing similar code multiple times in an application, you should extract the shared logic into a function or method instead of duplicating code between parts of a codebase.

You can use factory functions to follow the DRY principle (also known as *keeping the code DRY*). Moving duplicated object-creation logic into a factory function keeps the code DRY.

In Vue unit tests, it's common to call `shallowMount` with lots of options, like the code in the following listing.

> **Listing 8.3 Creating a wrapper**

```
const wrapper = shallowMount(TestComponent, {
  mocks: {
    $bar: {
      start: jest.fn(),
      finish: jest.fn()
    }
  }
})
```

If you have multiple tests that call `shallowMount` with the same options, you can move logic for calling `shallowMount` into a `createWrapper` function that calls `shallowMount` with the correct options. Rather than writing the same wrapper options in each test, you call the `createWrapper` function to get a wrapper of the mounted component:

```
const wrapper = createWrapper()
```

Now the logic for creating a wrapper with `shallowMount` is in one place and the code is kept DRY. If you add new dependencies to the component that you are testing, you can mock the dependency in one place in the factory function, rather than making changes in multiple places.

The other benefit of factory functions is that they give you a pattern to follow.

8.1.2 *Improving test code by following a pattern*

Most people don't think about patterns when they write test code. That works for a small test suite, but it can be damaging when your test suite grows large. Without a clear pattern, test code can grow into an unmaintainable mess.

Often, in large codebases, unplanned patterns appear. At first a developer might decide to write a function that mounts a component and checks that the root element has a class. Then other developers start using that function. One day a developer decides to pass some extra data into the function, so they add a new parameter. Before you know it, you have functions with a hundred parameters and names that read like tongue twisters, as follows:

```
mountComponentAndCheckRendersClass(store, useShallowMount, props, overrides)
    {
  // ..
}
```

I've seen this happen in many different codebases. Each team invents their own pattern to solve common problems without putting any thought into it. It's completely understandable—if you don't have a pattern to follow from the start, you'll end up creating your own.

In the previous chapter, I taught you the *before each pattern*. In the before each pattern, you rewrite common variables before each test in a `beforeEach` setup function. This approach avoids repetition in creating objects in tests and is a common pattern used in tests.

Factory functions are an alternative pattern you can use to avoid repetition. Whereas the before each pattern mutates variables that are used between tests, factory functions create new objects each time they are called. If done right, tests that use the factory function pattern are easier to follow than tests that use the before each pattern. That said, the factory function pattern does have some downsides.

8.1.3 *Understanding the trade-offs of factory functions*

Everything in life comes at a cost. The cost of using factory functions is that you increase the abstractions in your code, which can make tests more difficult for future developers to understand.

Many times, I've worked on a codebase and made a change that broke a dusty old test. When I opened the test file to read the broken test, I had to spend 20 minutes deciphering abstractions that I didn't understand.

When a future developer reads a test they didn't write, they won't know what a factory function does without looking at the internals of the function. This requires spending extra time in the file to understand how the test code behaves.

Considering this, in tests, repetition isn't always bad. If a test is self-contained without any abstractions, it will be easier for a future developer to understand. That's why I haven't had you writing factory functions or using the before each pattern from the start of this book.

But at this point in the test suite, the benefit of factory functions is worth the cost of extra abstractions. You're going to add factory functions to the `ItemList` component tests. The test code is already quite complex, and you'll add extra tests to this component in chapter 10. Adding factory functions now will make it much easier to write future tests.

> **NOTE** You won't refactor other test files to use factory functions, because the test code isn't complex enough to benefit from it.

The first factory function you'll write will create a Vuex store object.

8.2 *Creating a store factory function*

To create a Vuex store, you need to instantiate a Vuex instance with a configuration object. This is the kind of object creation that works well in a factory function.

A simple Vuex store factory function returns a store using a configuration object. The `ItemList` component requires a store with a `displayItems` getter and a `fetchListData` action. In src/views/__tests__/ItemList.spec.js, remove `let store` and `let storeOptions` from the code, and replace the `beforeEach` function with the `createStore` function in the following listing.

Listing 8.4   A `createStore` factory function

```
function createStore () {
  const defaultStoreConfig = {
    getters: {
      displayItems: jest.fn()
    },
    actions: {
      fetchListData: jest.fn(() => Promise.resolve())
    }
  }
  return new Vuex.Store(defaultStoreConfig)
}
```

This solution would work fine if the store should always behave in the same way. But in tests, you often need to control what the store returns. For example, take a look at the first test in src/views/__tests__/ItemList.spec.js—*renders an* Item *with data for each item in* displayItems. This test controls the displayItems getter return value. At the moment, the createStore function you wrote will always returns an empty array from the displayItems getter. You need a way to overwrite some of the default-StoreConfig values used by the createStore factory function.

8.3   *Overwriting default options in factory functions*

Sometimes you need to change the options used to create objects in factory functions. You can do this in many ways, but I'll show you what I think is the most intuitive way—merging options.

You have a createStore function that creates and returns a store with some default options, but you want to change the return value of the displayItems getter for one of your tests. One way to change the return value would be to add an items parameter to the createStore function, and set displayItems to return the items, like so:

```
const items = [{}, {}, {}]
createStore(items)
```

This solves the problem. You can control the displayItems return value. But what if you want to change the actions.fetchListData value in another test? Well, you could add another parameter, as follows:

```
const fetchListData = jest.fn()
createStore([], fetchListData)
```

Again, this works. But continually adding parameters isn't a good long-term solution. You can imagine other values you would want to overwrite in the future. I've seen factory functions in test code with 15 parameters!

Another option would be to pass in an object of values to use instead of the defaults, such as the following:

```
const fetchListData = jest.fn()
createStore({ actions: { fetchListData }})
```

```
const items = [{}, {}, {}]
createStore({ state: { items } })
```

Passing in an object is good API. It's easy to add extra options to pass in without editing older tests that use the function.

You can write the `createStore` function to overwrite only options that are passed in to the object. For example, imagine your default state has two values—`items` and `page`. You could write the `createStore` function to overwrite only the value passed in to the options and to leave the other property of state as the default, as shown next:

```
const store = createStore({ state: { items: [{}] } })
store.state.page // 1
store.state.items // [{}]
```

I find this approach easy to work with, especially when you need to override deeply nested objects. To overwrite existing properties in an object with properties from a new object without overwriting the entire object, you need to *merge the objects.*

> **NOTE** Merging an object means combining object properties recursively. In a merge, one object takes precedence over another, so the final object will always use the priority object when a clash of properties occurs.

Writing code to merge objects can be complicated, so why reinvent the wheel? The Lodash library has a merge option that does everything you want it to do. It recursively merges a source object into a destination object, as shown in the next listing.

Listing 8.5 Using Lodash merge

```
import merge from "lodash.merge"

const defaultOptions = {                      ◁——┐  The destination object
  state: {                                         │  to merge into
    items: null,
    page: 1
  }
}

const overrides = {           ◁——┐  A source object that
  state: {                         │  will be merged into
    items: [{}]                    │  the destination object
  }
}

merge(defaultOptions, overrides)
```

By default, it's not possible to override values with an empty array or an object. This can be a pain if you want to replace a default value with an empty object or an empty array, as shown in the next listing.

Listing 8.6　Using Lodash merge with an array or object

```
import merge from "lodash.merge"

const defaultOptions = {
  state: {
    arr: [{}],
    obj: {
      nestedProp: true
    }
  }
}

const overrides = {
  state: {
    arr: [],
    obj: {}
  }
}

merge(defaultOptions, overrides)
```

> The returned object will equal the defaultOptions object. The empty array and the empty object does not overwrite the defaultOptions object properties.

You can change the merge strategy by using the Lodash `mergeWith` function and providing a `customizer` function, as shown in listing 8.7. Lodash calls the `customizer` function each time there is a collision of properties during a merge. If `customizer` returns a value, Lodash will assign the property using the new value. If `customizer` returns undefined, Lodash will use the default merge strategy.

Listing 8.7　Using mergeWith with a customizer function

> Returns srcValue if it exists; otherwise returns objValue. srcValue is the value of a property in the source object that takes precedence over the target object. This customizer function would always reassign objValue with srcValue when there is a collision.

```
import mergeWith from "lodash.mergewith"

function customizer(objValue, srcValue) {
  return srcValue ? srcValue : objValue
}

mergeWith(defaultOptions, overrides, customizer)
```

> Merges using the customizer function

In your factory function, you'll use a `customizer` to overwrite properties if the source object properties are an empty object or an array. Add the following `customizer` function to the `ItemList` file, just after the `import` statements.

Listing 8.8　A customizer function to overwrite empty objects and arrays

```
function customizer(objValue, srcValue) {
  if (Array.isArray(srcValue)) {
    return srcValue
  }
```

> If the property that takes precedence is an array, overwrite the value rather than merging the arrays.

```
    if (srcValue instanceof Object && Object.keys(srcValue).length === 0) {  ◁─┐
      return srcValue                                                          │
    }                      If the property that takes precedence is an empty   │
}                          object, overwrite the property with an empty object.┘
```

Now install `lodash.mergewith` by running the following command in the command line:

```
npm install --save-dev lodash.mergewith
```

When `lodash.mergewith` has installed, you can use it in the `createStore` function. Add an `import` statement next to the other `import` statements in src/views/__tests__/ItemList.spec.js as follows:

```
import mergeWith from 'lodash.mergewith'
```

Edit the `createStore` function in src/views/__tests__/ItemList.spec.js to take an overrides parameter, and create the store using the result of `mergeWith`, as in the following code snippet:

```
function createStore (overrides) {
const defaultStoreConfig = {
getters: {
    displayItems: jest.fn()
  },
  actions: {
    fetchListData: jest.fn(() => Promise.resolve())
  }
}
return new Vuex.Store(
    mergeWith(defaultStoreConfig, overrides, customizer)
  )
}
```

Awesome—now you can change the store values in each test by passing in overrides to the `createStore` function. Replace the *renders an* `Item` *with data for each item in* `displayItems` test in src/views/__tests__/ItemList.spec.js with the code in the next listing.

Listing 8.9 Using a `createStore` factory function

```
test('renders an Item with data for each item in displayItems', () => {
  const $bar = {                              ◁─┐ $bar mock to avoid errors
    start: () => {},                             │ when mounting the component
    finish: () => {}
  }
  const items = [{}, {}, {}]     ◁─┘ Creates mock items
                                      to pass into the store
  const store = createStore({                 ◁─┐ Creates a store
    getters: {                                    │ using mock items
      displayItems: () => items
    }
  })
```

```
const wrapper = shallowMount(ItemList, {     ◁─┐ Creates
  mocks: {$bar},                                │ the wrapper
  localVue,
  store
})
const Items = wrapper.findAll(Item)
expect(Items).toHaveLength(items.length)     ◁─┐ Asserts that ItemList renders the
Items.wrappers.forEach((wrapper, i) => {       │ correct number of Item components
  expect(wrapper.vm.item).toBe(items[i])
})
})
```

If you run npm `run test:unit`, you'll see that the test you just refactored is passing. Unfortunately, lots of other tests aren't, because you deleted the `beforeEach` function. You can refactor those tests in a minute, but before you do that, there's another factory function for you to create.

8.4   *Creating a wrapper factory function*

In unit tests for Vue components, you can use Vue Test Utils to create a wrapper object of a mounted component. Often you need to add lots of mounting options to create a wrapper, which makes it a prime candidate to move into a factory function.

The wrapper factory function should return a wrapper with the default mounting options. To keep with the convention of `createStore`, it will be called `createWrapper`.

The `createWrapper` function will be similar to the `createStore` function. It takes optional overrides and returns a mounted component wrapper. Add the `createWrapper` function from the following listing to src/views/__tests__/Item List.spec.js, below the `createStore` function.

Listing 8.10   A `createWrapper` function

```
function createWrapper (overrides) {          ◁─┐ Accepts optional
  const defaultMountingOptions = {            ◁─┐ overrides
    mocks: {
      $bar: {                                  Defines the default
        start: jest.fn(),                      mounting options
        finish: jest.fn(),
        fail: jest.fn()
      }
    },
    localVue,
    store: createStore()     ◁─┐ Creates a default store with
  }                            │ the createStore function
  return shallowMount(         ◁─┐ Returns
    ItemList,                    │ a wrapper
    mergeWith(
      defaultMountingOptions,
      overrides,
      customizer
    )
  )
}
```

Now refactor the first test to use `createWrapper`. Open src/views/__tests__/Item List.spec.js, and replace the *renders an* `Item` *with data for each item in* `displayItems` test to use the code in the following listing.

Listing 8.11 Using `createStore` and `createWrapper` in a test

```
test('renders an Item with data for each item in displayItems', () => {
  const items = [{}, {}, {}]
  const store = createStore({
    getters: {
      displayItems: () => items
    }
  })

  const wrapper = createWrapper({ store })
  const Items = wrapper.findAll(Item)
  expect(Items).toHaveLength(items.length)
  Items.wrappers.forEach((wrapper, i) => {
    expect(wrapper.vm.item).toBe(items[i])
  })
})
```

> **Uses the createStore factory function to create a store with the correct displayItems getter** (annotation for the `createStore` block)
>
> **Uses the createWrapper factory function to return a wrapper, using the store you created as an override** (annotation for the `createWrapper` line)

Now run the test to make sure the refactored test still passes: npm run test:unit. As long as you added the correct code it will, but lots of other now-failing tests need your attention.

> **TIP** After you refactor tests, you should always check that they still pass. If you want to be extra careful (which I always am), you can edit the assertion to make sure it also still fails correctly.

In the next two tests, you don't need to mock the store, so you don't need to pass a store to the `createWrapper` factory function. But you do need to check that the methods inside the mock `$bar` object are called in the test.

One of the problems with factory functions is that you don't have a reference to functions or objects used as properties to create an object. This is problematic if you want to test that a mock function was called. The solution is to create mock functions in the test and pass them in as overrides to a factory function, as shown next.

Listing 8.12 Keeping a reference to a mock when using a factory function

```
test('calls onClose prop when clicked', () => {
  const propsData = {
    onClose: jest.fn()
  }
  const wrapper = createWrapper({ propsData })
  wrapper.trigger('click')
  expect(propsData.onClose).toHaveBeenCalled()
})
```

> **Creates a mock function** (annotation for the `onClose: jest.fn()` line)
>
> **Passes a mock function in propsData to override the default options** (annotation for the `createWrapper({ propsData })` line)
>
> **Asserts that the mock function was called** (annotation for the `expect(propsData.onClose).toHaveBeenCalled()` line)

In your test, you need to keep a reference to the $bar.start function. Replace the *calls $bar start on load* test with the code in the following listing.

Listing 8.13 Passing a mocks object to createWrapper

```
test('calls $bar start on render', () => {          Creates a mocks object
  const mocks = {                                    that contains the $bar object
    $bar: {
      start: jest.fn()                Sets $bar.start to a
    }                                  jest mock function
  }
  createWrapper({ mocks })                                        Creates a wrapper. There's no
  expect(mocks.$bar.start).toHaveBeenCalled()                    need to assign it to a variable.
})                                                               Creating the wrapper
              Uses the reference to $bar.start                    will mount the component
              to check whether it was called                      and call $bar.start.
```

Check that the test passes—npm run test:unit. Now you can refactor the next test to use the factory function. Replace the *calls $bar finish when load successful* test with the following code.

Listing 8.14 Using a createWrapper factory function

```
test('calls $bar finish when load successful', async () => {
  const mocks = {
    $bar: {
      finish: jest.fn()
    }
  }
  createWrapper({ mocks })
  await flushPromises()
  expect(mocks.$bar.finish).toHaveBeenCalled()
})
```

Check that the tests pass again with npm run test:unit. The next test to refactor is the *dispatches fetchListData with top* test. In this test, you need to create a store so that you can mock the store dispatch function. Then you pass the store to the createWrapper function, mount the component, and assert that dispatch was called with the correct arguments. Replace the test with the following code.

Listing 8.15 Mocking actions

```
                                    Creates a store          Mocks the store
                                                              dispatch function
test('dispatches fetchListData with top', async () => {      so you can check
  const store = createStore()                                that it was called
  store.dispatch = jest.fn(() => Promise.resolve())
  createWrapper({ store })
                                    createWrapper, which will
                                    mount the component using
                                    the store passed in
```

```
    await flushPromises()
    expect(store.dispatch).toHaveBeenCalledWith('fetchListData',
➥ { type: 'top' })
})
```

Asserts that the dispatch was
called with the correct arguments

The final test to refactor is the *calls $bar fail when load is unsuccessful*. Replace the
test with the following code.

Listing 8.16   Mocking actions to reject

```
test('calls $bar fail when fetchListData throws', async () => {
    const store = createStore({
        actions: { fetchListData: jest.fn(() => Promise.reject()) }
    })
    const mocks = {
        $bar: {
            fail: jest.fn()
        }
    }
    createWrapper({ mocks, store })
    await flushPromises()
    expect(mocks.$bar.fail).toHaveBeenCalled()
})
```

Creates a store with the
fetchListData action to
return a rejected promise

Asserts that $bar.fail
was called

Congratulations—you've refactored all the tests in ItemList.spec.js. In chapter 10
you'll see the awesome power of factory functions when you learn how to test Vue
Router.

Before you move on to the next chapter, let's recap what you learned in this chapter.

Summary

- Factory functions remove duplicate logic.
- Using factory functions can make test code more complex.
- The trade-off in using factory functions is not always worth the benefit of removing duplication.
- You can merge options in factory functions using the Lodash `mergeWith` function to easily overwrite default options.

Exercises

1   What does DRY stand for?
2   What are the benefits of using factory functions in tests?

Understanding Vue Router

When a single-page web app grows large, you might decide to split the UI into different views. You can use Vue Router to add client-side routing to handle navigation between views without causing a page reload.

This chapter is an introduction to Vue Router for readers who aren't familiar with the library. You'll learn about server-side routing, client-side routing, and Vue Router. At the end of the chapter, you'll add a bare-bones Vue Router setup to the Hacker News app.

> **NOTE** If you already have experience with Vue Router, you can skip ahead to chapter 10. You will need to check out the chapter-10 GitHub branch to follow along with that chapter.

If you've written a React or Angular application before, you might be familiar with the concept of client-side routing. If not, don't worry. The first section of this chapter is about understanding what client-side routing is. You'll learn about the traditional server-side routing of websites and compare that to the client-side routing approach.

After you've seen client-side routing at a high level, you'll learn about Vue Router and how to use it to add client-side routing to an application. Finally, you'll add a Vue Router setup to the Hacker News application. First, let's talk about routing.

9.1   *Understanding routing*

The definition of routing depends on the context in which you use it. In this chapter, routing means *using the path of a URL to serve content.*

> **DEFINITION**   A path is the part of a URL after the domain. For example, in the URL https://my-website.com/something/1, /something/1 is a path.

A typical website has several pages that map to URLs that you can navigate to by clicking links. This can happen in the following two ways:

- In server-side routing, a new page is requested from the server and rendered.
- In client-side routing, the page content is rendered on the client, without a new request to the server.

Don't worry if that brief explanation doesn't make sense to you, this section will go into more detail on the difference between the two. Let's begin by looking at server-side routing.

9.1.1   *Understanding server-side routing*

Server-side routing is the traditional method of matching a path to a file. As the name suggests, server-side routing is where the server does the routing work.

Think about the Hacker News website. When you enter the URL https://news.ycombinator.com/ into the browser address bar, a request is sent to a server, which responds with the correct content for the path. This is *server-side routing*. The server processes the request and uses the path (/) to respond with the correct content.

At the top of a Hacker News page are links for different Hacker News feeds. For example, figure 9.1 shows the live Hacker News nav bar, including a link to the Show feed.

Figure 9.1   Hacker News site with different feed links

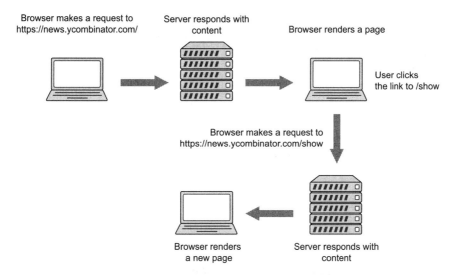

Figure 9.2 Server-sider routing

When a user clicks the Show link, the browser sends a new request to https://news.ycombinator.com/show. The server receives the request, processes it using the path (/show), and returns the matching document. When the browser receives the response, it loads the new document in the page (figure 9.2).

This is how navigation works on an app that uses server-side routing—each click sends a new request to the server, which processes the request and returns the correct content. This approach has worked since the dawn of the internet, and there's nothing broken about this system. But server-side routing does have one big problem: each time a browser loads a new document, it loses the current state of the application.

We have ways around this problem—cookies, local storage, and query parameters in the URL can all be used to save state between page requests. These solutions work fine, but they make development more complex. Vue applications often have a lot of state that can be difficult to maintain using the traditional solutions. That's where client-side routing comes into play.

9.1.2 *Understanding client-side routing*

In client-side routing, the routing work is done on the client. Client-side routing can be more difficult to get your head around (at least it was for me). The best way to explain it is to walk through the same example of clicking a link in the Hacker News app.

When an application uses client-side routing, you still make an initial request for the page, which is routed on the server side. If the Hacker News app were client-side routed, you would make an initial request to https://news.ycombinator.com/. The server would use the path to respond, and the browser would render the document it received.

The difference is, the server returns the same content whether the path is /new, /top, or /. The real routing work is done on the client. When the browser has loaded the JavaScript, a client-side routing library, like Vue Router, uses the path in the URL to render the correct content.

When the user clicks the /show link in the browser, the client-side router prevents the browser from making a new request to https://news.ycombinator.com/show. Instead, the router changes the URL without causing a page reload, and the page contents are rerendered with the show feed (figure 9.3). The point here is that *the page content updates, but the page maintains the same state.*

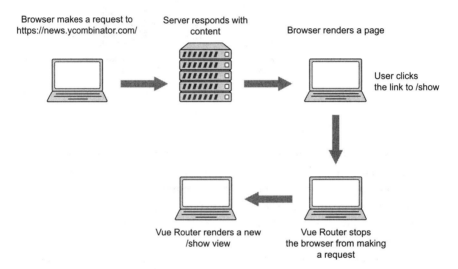

Figure 9.3   Client-side routing

Client-side routing makes the experience for the user faster, because they don't need to wait for an HTTP request to finish. It also improves the experience for the developer: it's much easier to develop apps that keep state between views using client-side routing.

In the Hacker News application, you're going to add support for multiple feeds using Vue Router. At the end of this section, you'll add a bare-bones router setup to the application. Before you add it to the project, you need to know some of the basic Vue Router concepts.

9.1.3   *Understanding Vue Router concepts*

Vue Router is the Vue client-side routing library. If you add client-side routing to a Vue project, then you're going to use Vue Router. It's by far the most advanced Vue routing library, and it's maintained by the Vue organization.

Vue Router matches the path of a URL to a component that it should render. You configure the paths that Vue Router should match with a *routes array*.

The routes array is an array of *route config* objects. A route config object can have lots of properties, but the most important are `path` and `component`. The `path` property is used to match against the current path in the URL, and `component` is the component that should be rendered for the matched path.

You can see an example of a routes array in the next listing. This routes array would match the path /item to an `ItemView` component, and the path / would match a `Main` component.

Listing 9.1   A routes array

```
import Main from './Main.vue'
import ItemView from './ItemView.vue'

const routes = [
  { path: '/', component: Main },
  { path: '/item', component: ItemView }
]
```

Matches the Main component for the / path

Matches the ItemView component for the /item path

By default, Vue Router just matches a route. You need to render a `RouterView` component, which is a Vue Router component that renders the currently matched route component.

You can think of `RouterView` as a placeholder. If the current route is /item, and /item matched the `ItemView` component, then a `RouterView` component would render an `ItemList` component as follows:

```
<template>
  <router-view />
</template>
```

Vue Router is a plugin like Vuex. To use the `RouterView` component, you need to install Vue Router on Vue, as shown in the next listing.

Listing 9.2   Using Vue Router to render an App component

```
import Vue from 'vue'
import VueRouter from 'vue-router'

const App = { template: '<div></div>' }

Vue.use(VueRouter)

const router = new VueRouter({
  routes: [{ path: '/', component: App }]
})

const app = new Vue({
  router,
  el: '#app',
  template: '<router-view />'
})
```

Installs Vue Router on Vue

Creates a router instance that will match the App component for the / path

Passes a router instance to Vue

Renders the matched component

You can use Vue Router to render components with a routes array and a `RouterView` component. Vue Router also links between pages without triggering a page load by using a `RouterLink` component. `RouterLink` accepts a `to` prop to link to a path, like so:

```
<router-link to="/item">item</item>
```

By default, a `RouterLink` component renders as an `<a>` element. When the element is clicked, Vue Router prevents the browser from reloading the page, updates the URL, and rerenders the `RouterView`.

> **NOTE** The `RouterLink` and `RouterView` components are registered as global components when Vue Router is installed on Vue, so there's no need to register the components locally.

That's the basic setup for Vue Router. The final Vue Router feature you need to know is dynamic route matching.

9.1.4   *Understanding dynamic route matching*

It's common to use part of a route to generate the content for a page. Think about a blog post with the path /item/1234; here, the second part of the path is the ID of the blog post. In server-side routing, the server would use this ID to generate the correct page. You can use the same technique in Vue Router using dynamic segments.

You define dynamic segments in a path, denoted by a colon (:). For example, a dynamic segment for `id` would look like this:

```
import ItemView from './ItemView.vue'

const routes = [
  { path: '/item/:id', component: ItemView }  ◁———┐ Matches an ItemView component
]                                                   for /item with a dynamic id segment
```

Matched dynamic segments are available in Vue instances on the `route` object (`$route.params`), which is added by Vue Router when you install it on Vue. You can use the dynamic segment value in a component as follows:

```
<template>
  <p>The ID is {{$route.params.id}}</p>
</template>
```

For fine-grained matching, you can use *regex* in the dynamic path.

> **NOTE** If you're unfamiliar with regex (regular expressions), you can read about them on MDN—http://mng.bz/edRZ.

The following rule matches any /top or /new paths and saves the value as a `type` property on the `$route.params` object. It also matches an optional page segment:

```
const routes = [
  { path: '/:type(top|new)/:page?', component: ItemView }
]
```

You can see an example of these advanced route patterns in table 9.1.

Table 9.1 Dynamic path matching

Pattern	Path	$route.params
/:type(top|new)	/top	`{type: 'top'}`
/:type(top|new)/:page	/new/123	`{type: 'new', page: '123'}`
/:type(top|new)/:page	/another-page/123	Unmatched

> **NOTE** You can read more about dynamic matching in the Vue Router docs—
> https://router.vuejs.org/en/essentials/dynamic-matching.html.

Now that you've learned the basic concepts, you can add Vue Router to the Hacker News application.

9.1.5 *Adding Vue Router to an application*

In this section, you'll add Vue Router to the application. By the end of the section, the app will be using Vue Router to render the `ItemList` component.

First, you need to install Vue Router. Run the following command in the command line to install Vue Router as a dependency:

```
npm install --save vue-router
```

Now you need to create the routes array file. The Hacker News app will support five paths: /top, /new, /show, /ask, and /job. Each of these paths is a different Hacker News list.

You'll use dynamic path-matching to match each of these routes as a `type` segment. The path will also match an optional `page` segment. So a path of /top/3 would create a `$route.params` object of `{ type: 'top', page: '3' }`. The second object in the routes array redirects a request from the root (/) to /top so that you have always access to a `type` parameter, even on the default route.

Create a file named src/router/routes.js, and add the following code.

Listing 9.3 An array of `RouteConfig` objects

```
import ItemList from '../views/ItemList.vue'

export default [
  { path: '/:type(top|new|show|ask|job)/:page?', component: ItemList }
  { path: '/', redirect: '/top' }
]
```

Sets the dynamic type segment that matches top, new, show, ask, and job. Also supports the optional page segment.

Redirects the root request to top so the app has the correct property

Next, you'll create a router configuration file. The configuration file will export an object that you'll use to create the router instance. It's similar to the store config file you added in chapter 7.

The configuration object will have two properties, `mode` and `routes`. `mode` sets how Vue Router controls the URL. You'll use the history mode, which tells Vue Router to use the `window.history.pushState` method under the hood to set the URL without triggering a page load. `routes` is the routes array that defines which routes should be matched.

Create a file named src/router/router-config.js, and add the code from the following listing.

Listing 9.4   Router config file

```
import routes from './routes'

export default {
  mode: 'history',
  routes
}
```

Now you can create a router instance using the route config. Open the src/main.js entry file, and add the following `import` statements to the file below the existing `import` statements:

```
import Router from 'vue-router'
import routerConfig from './router/router-config'
```

Add the following code to src/main.js, below the code that creates a store instance, but before the code that creates the Vue instance:

```
Vue.use(Router)
const router = new Router(routerConfig)
```

> **NOTE**   If you are having trouble adding this code to the file, you can see the finished file in the chapter-10 branch src/main.js.

As with Vuex, you need to pass the router instance to Vue when it's instantiated in the entry file. Replace your Vue instantiation in src/mains.js with the following code:

```
new Vue({
  el: "#app",
  store,
  router,
  render: h => h(App),
})
```

Now that Vue Router is set up to match the path, you need to render a `RouterView` component in order to render the currently matched component. You'll replace the `ItemList` component in src/App.vue with a `RouterView` component.

While you're editing the `App` component, you should add `RouterLink` components to link to the different type of feeds. Open src/App.vue, and replace the `<template>` block with the code shown next.

Listing 9.5 Using `RouterView` to render components

```
<template>
  <div id="app">
    <header class="header">
      <nav class="inner">
        <router-link to="/top">Top</router-link>        ◁─┐  Adds links to
        <router-link to="/new">New</router-link>            different routes
        <router-link to="/show">Show</router-link>
        <router-link to="/ask">Ask</router-link>
        <router-link to="/job">Jobs</router-link>
      </nav>
    </header>
    <div class="view">
      <router-view :key="$route.params.type" />            ◁─
    </div>
  </div>
</template>
```

Renders the app using the `<router-view>`
component, and adds a unique key so the
component rerenders when the type changes

Great—Vue Router is set up and running! Now, when you land on /top/2, the app will render the `ItemList` component. It's the same as before, except now you have access to the `type` and `page` parameters, which you can use to dynamically render different lists.

It's worth mentioning that so far you have no unit tests for the route configuration. Configuration is an example of something you should never test explicitly. Configuration doesn't contain much logic, and unit tests for configuration often require extreme mocking. You'll test the configuration implicitly with end-to-end tests later in the book; but as I mentioned in chapter 7, it's just not worth the time investment to test configuration explicitly with unit tests.

In the next chapter, you'll refactor the app to use the route parameters to render different feeds.

Summary

- Vue Router handles client-side routing in a Vue app.
- Vue Router is configured with a routes array.
- Vue Router renders the matched component in the `RouterLink` component.
- Dynamic path-matching adds matched values to the `$route.params` object.

Testing Vue Router

10

Vue Router is the official client-side routing library. If you add client-side routing to a Vue application, you'll use Vue Router. Therefore, you should learn how to test applications that use Vue Router.

To learn Vue Router testing techniques, you'll work on the Hacker News application. So far, the Hacker News application renders a single feed. You'll refactor the app to support multiple feeds and add *pagination*, so that users can navigate between pages of feed items.

> **DEFINITION** Pagination is adding paged content. A Google search page is paginated; you can click through many different pages of results (although you probably never do!).

In chapter 9, you added a Vue Router setup to the application. The router matches any of the Hacker News feeds—/top, /new, /show, /ask, and /jobs—and adds the values to the $route.params object as type. The router also matches an optional page parameter. For example, the path /top/2 will match with a $route.params object of

```
{ type: 'top', page: '2' }
```

You can use these values to render different feeds and different pages of items. To add these features, you'll learn how to test Vue Router instance properties, how to test RouterLink components, and how to access Vue Router properties in a store.

By the end of the chapter, you'll have added six item feeds and pagination to the Hacker News app. The first Vue Router features you'll learn to test are router properties.

> **NOTE** You're following on from the app you made in chapter 9. If you don't have the app, you can check out the chapter-10 Git branch following the instructions in appendix A.

10.1 *Testing router properties*

Vue Router adds two instance properties when you install it on Vue: the $route property and the $router property. These properties should come with a giant warning sign, because they can cause a lot of problems in tests. $route *and* $router *are added as read-only properties to the Vue instance.* It's impossible to overwrite their values after they've been added. I'll show you how to avoid this problem in the final part of this section.

The $route property contains information about the currently matched route, which includes any router parameters from dynamic segments. In the Hacker News app, you'll use the dynamic parameters to fetch different list types. If the path is /top, you'll fetch items for the top list; if the path is /new, you'll fetch items for the new list.

The other Router property is $router, which is the router instance that you pass to Vue in the entry file. The $router instance includes methods for controlling Vue Router. For example, it has a replace method you can use to update the current view without causing a page refresh.

The first property you'll write tests for is the $route property, to render different feed types and to render the current page.

10.1.1 *Testing the $route property*

If a component uses the $route instance property, then the property becomes a dependency of the component. When you test components with dependencies, you need to mock the dependencies to prevent errors.

The technique for mocking Vue Router instance properties is the same as for testing other instance properties. You can use the Vue Test Utils `mocks` mounting option to add it as an instance property in tests, as shown in the next listing.

Listing 10.1 Mocking a `$route` property

```
test('renders id param', () => {
  const wrapper = shallowMount(TestComponent, {
    mocks: {                              ←——  Adds the mock $route
      $route: {                                instance property
        params: {
          id: 123
        }
      }
    }
  })
  expect(wrapper.text()).toContain('123')  ←——┐ Asserts that the component
})                                             └ renders the id param as text
```

In the Hacker News app, you will use the `$route.params` properties to fetch items for the current type and to render the current page value.

You'll add tests for the following specs:

- `ItemList` dispatches `fetchListData` with `$route.params.type`.
- `ItemList` renders page 1/5 when the page parameter is 1 and `maxPage` is 5.
- `ItemList` renders page 2/5 when the page parameter is 2 and `maxPage` is 5.

The first test you write will be a refactor of an existing test to dispatch the `$route.params.type` value in the `fetchListData` action. Currently, in the `Item-List` component, you dispatch a `fetchListData` action with a `type` of `top` when the component mounts. The `ItemList` always fetches items for the top list.

You'll refactor this test and the component to use the `$route.params.type` value instead, so that it fetches a different list depending on the URL. Remember, a URL of /new/2 will have a `$route.params` object of `{ type: 'new', page: '2' }`.

In the test, you can add `$route` as an instance property using the `mocks` option and then assert that `dispatch` was called with the correct arguments. Open src/views/__tests__/ItemList.spec.js, and find the *dispatches* `fetchListData` *with top* test. Replace the test with the following code.

Listing 10.2 Passing props into a component

```
                                                     ┌ Creates a store using
                                                     └ the factory function
test('dispatches fetchListData with $route.params.type', async () => {
  expect.assertions(1)
  const store = createStore()                     ←——┘
  store.dispatch = jest.fn(() => Promise.resolve())  ←——┐ Replaces the store dispatch
                                                        └ method with a mock function
```

```
const type = 'a type'
const mocks = {                    ⟵——┐ Mocks the
  $route: {                             $route.params.type value
    params: {
      type
    }
  }
}                                            Asserts that dispatch was
createWrapper({ store, mocks })            called with the correct arguments
await flushPromises()
expect(store.dispatch).toHaveBeenCalledWith('fetchListData', { type })  ⟵——┘
})
```

Now refactor the dispatch call in src/views/ItemList.vue to use the $route.params
.type prop value, as follows:

```
this.$store.dispatch('fetchListData', {
  type: this.$route.params.type
})
```

Check that the test passes by running npm run test:unit. Oh no, failing tests! The
test you just wrote is actually passing, but all the other tests are now failing! The problem is, all the existing tests don't have $route.params as an instance property, so
they create an error when ItemList tries to access $route.params.type. For these
failing tests, you need to add $route as an instance property so that the code doesn't
throw an error when it tries to access $route.params.type.

Methods for patching $route and $router

Remember the leaky bucket analogy? A component that accesses properties that are
injected by Vue Router has lots of holes to patch. You can use two techniques to add
$route and $router to components in tests.

First, you can install Vue Router using a localVue. This technique is useful if you're
testing a component that accesses properties and methods on $route and
$router, but you don't need to control the values of $route and $router in the
tests. Remember, installing Vue Router sets $route and $router as read-only
properties, so you can't control their values in the test.

To control the data included in the $route and $router object, you need to use
the mocks mounting option. The mocks mounting option makes properties available
inside each mounted component.

This is where factory functions start to shine! Instead of editing the existing tests, you
need to edit only the factory function to add a new default option. You add a $route
object to the mocks object that the createWrapper factory function uses.

Open src/views/__tests__/ItemList.spec.js, and in the createWrapper function
in the mocks object, add a $route object. Set a default type value, as shown next,

because the `ItemList` will always have a `type` parameter in production; but leave
`page` undefined because it can sometimes be `undefined` in production:

```
$route: {
  params: { type: 'top' }
},
```

Now run the tests with `npm run test:unit`. Fantastic—you filled in the leaky bucket, and all the tests are passing!

With that small change, you've added support for multiple lists! Open the dev server and take a look: `npm run serve`. If you click the links in the header, the app will render different lists—magic!

You're only a few pages in, and you've already added support for different lists. The rest of the chapter will be spent adding pagination.

Because the app receives an unknown number of items from the API and will display 20 items per page, the app should indicate how many pages (of 20 items each) exist. The app will render the current page and the max page in `ItemList`. For example, if you were on page 2 and there were 21 pages worth of items in the store, the app would render the text "2/21." You can access the current page on the `$route` `.params` object, and you can get the maximum page value from the `maxPage` getter that you wrote in chapter 7.

There are two tests you should write to test that you're rendering the correct page information. One test will set `$route.params.page` and the `maxPage` getter. The other test handles cases where the `$route.params` object is `undefined`.

First you'll add a test for when `$route.params.page` is `undefined`. The page parameter is `undefined` if the current path doesn't include a page segment, so if the path is /top, the `page` parameter would be `undefined`. In this case, you should default to the first page of items.

In the test, you'll create a store with a `maxPage` getter that returns 5 and then assert that the component text includes "1/5." Add the test from the next code listing to the `describe` block in src/views/__tests__/ItemList.spec.js.

Listing 10.3 Creating a store with a `maxPage` getter

```
test('renders 1/5 when on page 1 of 5', () => {
  const store = createStore({
    getters: {
      maxPage: () => 5           Sets the maxPage getter
    }                            to return 5
  })
  const wrapper = createWrapper({ store })              Asserts that ItemList
  expect(wrapper.text()).toContain('1/5')               renders "1/5"
})
```

The second test will check that you use the `$route.params.page` property to display the correct page if it exists. To check this, you'll mock the `$route.params` object. Add the next code to src/views/__tests__/ItemList.spec.js.

Listing 10.4 Mocking `$route.params`

```
test('renders 2/5 when on page 2 of 5', () => {
  const store = createStore({
    getters: {
      maxPage: () => 5
    }
  })
  const mocks = {
    $route: {
      params: {
        page: '2'
      }
    }
  }
  const wrapper = createWrapper({ mocks, store })
  expect(wrapper.text()).toContain('2/5')
})
```

Make sure the tests fail: `npm run test:unit`. Now make the tests pass by rendering the correct page/max page values in the `ItemList`. Open src/views/ItemList.vue, and add the next code to the `<template>` block.

Listing 10.5 Using the `$route.params` value in the template

```
<span>
  {{$route.params.page || 1}}/{{$store.getters.maxPage}}          ◁─────┐
</span>
```
Displays page/maxPage using route params and maxPage; defaults to 1 if there is no page param

Run the tests with `npm run test:unit`. Great—the tests are passing.

You're making the assumption that the page parameter is always valid. Making those kind of assumptions is dangerous, especially because the user can control the page param by changing the URL. You should add some code to handle invalid values and redirect to a valid page if the `page` value is invalid. To do that, you'll learn how to test the `$router` property.

10.1.2 *Testing the $router property*

`$router` is the router instance, and it contains helper methods to control the routing programmatically. `$router` is an instance property, so you can control the `$router` value in tests by using the Vue Test Utils `mocks` mounting option.

In your app, you're using the page URL to render the current page. So, when a user lands on /top/5, and there are 40 pages of items, they'll see that they are on page 5 out of 40 (5/40).

But what happens if the user lands on page /top/500 when there are only 10 pages of items? Right now, the `ItemList` would render 500/10. That's going to look pretty buggy to the user. Instead of leaving them on a buggy page, you should redirect them to the first page of items.

To send users to a different page, you can use the `$router.replace` method. `$router.replace` replaces the current URL and updates the `RouterLink`. It's like a redirect in your code.

You'll add a test that checks that the component calls `replace` with the first page of the current list the user is on if the `page` parameter is larger than the max page. Add the code that follows to the `describe` block in src/views/__tests__/ItemList.spec.js.

Listing 10.6   Testing a `router.replace` call

```
test('calls $router.replace when the page parameter is greater than the max
    page count', async () => {
  expect.assertions(1)
  const store = createStore({
    getters: {
      maxPage: () => 5
    }
  })
  const mocks = {              ◁────  Create mocks to pass
    $route: {                          to createWrapper
      params: {
        page: '1000'
      }
    },
    $router: {
      replace: jest.fn()
    }
  }                                        Assert $router.replace was
  createWrapper({ mocks, store })          called with the correct arguments
  await flushPromises()
  expect(mocks.$router.replace).toHaveBeenCalledWith('/top/1')   ◁────
})
```

Check that the test fails with an assertion error: `npm run test:unit`. Now you need to update the component to perform the redirect. You'll add the `$router.replace` call inside the `loadItems` method, after the initial call to `fetchListData`. If you call it before `fetchListData` has completed, you won't have the correct data in the store to calculate how many pages there are.

Open src/views/ItemList.vue, and replace the `loadItems` method with the following code.

Listing 10.7   Calling `$router.replace`

```
loadItems () {
  this.$bar.start()
  this.$store.dispatch('fetchListData', {
    type: this.$route.params.type
```

```
    }).then(() => {
        if (this.$route.params.page > this.$store.getters.maxPage) {
            this.$router.replace(`/${this.$route.params.type }/1`)
            return
        }
        this.$bar.finish()
    })
    .catch(() => {
        this.$bar.fail()
    })
}
```

Now the unit tests will pass again: `npm run test:unit`. You could write other tests here to check that different page parameters are handled. For example, what would happen if the path was /top/abcd, or /top/–123? The tests would be similar to the test that you just wrote, so I won't show you how to write them here.

Congratulations, you've successfully added tests for logic that uses the `$route` and `$router` properties—the most notorious instance properties to write tests for. They are notorious because they have a common gotcha that catches a lot of developers out.

10.1.3 Avoiding common gotchas

The `$route` and `$router` properties are added as read-only properties to the Vue constructor prototype when Vue Router is installed. Whatever you do, *there's no way to overwrite Vue Router properties after they've been added to the Vue prototype.* I've seen many people stung by this—it's probably the most common issue people come to me with!

Remember in the last chapter when I talked about how the base Vue constructor is like a master copy? You shouldn't write on the master copy, because everything that's copied from it will include that writing. Installing Vue Router on the base constructor is like taking a permanent marker and scribbling all over the master copy. The Vue Router properties are never coming off, and you can't overwrite them no matter what you do.

I've already spoken about why you should use a `localVue` constructor and avoid installing on the base constructor. This is especially important for Vue Router. *Always use a `localVue` to install Vue Router in tests.* You must make sure that no file in your test suite imports a file that calls `Vue.use` with Vue Router. It's easy to accidentally import a file that includes `Vue.use`. Even if you don't run a module, if the module is imported, then the code inside it will be evaluated. You can see an example in figure 10.1.

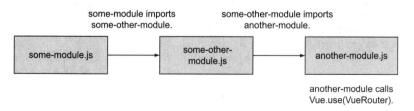

Figure 10.1 Unintentionally calling `Vue.use` when importing a module

I hope that you now share my wariness of Vue Router in tests. Now that you know to avoid installing Vue Router on the Vue base constructor, it's time to learn how to test the RouterLink component.

10.2 *Testing the RouterLink component*

RouterLink components add Vue Router–friendly links to navigate between views. If you use logic to render RouterLink components, then you should write tests for them.

To learn how to test RouterLink components, you're going to add pagination links to the Hacker News app. The app will render a RouterLink component that links to the previous page or the next page. For example, if you're on /top/3, you would render one RouterLink component that links to /top/2, and one that links to /top/4 (figure 10.2). If there are no previous pages (or no more pages) to navigate to, you'll render an <a> tag without an href (figure 10.3).

< prev   3/19   more >   < prev   1/18   more >

Figure 10.2 Pagination on the third page    **Figure 10.3 Pagination on the first page**

You can write the following four tests for ItemList to check that the pagination links are rendered correctly:

- ItemList renders a RouterLink to the previous page if one exists.
- ItemList renders an a tag without an href if there are no previous pages.
- ItemList renders a RouterLink to the next page if one exists.
- ItemList renders an a tag without an href if there are no next pages.

To create a RouterLink component that links to another view, you pass the Router-Link a to prop with a path like so:

```
<router-link to="/top/2">top</router-link>
```

To test that you render a RouterLink to another page, you need to assert that a RouterLink component receives the correct to prop. Remember, you can test component props with the wrapper find method. find uses a selector to get a matching node wrapper from the rendered output, as shown in the next listing.

Listing 10.8 Testing that a ChildComponent receives a prop

```
import { shallowMount } from '@vue/test-utils'
import ChildComponent from './ChildComponent.vue'
import ParentComponent from './ParentComponent.vue'                    Asserts that
                                                              ChildComponent receives
test('renders Child', () => {                                     a to prop of /path
  const wrapper = shallowMount(ParentComponent)
  expect(wrapper.find(ChildComponent).props().to).toBe('/path')    ◁——
})
```

The problem is, Vue Router does not export the `RouterLink` or `RouterView` components, so you can't use the `RouterLink` as a selector. The solution is to control the component that is rendered as a `RouterLink` and use the controlled component as a selector instead. You can control the rendered component with Vue Test Utils. When a parent Vue component renders a child component, Vue attempts to resolve the child component on the parent component instance. With the Vue Test Utils `stubs` option, you can override this process. For example, you could set the component to resolve all `RouterLink` components as `<div>` elements, as shown in the following listing.

Listing 10.9　Stubbing `RouterLink` in a test

```
const wrapper = shallowMount(TestComponent, {
  stubs: {
    RouterLink: 'div'
  }
})
```

◁── Sets all RouterLink components to render as <div> elements

> **TIP** You can use the component name, a camelCase version of the name, or a PascalCase (capitalized) version of the name in the `stubs` mounting option. So `router-link`, `routerLink`, and `RouterLink` would all stub the `RouterLink` component.

Vue Test Utils exports a `RouterLinkStub` component that behaves like a `RouterLink` component. You can stub all `RouterLink` components to resolve as the `RouterLinkStub` component and use `RouterLinkStub` as a selector, as shown next.

Listing 10.10　Using a `RouterLinkStub`

```
import { shallowMount, RouterLinkStub } from '@vue/test-utils'
import ParentComponent from './ParentComponent.vue'

test('renders RouterLink', () => {
  const wrapper = shallowMount(ParentComponent, {
    stubs: {
      RouterLink: RouterLinkStub
    }
  })
  expect(wrapper.find(RouterLinkStub).props().to).toBe('/path')
})
```

◁── Stubs the RouterLink component with a RouterLinkStub component

> **NOTE** You can read more about the stubs mounting option in the vue-test-utils docs at https://vue-test-utils.vuejs.org/api/options.html#stubs.

You'll use this stubbing technique to test that you render a `RouterLink` with the correct props. In your `ItemList` test file, add `RouterLink` to the `stubs` option in the `createWrapper` factory function. In src/views/__tests__/ItemList.spec.js, import `RouterLinkStub` from Vue Test Utils as shown next:

```
import { shallowMount, createLocalVue, RouterLinkStub } from '@vue/test-utils'
```

Next, in the `createWrapper` factory function, add a `stubs` property to the `defaultMountingOptions` object to stub all `RouterLink` components with the `RouterLinkStub`:

```
stubs: {
  RouterLink: RouterLinkStub
}
```

Now you can use the `RouterLinkStub` component as a selector to find rendered `RouterLink` components. The first test to write checks that `ItemList` renders a `RouterLink` with the previous page if one exists. In the test, you should find a `RouterLinkStub` and check that it has the correct `to` prop and text.

Add the code from the next listing to the `describe` block in src/views/__tests__/ItemList.spec.js.

Listing 10.11   Using `RouterLinkStub` to find a component

```
test('renders a RouterLink with the previous page if one exists', () => {
  const mocks = {                        ◁─────┐   Creates mocks to pass to the
    $route: {                                  │   createWrapper factory function
      params: { page: '2' }
    }
  }
  const wrapper = createWrapper({ mocks })          Finds the stubbed router-link
                                                    with a RouterLinkStub selector

  expect(wrapper.find(RouterLinkStub).props().to).toBe('/top/1')   ◁────────
  expect(wrapper.find(RouterLinkStub).text()).toBe('< prev')
})
```

You can write another test to make sure the `ItemList` component renders a RouterLink for the next page. To do this, you'll need use the `createStore` factory function to create a store that has enough items to generate a next page. Add the two tests from the following listing to your test suite.

Listing 10.12   Using `RouterLinkStub` as a selector

```
test('renders a RouterLink with the next page if one exists', () => {
  const store = createStore({
    getters: {
      maxPage: () => 3
    }
  })
  const mocks = {
    $route: {
      params: { page: '1' }
    }
  }
  const wrapper = createWrapper({ store, mocks })
  expect(wrapper.find(RouterLinkStub).props().to).toBe('/top/2')
  expect(wrapper.find(RouterLinkStub).text()).toBe('more >')
})
```

```
test('renders a RouterLink with the next page when no page param exists', () => {
  const store = createStore({
    getters: {
      maxPage: () => 3
    }
  })
  const wrapper = createWrapper({ store
})
  expect(wrapper.find(RouterLinkStub).props().to).toBe('/top/2')
  expect(wrapper.find(RouterLinkStub).text()).toBe('more >')
})
```

Before you add the code to the `ItemList` component, you should write the tests for when a previous page or next page doesn't exist.

When there isn't a previous page, the `ItemList` should render an `<a>` tag without an href, which you'll style to appear disabled. You'll do the same thing if there isn't a next page. Add the tests from the following code to the `describe` block in src/views/__tests__/ItemList.spec.js.

Listing 10.13 Testing that `router-link` is rendered

```
test('renders an <a> element without an href if there are no previous pages',
    () => {
  const wrapper = createWrapper()                      Asserts that the <a> element
                                                       doesn't have an href
  expect(wrapper.find('a').attributes().href).toBe(undefined)
  expect(wrapper.find('a').text()).toBe('< prev')      Asserts that the <a> element
})                                                     contains correct text
test('renders an <a> element without an href if there are no next pages', ()
    => {
  const store = createStore({
    getters: {
      maxPage: () => 1                   Sets maxPage to 1, so there
    }                                    isn't a next page to link to
  })
  const wrapper = createWrapper({ store })

  expect(wrapper.findAll('a').at(1).attributes().href).toBe(undefined)
  expect(wrapper.findAll('a').at(1).text()).toBe('more >')
})
```

Now make the test pass by rendering `RouterLink` components in the `ItemList` template. Add the code from the next listing to src/views/ItemList.vue in the `<template>` block. Warning: this code block is ugly.

Listing 10.14 Using `router-link` in the template

```
<router-link                               Creates a link to the previous page
  v-if="$route.params.page > 1"            using type and page params
  :to="'/' + $route.params.type + '/' + ($route.params.page - 1)">
```

Escapes the < character, to avoid
potential HTML parse errors

Renders an <a> element
if no previous page exists

```
   &lt; prev
</router-link>
<a v-else>&lt; prev</a>
<span>{{ $route.params.page || 1 }}/{{ $store.getters.maxPage }}</span>
<router-link
   v-if="($route.params.page || 1) < $store.getters.maxPage"
   :to="'/' + $route.params.type + '/' + ((Number($route.params.page) || 1) + 1)">
      more &gt;
</router-link>
<a v-else>more &gt;</a>
```

Constructs a link for the
next page if one exists

Run the tests and watch them pass. As a side note: the code in the template is just bad. There's a lot of repetition, and it's difficult to read—this is a prime candidate for refactoring. The reason I had you add it is because it's simple and it makes the test pass. Now that the test passes, you're free to refactor the component. Refactoring is easy when you have unit tests. I won't show you how to refactor in this chapter, but you can refactor yourself and compare to a refactored version in the chapter-11 branch.

Rendering Vue Router components in tests

Vue Router components are registered as global components when you install Vue Router. They are available for a component to render only if Vue Router was installed on a Vue constructor before the Vue instance was instantiated. If you mount a component that renders a `RouterLink` or `RouterView` component without either stubbing them or installing Vue Router on a `localVue` constructor, you will get warnings in your test output.

I recommend that you stub these components with the `stubs` mounting option in a wrapper factory function rather than installing Vue Router on a `localVue` constructor, so that you can overwrite Vue Router properties if required.

Now you've rendered pagination links and the current page in the `ItemList` component. There's one problem, though—the paginated pages don't change the content that's rendered. To change the items that are rendered, you need to edit the `displayItems` getter to use the route `page` parameter. You can do that by syncing Vuex and Vue Router.

10.3 *Using Vuex with Vue Router*

It can be useful to use Vue Router properties in a Vuex store. You can use the library `vuex-router-sync` to synchronize Vuex and Vue Router to make the `route` object available in the store.

In the Hacker News app, you're going to use the current page number, defined in `route.params`, to display the correct items and add pagination. You'll do that by updating the `displayItems` Vuex getter to use the current `page` parameter from the `route` object.

10.3.1 *Adding the route to the store*

You need to add the route to the store, so that you can access the `$route.params` object in a store getter. You can use the `vuex-router-sync` library to add the `route` object for you.

The first step is to install the package as a dependency. Run the following `install` command:

```
npm install --save vuex-router-sync
```

Add the following `import` statement to src/main.js:

```
import { sync } from 'vuex-router-sync'
```

In src/main.js, after you create the store and router instances, call `sync` to sync them together as follows:

```
sync(store, router)
```

Now the store will include a `route` object, which has the same value as `$route` in component instances.

10.3.2 *Using router parameters in the store*

To add pagination, you need to display a range of items depending on the current `page` parameter. For example, if you're on page 2, you should display the items from 20–40. If you're on page 10, you'll display the items from 200–220. This way, the user will feel like they're navigating between pages.

In your app, you use the `displayItems` getter to return the items to render. Right now, `displayItems` return the first 20 items from `state.items`. To achieve pagination, you'll update the getter to use the `route.params.page` value to calculate which items to return.

You need to add a new test for the `displayItems` getter to check that you return the items from index 20 to index 40 if the route page parameter is 2. In the test, you'll create an array of numbers to use as mock items and then create a mock `state` object. You call the `displayItems` getter with the mock state and check that the getter returns the correct items. Add the code from the next listing to src/store/__tests__/getters.spec.js, inside the `describe` block.

> **Listing 10.15 Testing a getter that uses the `route` object**

```
test('displayItems returns items 20-40 if page is 2', () => {
  const items = Array(40).fill().map((v, i) => i)           ⟵  Creates an array of 40 items.
  const result = getters.displayItems({          ⟵              Each item will be a number of
    items,                      Calls displayItems                the item index, so the array
    route: {                    with a mock state                 will be 0, 1, 2, 3 up to 39.
      params: {
        page: '2'        ⟵  Sets the mock page
    }                        parameter to 2
```

```
    }
  })
  const expectedResult = items.slice(20, 40)
  expect(result).toEqual(expectedResult)
})
```
> Asserts that displayItems returns items with numbers from 19 to 39

You'll add another test case to make sure the getter returns the remaining items if there isn't a full page of items remaining. Add the code from the next listing to the `describe` block in src/store/__tests__/getters.spec.js.

```
test('displayItems returns remaining items if there are insufficient
 items', () => {
  const numberArray = Array(21).fill().map((v, i) => i)
  const store = {
    items: numberArray,
    route: {
      params: {
        page: '2'
      }
    }
  }
  const result = getters.displayItems(store)
  expect(result).toHaveLength(1)
  expect(result[0]).toEqual(numberArray[20])
})
```
> Creates an array of 21 items. Each item will be a number of the item index, so the array will be 0, 1, 2, 3 up to 20.

> Asserts that the item is the last item in the items array

To make the test pass, you need to update the `displayItems` getter. Open src/store/getters.js, and replace the `displayItems` getter with the code shown in listing 10.17. This code uses the OR operator to default to a value of 1 for `page`. If `Number(state.route.params.page)` returns a number, the expression will be evaluated as truthy and will return the number. If `Number(state.route.params.page)` returns undefined, the expression will evaluate to false and return the value 1.

NOTE   If this usage of the OR operator confuses you, check out the guide on MDN. It explains how logical operators return values—http://mng.bz/zMMg.

> Casts the state.route.params.page value to a number; defaults to 1 if the page value is undefined

```
displayItems (state) {
  const page = Number(state.route.params.page) || 1
  const start = (page - 1) * 20
  const end = page * 20
```
> Calculates where the array should be sliced from

> Calculates what position in the array the last item should be

```
    return state.items.slice(start, end)
},
```

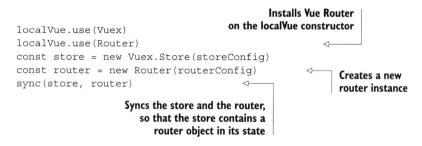 Returns an array containing the correct items

Now run your tests. Great—the new test passed, but another unit tests is failing with ugly type errors.

The problem is that previous tests that call the `displayItems` getter don't have a `route` object in the state. That means there's a type error when `displayItems` tries to access `route.params`. To fix this, you need to update previous tests to include a `route` object that contains an empty `params` object.

Open src/store/__tests__/getters.spec.js. You need to update the test `display-Items` *returns the first 20 items from the list matching state* .`displayItems`. In the `state` object, add a `route` object that with an empty `params` object as follows:

```
const state = {
  // ..
  route: {
    params: {}
  }
}
```

Now run the tests. You still have a failing test: the test in src/store/__tests__/store-config.spec.js is creating an error. Leaky buckets everywhere! It's the same problem—`route` isn't defined. In this test, though, you aren't mocking the state, so you need to sync the router and store in the test with `vuex-router-sync`.

You'll create a `router` instance and call the `vuex-router-sync` sync method before you create the `store` instance. Open src/store/__tests__/store-config.spec.js, and import sync from `vuex-router-sync` as follows:

```
import Router from 'vue-router'
import { sync } from 'vuex-router-sync'
import routerConfig from '../../router/router-config'
```

Add the code from the following listing to src/store/__tests__/store-config.spec.js. The purpose is to create an initial state just like the initial state you create in the app entry file.

Listing 10.18 Syncing Vuex and Vue Router on a `localVue`

```
localVue.use(Vuex)
localVue.use(Router)
const store = new Vuex.Store(storeConfig)
const router = new Router(routerConfig)
sync(store, router)
```

Installs Vue Router on the localVue constructor

Creates a new router instance

Syncs the store and the router, so that the store contains a router object in its state

Now you've set up the `displayItems` getter to handle pages. That means the app will support pagination. Run the development server—npm run serve—and then open the development server and take a look.

The app is looking good now. It renders different feeds, and it has pagination to navigate between pages of feed items. In the next chapter, you'll learn how to write and test mixins and filters to add the finishing touches to the UI.

Summary

- The `$route` and `$router` properties cause difficult-to-debug problems when they are installed on the base Vue class.
- `RouterLink` components can be tested using the Vue Test Utils `stubs` mounting option.
- You can sync Vuex and Vue Router using the `vuex-router-sync` library.

Exercises

1 Write a test to check that the following component calls `injectedMethod` with the `$route.path` Vue instance value:

```
// TestComponent.vue
<script>
export default {
  beforeMount() {
    this.injectedMethod(this.$route.path)
  }
}
</script>
```

2 What library can you use if you want to use the current `$route` values inside a Vuex store?

Testing mixins and filters

This chapter covers

- Using Vue mixins and filters in a project
- Writing unit tests for Vue mixins and filters
- Writing unit tests for components that use Vue mixins and filters

Mixins and filters are great ways to add reusable functionality to Vue components. In this chapter, you'll learn what mixins and filters are and how to write unit tests for them.

At this point in the book, the Hacker News application is looking good. You have Vue, Vue Router, and Vuex—the holy trinity of Vue applications—working together to create a dynamic Hacker News feed. In this chapter, you'll add some finishing touches to improve the UI.

The first section is about mixins. You'll learn what mixins are and how to test them by creating a mixin to set the document title depending on the view that's currently rendered. You'll learn how to write unit tests for the mixin itself and how to write unit tests for components that use the mixin.

After you've added mixins, I'll teach you how to test filters. In the same way, you'll learn what filters are, how to write unit tests for filters, and how to write unit tests for components that use filters.

Let's start by looking at mixins.

11.1 Testing mixins

Mixins add functionality to Vue components (there's a more robust definition of mixins later in this chapter). They can contain complicated logic, so it's important to learn how to test them.

Currently, the document title of the Hacker News app is vue-hackernews—not very professional! You'll write a mixin to add a different document title depending on the view component that's rendered.

Don't worry if you aren't familiar with mixins. Before you write any code, I'll show you what mixins actually are and why you use them in applications.

11.1.1 Understanding mixins

Mixins extend Vue components with extra options. A mixin can contain any component options, like methods or hooks, that get *mixed in* to a component.

When you create a component, any registered mixins are combined with the component's options. You can see an example mixin in the next listing.

Listing 11.1 An example mixin

```
const logHelloOnCreateMixin = {          A mixin
  created ()
    console.log('hello')
  }
}
                                         Creates and mounts a Vue instance that
                                         uses the logHelloOnCreate mixin. The
new Vue({                                component will log hello when it's created.
  mixins: [logHelloOnCreateMixin ],
  template: '<div />'
}).$mount()
```

Mixins work by *merging* options into a component's options. When conflicting options occur in a component and a mixin, Vue follows a merge strategy to combine the options. Different properties have different strategies. For example, lifecycle hooks are merged into an array and called one after the other. Object properties like methods and components are combined into a single object. If conflicting properties exist, the component property will override the mixin property.

> **NOTE** You can read in detail about the merge strategy in the Vue docs— https://vuejs.org/v2/guide/mixins.html#Option-Merging.

You can register mixins to be used by components in two ways: globally or locally. To register a global mixin, you call Vue.mixin with the mixin you want to register:

```
Vue.mixin(logHelloOnCreateMixin)
```

Global mixins add options that are available to *every* future component created, so you should be careful that you want this behavior when you register a global mixin.

You can also register a mixin locally on a component by defining it in the component options object, as shown next:

```
const TestComponent = {
  mixins: [logHelloOnCreateMixin]
}
```

A locally registered mixin will apply only to the component that it's registered on. Both ways of registering mixins are valid, so I'll teach you how to test components that use local mixins, as well as components that use global mixins. Before you write tests for components that use mixins, you need to learn how to write and test a mixin itself.

11.1.2 *Writing tests for mixins*

The process of testing a mixin is simple. You register the mixin on a component, mount the component, and then check that the mixin produced the expected behavior.

Imagine you want to test that a `logHelloOnCreateMixin` calls `console.log` with "hello" when a component that uses the mixin is mounted. You could write a test that spies on `console.log`, mount a minimal component with the mixin, and assert that `console.log` was called, as shown in the following listing.

Listing 11.2 Testing a mixin

```
test('logHelloOnCreateMixin logs hello', () => {
  jest.spyOn(console, 'log')                          ◁── Spies on console.log
  const Component = {
    render() {},                                      ◁── Adds an empty render function to avoid Vue
    mixins: [logHelloOnCreateMixin]                       warnings when mounting the component
  }                                                   ◁── Registers the mixin
  shallowMount(Component)                                  on the component
  expect(console.log).toHaveBeenCalledWith('hello')   ◁──                    Mounts the
})                                                            Asserts that the console   component
                                                              log was called with "hello"
```

You can use the same technique to test any mixin. Create a simple component with the mixin registered, mount the component, and assert the output.

For the Hacker News app, you're going to write a mixin that sets the document title using a `title` property defined on a component. For example, when a component has a `title` property of `Home`, the page title should be set to *Vue HN | Home*, shown in the next listing.

Listing 11.3 Creating an instance with a mixin

```
new Vue({                                                              ◁── Creates a
  mixins: [titleMixin],          ◁── Registers titleMixin to change        new instance
  template: '<div />',               the document title using the
                                     component title property
```

```
    title: 'Home'
}).$mount()
```

You should write two tests for the mixin—one to check that the mixin sets the document title using the `title` property and another to test that it does not set the document title if no `title` property exists on the target component.

As I mentioned, to test that a mixin works correctly, you register it on a component, mount the component, and then assert that it produces the expected output. You should always be thrifty with your test code—the less test code there is, the easier it is to understand. In mixin tests, therefore, you should create a component with the minimum options you need to check that the mixin works correctly.

In your test, the minimum options are a `title` property, an empty `render` function to stop Vue errors, and a mixin array to register the mixin. After you create the component with those options, you can mount it and test that the `document.title` was updated with the value of the `title` property.

Create a test file, src/util/__tests__/mixins.spec.js, and add the code from the next listing.

Listing 11.4   Testing a mixin

```
import { mount } from '@vue/test-utils'
import { titleMixin } from '../mixins'

describe('titleMixin', () => {                          Creates a test
  test('set document.title using component title property', () => {    component
    const Component = {
      render() {},
      title: 'dummy title',
      mixins: [titleMixin]        Registers a mixin
    }                             on the component
    mount(Component)
    expect(document.title).toBe('Vue HN | dummy title')
  })                                             Asserts that document.title has
                                                 been updated to the correct value

  test('does not set document.title if title property does not exist', () =>
    {
    document.title = 'some title'        Sets the document title so that you
    const Component = {                  can assert that it hasn't updated
      render() {},                       after mounting the component
      mixins: [titleMixin]
    }
    mount(Component)
    expect(document.title).toBe('some title')
  })
})
```

NOTE   Editing the `document.title` in a test changes the `title` value for all other tests running in the current context (in Jest, each test file runs in its own context). That means you need to be careful that you don't run a test that asserts the `document.title` value is the same as a previous test; otherwise, one test could set the title correctly, and another test might not set the title at all but still pass because the previous test set it to the same value that the current test is asserting.

Now you need to add the code to make the test pass. Create a file for the mixin named src/util/mixins.js. Add the following code to the file to add the mixin and make the tests pass.

Listing 11.5 A title mixin

```
export const titleMixin = {
  mounted () {
    const title = this.$options.title
    if (title) {
      document.title = `Vue HN | ${title}`
    }
  }
}
```

Check that the test passes: `npm run test:unit`. So far, so good—you can register this mixin in your application and define a `title` property on a component to set the document title.

This works fine for a static title value. The problem is, you have an `ItemList` component that renders dynamic feeds. It would be great if the document title updated each time you switched feeds, so switching between top and new would change the title from *Vue HN | Top* to *Vue HN | New.*

To change the title to the list type, you need to access the $route object. You can't set the `title` property to be `this.$route.params.type`, because you can't access an object from inside itself. The solution is to add `title` as a function that gets called, as follows:

```
title () {
  return this.$route.params.type
}
```

To enable this functionality, you need to update the `titleMixin` to support `title` as a function. If `title` is a function, the mixin should call `title` with `this` set to the component instance.

Create a new test that checks that the mixin uses the return from a function. Add the code from the next listing to src/util/__tests__/mixins.spec.js.

Listing 11.6 Testing a mixin

```
test(' sets document.title using result of title if it is a function ', () => {
  const Component = {
    render() {},
```

```
    data () {                          ◁─────────────┐  Creates the titleValue
      return {                                       │  property on the instance
        titleValue: 'another dummy title'
      }
    },
    title () {                                          ┐  Returns the
      return this.titleValue          ◁─────────────────┘  titleValue
    },                                   ┐  Registers the
    mixins: [titleMixin]          ◁──────┘  titleMixin
  }                                                 ┐  Mounts the
  mount(Component)                  ◁───────────────┘  component
  expect(document.title).toBe('Vue HN | another dummy title')   ◁──────┐
})                                                                       │
                                                        Asserts that the title
                                                        was set using titleValue
```

You can make it pass by refactoring the mixin to use a `getTitle` function that calls `title` if it's a function and returns the value if it's not. In src/util/mixins.js, add the following code.

Listing 11.7   Calling the instance property if `title` is a function

```
function getTitle (vm) {
  const { title } = vm.$options          ◁───────┐  Destructures the title value
  if (title) {                                    │  from the component options
    return typeof title === 'function'  ◁────┐
      ? title.call(vm)                        │
      : title                         If title is a function, calls it with the
  }                                   component instance as the this value;
}                                     otherwise, returns the value of title
```

In src/util/mixins.js, replace the line in `titleMixin` where you define the `title` const with the next code:

```
const title = getTitle(this)
```

Run the tests: `npm run test:unit`. Great, now the mixin supports `title` as a function, which means you can access instance values to set the title. When you register the mixin on the `ItemList` component, you can set the document title using the `$router.params.type` value in a `title` function on the component.

The next step is to use the mixin in the `ItemList` component. As I mentioned earlier, you have two ways to register mixins in your application—locally and globally. I'll show you how to test components that register mixins locally first.

11.1.3 *Testing local mixins in components*

A mixin is one of many ways that you can add functionality to a component. In other words, a mixin is an implementation detail. Unit tests for components that use mixins should be unaware of the mixin—the tests should just test the output of the mixin.

There is no special technique for writing tests for components that use mixins. You write a test that checks for the desired output in a component, and then use a mixin to implement the functionality to produce the output.

For example, the `titleMixin` mixin sets the document title. The test will mount the component and then assert that the document title is set to the correct value. You could use a method, or a mixin, to add the functionality that will make the test pass.

Add the code from the next listing to the bottom of the `describe` block in src/ views/__tests__/ItemList.spec.js to test that the document title is updated.

Listing 11.8 Testing a mixin in a component

```
test('sets document.title with the capitalized type prop', () => {
  createWrapper({                            ◁──┐
    mocks: {                                     Shallow-mounts ItemList with the
      $route: { params: { type: 'top' } }        correct data and the propsData type
    }                                            that will be used to create the title
  })
  expect(document.title).toBe('Vue HN | Top')  ◁──┐
})                                                 Asserts that document.title
                                                   was updated using the mixin
                                                   and the type prop value
```

To pass this test, you need to register the mixin on the `ItemList` component and add a `title` function that returns `$route.params.type` capitalized.

Open src/views/ItemList.vue. Add the following `import` statement at the top of the `<script>` block to import `titleMixin`:

```
import { titleMixin } from '../util/mixins'
```

Then create a function after the `import` statements, just before the component options object. This helper function returns a string with the first letter uppercased, as shown in the next code snippet. You'll use it to capitalize the `$route.params.type` value:

```
function capitalizeFirstLetter (string) {
  return string.charAt(0).toUpperCase() + string.slice(1)
}
```

Now register the mixin on the component, and create a `title` method that returns the capitalized `type` value. Add the following options to the component options object in src/views/ItemList.vue as top-level properties:

```
export default {
  // ..

  title () {
    return `${capitalizeFirstLetter(this.$route.params.type)}`
  },

  mixins: [titleMixin],

  // ..
}
```

Run the tests with the command `npm run test:unit`. Great! You've added a local mixin and tests. Next I'll show you how to test global mixins in components. Spoiler: it's pretty much the same as testing a local mixin.

11.1.4 *Testing global mixins in components*

Just like local mixins, global mixins are an implementation detail. You can use the same test for a mixin whether it's registered globally or locally, because it will produce the same output.

You don't need to rewrite your existing test that checks that the document title is set to the `type` value. You can change how the mixin is registered, and the test will pass. This is the beauty of a test that doesn't check the implementation details—you're free to change how you add the functionality.

The difference between global mixins and local mixins is that global mixins need to be registered before a component is mounted. In production, you'll register `titleMixin` globally in the main entry file (src/main.js). This method works fine for the app, but you need a different strategy to register mixins before the tests run.

Before I show you how to register mixins before tests, you should register the mixin globally in the entry file and remove the local mixin from `ItemList`. Open src/main.js, and add the following code, so that you import `titleMixin`:

```
import { titleMixin } from './util/mixins'
```

To register global mixins, use the `Vue.mixin` method. Add the following code to the src/main.js file, somewhere after the `import` statement but before the Vue instance is created:

```
Vue.mixin(titleMixin)
```

Now the production application will apply `titleMixin` to every component. You can remove the existing code that registers `titleMixin` in the `ItemList` component. Open src/views/ItemList.vue, and remove the `mixins` option and the `titleMixin` import statement.

Run the tests again with `npm run test:unit`. The component mixin test will fail. The problem is, the mixin isn't registered in the test, as it will be in production. You have the following possible solutions:

- Create a `localVue` constructor, install the mixin on the `localVue`, and mount the component with the `localVue` constructor.
- Run a file before the tests to register global mixins on the Vue base constructor.

The best option is to register the mixin on the Vue base constructor before the tests run. It's less code, and you can use mixins in future tests without extra setup.

> ### Avoiding polluting the Vue base class
>
> I've told you that no matter what you do, you should never install a plugin or mixin on the Vue base constructor in tests. But the truth is less clear-cut. It's sometimes OK to pollute the Vue base constructor.
>
> In school, I was taught that you could never start a sentence with *and* or *but*. In general, this rule is good because it teaches you to be careful that your writing uses connectives correctly. *But* as I grew older, I learned that this rule isn't as strict as my teacher taught me. There are times where it's acceptable to begin a sentence with *but*.
>
> The rule I taught you earlier about never polluting the Vue base constructor is like the rule my teacher taught me. When you don't understand what you're doing, you should follow the rule; but as you get more experienced and begin to understand why the rule is important, you'll find cases where it's appropriate to break the rule.
>
> Mixins and filters are an example where you can break the rule. Before the tests run, you can add the mixins and filters that you'll use in the tests to the Vue constructor. That means they'll always be registered for each Vue instance created in the tests, but that's fine. In the live environment, you also always have the mixins and filters registered.
>
> The one time you shouldn't add mixins or filters globally is when they perform side effects that would slow down tests or when they are complicated enough that you need to control what they return.

You can configure Jest to run files before it runs the tests, so you can create a file to register mixins before the tests are run. Create a file named test-setup.js in the root of the project. Add the code from the next listing to the file.

Listing 11.9 A test setup file

```
import Vue from 'vue'
import {
  titleMixin
} from './src/util/mixins'

Vue.config.productionTip = false

Vue.mixin(titleMixin)
```

Sets the Vue production tip to be false; this stops Vue from logging a warning that you are using the development build when you run your tests.

Registers the mixin

You need to update your Jest config to tell Jest to run the file before it runs the tests. To do that, use the `setupFiles` option. Open the package.json file, and find the `jest` field. Update the `jest` field to include the following code:

```
"jest": {
  "transform": {
    "^.+\\.js$": "babel-jest",
```

```
    "^.+\\.vue$": "vue-jest"
  },
  "setupFiles": ["./test-setup.js"]
}
```

Jest will run the test-setup.js file before each of your tests, which will register the mixin globally. Because the mixin is registered globally, the existing mixin test will pass: npm run test:unit.

The trick to testing mixins is to make sure the tests check output. That way, you're free to refactor the implementation. When you're testing a locally registered mixin, you don't need to do any extra setup. If you use a globally registered mixin, however, you need to register it before the tests run.

Now that you've seen how to test local mixins and global mixins, it's time to learn about Vue filters and how to test them.

11.2 Testing filters

You can think of filters as transforms that are applied to values in a Vue template. Like mixins, filters are registered both globally and locally.

After you register a filter, you can use it in a template using the pipe operator (|). An example that would convert the msg value to uppercase follows.

> **Listing 11.10 Applying a filter in a template**

```
<template>
  <div>
    {{ msg | upperCase }}          ◁──┐  The msg data will be output in uppercase, after it's
  </div>                               passed to the uppercase filter, which is a function
</template>                            that takes msg as an argument and returns a value.
```

Filters are functions that take a value and return another value. The upperCase filter would look like this:

```
export function uppercase (str) {
    return str.toUpperCase()
}
```

Because filters are just functions, they are easy to write unit tests for. In this section, you'll write unit tests for two filters and then write unit tests for components that use the filters.

The first filter you create will take a URL as input and return a cleaned URL. The second filter will take a UNIX timestamp and convert it into readable text. Before you use the filters in components, you need to write the tests for the filter functions themselves.

11.2.1 Writing tests for filters

Filters are functions that return a value, so you can test them by calling them with arguments and asserting they return the correct value. Simple!

> ### The anatomy of a URL
>
> Let's dissect the URL https://subdomain.domain.com/some-path/:
>
> - https:// is the *protocol*.
> - domain.com is the *domain*.
> - subdomain is the *subdomain*.
> - /some-path/ is the *path*.
>
> The combination of the subdomain and the domain is called the *hostname*.

The first filter that you write will convert a URL to a *hostname*. Currently, the app renders a full item URL (see figure 11.1).

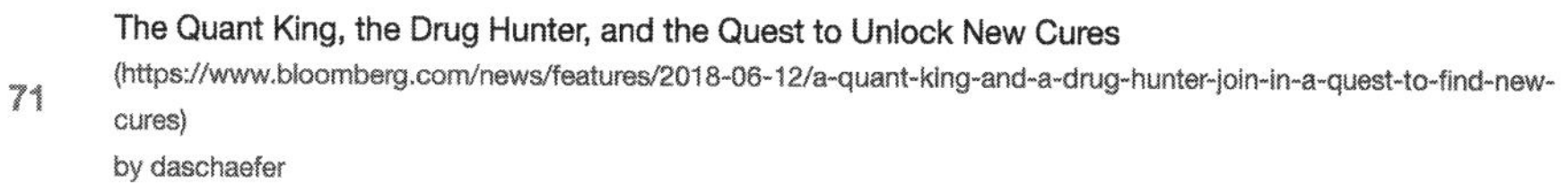

71 The Quant King, the Drug Hunter, and the Quest to Unlock New Cures
(https://www.bloomberg.com/news/features/2018-06-12/a-quant-king-and-a-drug-hunter-join-in-a-quest-to-find-new-cures)
by daschaefer

Figure 11.1   Before filtering

This URL can be difficult to read, so you'll add a filter that makes it easier to parse by removing extra information, like the path (see figure 11.2).

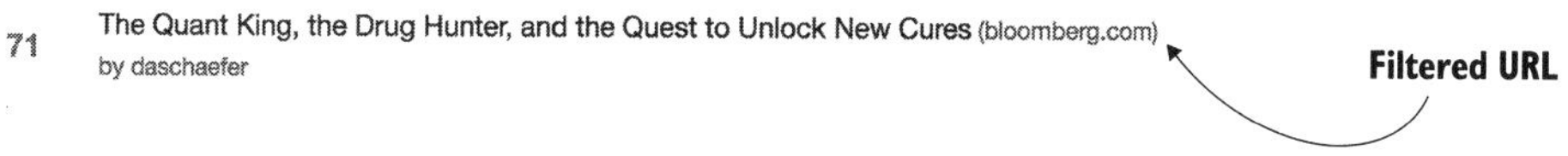

71 The Quant King, the Drug Hunter, and the Quest to Unlock New Cures (bloomberg.com)
by daschaefer   **Filtered URL**

Figure 11.2   After filtering

URLs can be quite complicated, so you should test lots of cases. The filter should

- Return the hostname from a URL beginning with http://
- Return the hostname from a URL beginning with https://
- Return the subdomain in the hostname
- Remove the path from a URL
- Remove *www* from a URL
- Return the last subdomain

Although lots of test cases are possible, the tests themselves are simple, so you'll add all these test cases in one go. Create a test file, src/util/__tests__/filters.spec.js. Open the test file, and add the code from the next listing.

Listing 11.11 Testing a filter

```
  import { host, timeAgo } from '../filters'

describe('host', () => {
  test('returns empty string if url is undefined', () => {
    expect(host(undefined)).toBe('')
  })

  test('returns the host from a URL beginning with http://', () => {
    const url = 'http://google.com'
    expect(host(url)).toBe('google.com')
  })

  test('returns the host from a URL beginning with https://', () => {
    const url = 'https://google.com'
    expect(host(url)).toBe('google.com')
  })

  test('removes path from URL', () => {
    const url = 'google.com/long/path/ '
    expect(host(url)).toBe('google.com')
  })

  test('removes www from URL', () => {
    const url = 'www.blogs.google.com/'
    expect(host(url)).toBe('blogs.google.com')
  })

  test('keeps the subdomain', () => {
    const url = 'https://blogs.google.com/long/path/ '
    expect(host(url)).toBe('blogs.google.com')
  })

  test('returns one subdomain and removes others', () => {
    const url = 'personal.blogs.google.com/long/path/ '
    expect(host(url)).toBe('blogs.google.com')
  })
})
```

Now let's add the filter code. Create a src/util/filters.js file, and add the code from the following listing into the file to add the code for the host filter.

Listing 11.12 A host filter

```
export function host (url) {
  if (!url) {
    return ''
  }
  const host = url.replace(/^https?:\/\//, '').replace(/\/.*$/, '')    ◁——  Removes the protocol and the paths
  const parts = host.split('.').slice(-3)    ◁——  Returns the last three parts of the domain that are separated by dots
  if (parts[0] === 'www') {
    parts.shift()    ◁——  Removes www if it exists
  }
  return parts.join('.')    ◁——  Joins the array into a string and returns the string
}
```

Check that the tests are passing by running the unit script, `npm run test:unit`. Great—you've written your first filter. That was easy, wasn't it?

Compared with components, testing filters is easy because they're plain old JavaScript functions that take an input and return an output. Now you'll write your second filter. This one is a bit more complicated, because it relies on the current time using `Date.now`.

11.2.2 *Testing filters that use Date.now*

`Date.now` is a method on the JavaScript `Date` object that returns the number of milliseconds that have elapsed since January 1 1970, 00:00 UTC. You can use it to calculate the current time.

Testing functions that use `Date.now` presents a problem. The value returned by `Date.now` is constantly changing, which means unit tests that use `Date.now` won't be predictable. The solution is to mock the `Date.now` method. You'll learn how to do that by writing tests for the `timeAgo` filter.

The `timeAgo` filter takes a UNIX timestamp and converts it into readable text that tells how long ago the timestamp was. It will convert `1513527632` into *4 minutes*.

> **DEFINITION**   The UNIX timestamp, also known as the UNIX epoch, is a standard way of measuring time on systems. It returns the seconds elapsed since January 1 1970, 00:00 UTC. Computers can use this data to calculate the date.

The Hacker News API returns a UNIX timestamp for the time that an item was posted. You'll use this value and transform it with the filter to display how long it has been since an item was posted.

To calculate how long ago a UNIX timestamp was, you can use the `Date.now` method to get the current time and then subtract the UNIX timestamp from it to get the time difference. When you've got the difference in seconds, you can convert that to a readable number.

The filter converts the UNIX time into the number of minutes, hours, or days it has been since the UNIX timestamp. If you convert that into specs, the filter should do the following:

- Return a singular minute
- Return plural minutes
- Return a singular hour
- Return plural hours
- Return a singular day
- Return plural days
- Return the time rounded to the nearest whole number

In the tests, you'll call the `timeAgo` function with a value and expect that it returns the correct human-readable time.

Because the `timeAgo` filter will use `Date.now`, you need to stub `Date.now` to return the same value in each test. You'll generate a UNIX time value to pass in, using the value you return from `Date.now`. Then you'll call the `timeAgo` filter with a UNIX timestamp from one minute prior to the mocked `Date`.

Unfortunately, UNIX timestamps are the *number of seconds* that have passed since 1970, but `Date.now` returns the *number of milliseconds*, so you need to include that in your calculations. Add the `describe` block from the next listing to src/util/__tests__/filters.spec.js, after the previous `describe` block.

Listing 11.13   Stubbing `Date.now`

```
describe('timeAgo', () => {

  Date.now = () => new Date('2018')         ←— Mocks Date.now to always
  const unixTime = Date.now() / 1000        ←   return the same date
                                             └— Converts Date.now
  test('returns singular minute', () => {       to UNIX time
    expect(timeAgo(unixTime - 60)).toBe('1 minute')  ←— Asserts that timeAgo returns the
  })                                                      correct value when called with a
})                                                        timestamp from one minute ago
})
```

You'll add the rest of the tests before you write the code for the filter. You can write similar tests by subtracting the time you want to test from the `unixTime` variable. This quickly becomes math heavy. *How many seconds is 5 days?* Instead of doing the math, you can use helper functions to do the math for you. Add the following helper functions to the `timeAgo` describe block in src/util/__tests__/filters.spec.js:

```
const seconds = (second) => second * 1
const minutes = (minute) => minute * seconds(60)
const hours = (hour) => hour * minutes(60)
const days = (day) => day * hours(24)
```

Update the existing *returns singular minute* test in src/util/__tests__/filters.spec.js to use the `minutes` helper function as follows:

```
test('returns singular minute', () => {
  expect(timeAgo(unixTime - minutes(1))).toBe('1 minute')
})
```

You'll add the remaining tests using the helper functions. Add the tests from the following listing to src/util/__tests__/filter.spec.js.

Listing 11.14   Testing a filter function

```
test('returns plural minutes', () => {
  expect(timeAgo(unixTime - minutes(5))).toBe('5 minutes')
})

test('returns singular hour', () => {
  expect(timeAgo(unixTime - hours(1))).toBe('1 hour')
})
```

```
test('returns plural hours', () => {
  expect(timeAgo(unixTime - hours(5))).toBe('5 hours')
})

test('returns singular day', () => {
  expect(timeAgo(unixTime - days(1))).toBe('1 day')
})

test('returns plural days', () => {
  expect(timeAgo(unixTime - days(5))).toBe('5 days')
})

test('returns day rounded to nearest value', () => {
  expect(timeAgo(unixTime - (days(2) + hours(10)))).toBe('2 days')
})
```

Now that the tests are written, it's time to add the `timeAgo` filter code. This code will get the current time using `Date.now`, convert it to seconds, and subtract the time to get the difference. Then it returns *minute*, *hour*, or *day*, depending on the time difference, appended with an *s* if the number of time is greater than 1. Open src/util/ filters.js, and add the following code to the file.

Listing 11.15 Writing a `timeAgo` filter

Gets the difference between the time value passed in to the function and Date.now, the current time, as seconds

```
export function timeAgo (time) {
  const between = Date.now() / 1000 - Number(time)
  if (between < 3600) {                                    ◁
    return pluralize((between / 60), ' minute')    ◁
  } else if (between < 86400) {
    return pluralize((between / 3600), ' hour')
  } else {
    return pluralize((between / 86400), ' day')
  }
}

function pluralize (time, label)                            ◁
  const roundedTime = Math.round(time)       ◁
  if (roundedTime === 1) {
    return roundedTime + label
  }
  return roundedTime + label + 's'
}
```

Returns the value as minutes, if the difference between the time and current time is less than an hour

Returns the correctly pluralized result

Helper function to add a plural to the label if the value isn't 1

Rounds the value to the nearest integer

Check that the tests pass by running `npm run test:unit`. That's great—you've written the second filter. The final step is to use both filters in a component.

11.2.3 *Testing filters in components*

Testing filters in components is similar to testing mixins in components. You shouldn't test that the filter is used explicitly. Instead, you test that the component produces the correct output and use the filter to produce the correct output.

Filters can be registered globally or locally. The test strategy is the same for testing mixins, so instead of testing them locally and globally, you'll just test globally registered filters. Before you use filters in a component, you need to register them globally in the entry file and also in the test-setup file so you can use them in the test without extra setup.

Add the following lines to src/main.js:

```
import {
  timeAgo,
  host
} from './util/filters'
And to test-setup.js:
import {
  timeAgo,
  host
} from './src/util/filters'
```

And add the code to register the filters in both src/main.js and test-setup.js:

```
Vue.filter('timeAgo', timeAgo)
Vue.filter('host', host)
```

You'll start by testing that the component renders the filtered time value. You'll pass the Item a UNIX time value that's 10 minutes before the current time and assert that it generates an output that contains the correctly transformed value.

Open src/components/__tests__/Item.spec.js, and add the code from the next listing to the describe block after the existing tests.

Listing 11.16   Mocking `Date.now` in a test

```
test('renders the time since the last post', () => {
  const dateNow = jest.spyOn(Date, 'now')        ◁——— Spies on the
  const dateNowTime = new Date('2018')                 Date.now function

  dateNow.mockImplementation(() => dateNowTime)   ◁——— Mocks dateNow to always
                                                       call the same time
  const item = {                                  ◁——— Creates a mock
    time: (dateNowTime / 1000) - 600   ◁                item to pass in
  }                                     │
  const wrapper = shallowMount(Item, {  └─── Creates a UNIX time value
    propsData: {                             that is 10 minutes ago from
      item                                   the mocked current time
    }
  })                             ┌─── Restores the dateNow mock
  dateNow.mockRestore()    ◁─────┘    before running the assertion
  expect(wrapper.text()).toContain('10 minutes ago')   ◁─── Asserts that the wrapper
})                                                          output contains
                                                            10 minutes ago
```

> **NOTE** When you stub a global function, as you have with `Date.now` in listing 11.16, you should be aware that it will affect future tests in the test file. Often, you don't need to reset the value, but you will need to if future tests rely on the original `Date.now` functionality.

Now you can add the code to the `Item` component. The test is lenient—it doesn't check that the text is output in a particular element; it just checks that it's rendered *somewhere* in the component. Add the following code to the `<template>` block in src/components/Item.vue:

```
{{ item.time | timeAgo }} ago
```

Next, let's test that you're rendering the host name, instead of the full URL. In this test, you'll pass in an item with a `url` property. Then you'll test that somewhere in the text you render just the hostname of the URL. Replace the *renders* `item.url` test in src/components/__tests__/Item.spec.js with the test in the next listing.

Listing 11.17 Testing a filter in a component

```
test('renders the hostname', () => {
  const item = {
    url: 'https://some-url.com/with-paths'
  }
  const wrapper = shallowMount(Item, {
    propsData: {
      item
    }
  })
  expect(wrapper.text()).toContain('(some-url.com)')
})
```

To update this, you just need to add a `<span>` tag to the `Item` component. Open src/components/Item.vue, and replace the code that renders `item.url` with the following code:

```
<span class="host"> ({{ item.url | host }})</span>
```

Run the test to make sure it passes: `npm run test:unit`. Great—you've added filters and mixins to the application.

You're ready to move on to the next chapter, where you'll learn about snapshot testing. I love snapshot testing, and I'm really excited to teach you about it!

Summary

- Mixins can be tested by creating a mock component and registering the mixin on the component.
- Mixins can be applied globally or locally on a component.
- You can register filters and mixins before running unit tests.
- You can test filters and mixins in components by testing component output.

Exercises

1   Write a test for the follow mixin that calls a method before the component mounts:

```
const testMixin = {
  beforeMount() {
    this.myMethod()
  }
}
```

2   Write a filter that passes this test:

```
test('converts first letter to uppercase', () => {
  expect(capitalize('test')).toBe('Test')
})
```

3   Write a test that checks that the uppercase filter works correctly in the following component. You should include a test-setup.js file:

```
// uppercase.js
function uppercase(string) {
    return string.charAt(0).toUpperCase() + string.slice(1);
}
// TestComponent.vue
<template>
  <div>
    {{ name | uppercase }}
  </div>
</template>

<script>
export default {
  props: ['name']
}
</script>
```

Writing snapshot tests

12

In this chapter, you'll learn what snapshot tests are, how they fit in to the testing workflow, and how to use them to make sure components aren't changed unintentionally.

> **DEFINITION** Snapshot testing is a way of comparing two pictures of an application automatically.

Up until this chapter, you've learned to write unit tests. Now it's time to add a new type of test to your testing tool belt. If you remember from back in chapter 1, I showed you how to use the frontend pyramid as a guide for how to structure a test suite (figure 12.1). The next type of tests in the pyramid after unit tests are snapshot tests.

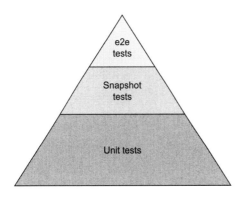

Figure 12.1   The frontend testing pyramid

In the first section of this chapter, you'll learn what snapshot testing is. When you've got an understanding of it, I'll show you how it fits into your testing workflow and how you can use snapshot tests to catch unintended changes to components

In the second section of the chapter, you'll learn how to write effective snapshot tests for both static and dynamic components.

Before you go further, you need to download the finished chapter-12 application. This application has new views that I added outside of this book. Follow the instructions in appendix A to download the Git repository if you haven't already, and switch to the chapter-12 branch.

After you have downloaded the Git repository, you can begin. The first thing to do is learn what snapshot tests are.

12.1   *Understanding snapshot tests*

A simple explanation of snapshot tests is that they take a snapshot of your code and compare it against a previously saved snapshot. If the new snapshot doesn't match the previous one, the tests will fail.

Snapshot testing is like having someone play a game of Spot the Differences between your latest output and a saved file of your output. The computer spots the differences between the old and new snapshots, highlights them, and reports back to you. If there's a difference between the snapshots, the test fails.

You're going to write snapshot tests using Jest. Jest snapshot tests compares *serializable values.* A serializable value is basically any JavaScript value that can be converted to a string.

To add a snapshot test in Jest, you use the `toMatchSnapshot` matcher as follows:

```
expect('value').toMatchSnapshot()
```

You can also pass DOM nodes to the snapshot, like so:

```
expect(document.querySelector('div')).toMatchSnapshot()
```

The first time a snapshot test runs, Jest creates a snap file with the value passed to `expect`. Imagine that you wrote a snapshot test for a `ListItem` component that rendered an `<li>` tag. You would mount the component and then create a snapshot using the wrapper DOM node shown next.

Listing 12.1 A snapshot test

```
test('renders list item correctly', () => {
  const wrapper = shallowMount(List)
  expect(wrapper.element).toMatchSnapshot()
})
```

◁─────── **Mounts the
ListItem component**

◁─── **Creates a snapshot test**

When you run the snapshot test in Jest, Jest generates a formatted file using the DOM node that `expect` was called with. A snap file, shown in the next listing, is a way for Jest to store output that it will compare against in future tests.

Listing 12.2 A snap file

```
exports[`renders list item correctly`] = `
<li>
  List item
</li>
`;
```

◁─── **Snapshot for the test renders
the list item correctly**

◁─── **The snapshot output
that is compared against**

The next time the snapshot test runs, it will compare the new value that `expect` was called with, with the saved value in the snap file. If the output matches, then the snapshot test will pass. If the DOM node generated by the component had changed, then the new value would be different from the saved value, and the snapshot test would fail with a diff.

> **NOTE** A *diff* is a comparison between the previous output and the latest output that helps you see which part has changed

For example, if the `List` item text were changed to *Not list*, the test would fail with the following diff:

```
- Snapshot
+ Received

  <li>
-   List item
+   Not list
  </li>
```

You can see the flow chart that Jest follows when it runs a snapshot test in figure 12.2.

If the changes between the saved snap file and the new output are intended, then you can overwrite the saved snapshot with the new output. If the detected changes aren't intended, then you have a chance to fix the problem.

Jest manages snap files for you. The snap files are generated with a .snap extension in the __snapshots__ directory, which is created in the same directory as the test file. Snap files are the single source of truth for the output of a snapshot test, so you should include the snap files in your source control for Jest to use if you run the tests on different devices.

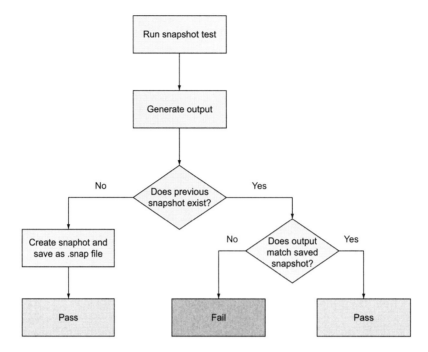

Figure 12.2   The snapshot test flow

Now that you've seen a high-level overview of snapshot testing, you're ready to write some snapshot tests yourself!

12.1.1   *Writing snapshot tests for components*

Snapshot tests are most effective for testing the output of components. They give you a lot of bang for your buck—a single snapshot test can test the markup of a component that's hundreds of lines long.

The technique for writing component snapshot tests depends on the kind of component you are testing. In this section, you'll learn how to write snapshot tests for both static and dynamic components.

12.1.2   *Writing snapshot tests for static components*

A *static component* is a component that always renders the same output. It doesn't receive any props, and it doesn't have any state. There's no logic in the component, and it always renders the same HTML elements.

Static components sound rather boring—and they are. Writing unit tests for static components is unnecessary, because they don't really do anything. It can be useful, however, to make sure the static component doesn't change in the future after it was originally written and manually tested.

There is a static `Spinner` component in the Hacker News app. Open src/components/Spinner.vue, and take a look at the code, shown in the next listing.

Listing 12.3 A static component

```
<template>
  <transition>
    <svg class="spinner" width="44px" height="44px" viewBox="0 0 44 44">
      <circle class="path" fill="none" stroke-width="4" stroke-
    linecap="round" cx="22" cy="22" r="20"></circle>
    </svg>
  </transition>
</template>
```

Create a file in src/components/__tests__/Spinner.spec.js for the snapshot test.

To create a snapshot test for the DOM nodes of a component, you need to mount a component and then use the root DOM node (accessible as `wrapper.element`) as input for the snapshot test. Add the code from the next listing to src/components/__tests__/Spinner.spec.js.

Listing 12.4 Writing a snapshot test

```
import { shallowMount } from '@vue/test-utils'
import Spinner from '../Spinner.vue'

describe('Spinner.vue', () => {
  test('renders correctly', () => {
    expect(shallowMount(Spinner).element).toMatchSnapshot()    ◁──
  })
})
```

> Generates a snapshot with the root DOM node of the mounted Spinner component

Now run the test suite with `npm run test:unit`. Check the output of the console; you'll see that Jest created a snap file. Open the snap file in src/components/__tests__/__snapshots__/Spinner.spec.js.snap, where you can see that Jest saved the `element` value to this file.

To understand the power of a snapshot test, you need to see it fail. In src/components/Spinner.vue, change the values in the `<svg>` tag as follows:

```
<svg class="spinner" width="50px" height="50px" viewBox="0 0 50 50">
```

Run the tests again with `npm run test:unit`. The snapshot test will fail with some output showing you a diff of the saved snapshot and the received output

A failing snapshot test is a warning that tells you component output has changed. If the change is accidental, the test will catch unintended changes to the output. If it's an intended change, then you need to update the snapshot file. In this case, the change you made was intentional.

You can rewrite a snap file by calling Jest with the `--update` flag. To do that in your test suite, call your `test:unit` script with an extra `updateSnapshot` parameter, as follows:

```
npm run test:unit -- --updateSnapshot
```

The `updateSnapshot` parameter is quite long to type. So instead, you can use the alias –u to update, like so:

```
npm run test:unit -- -u
```

This command will tell Jest to rewrite *all* failing snapshots. It's useful if you want to rewrite multiple snapshots at a time, but it can be dangerous. You might accidentally add an incorrect snapshot. To avoid adding a buggy snapshot, you can run Jest in interactive mode. Use the following command to run the interactive update snapshot mode:

```
npm run test:unit -- --watch
```

When the prompt appears in the terminal, press the i key to go through the failing snapshots. You can press the u key to update the saved snapshot file with the latest value. Interactive mode is a safe way of verifying multiple snapshots at once.

Writing snapshot tests for static components is useful, because it stops you from accidentally changing the rendered output of a component. Snapshot tests are even more useful for dynamic components.

12.1.3 *Writing snapshot tests for dynamic components*

Dynamic components are components that include logic and state. For example, they might take props or update data when a button is clicked.

When you write snapshot tests for dynamic components, you should try to capture as many different combinations of state as possible. This way, the snapshot test covers as much functionality as possible.

> **NOTE** Here I define dynamic components as components that include logic or take props, which is different from the dynamic components in the Vue documentation—https://vuejs.org/v2/guide/components.html#Dynamic-Components.

Let's add some snapshots for the `Item` component. The `Item` component takes an `item` prop and uses that object to render the markup. For the snapshot test, you need to create an `item` prop with realistic data. This makes the test more reliable, because it will produce output that's closer to the production output.

One rule of snapshot tests is that they must be deterministic. In other words, if the code used to generate the output hasn't changed, the output should always be the same, no matter how many times you run the test. This can be a problem when you use nondeterministic functions, like `Date.now`.

Remember, your `Item` component renders information about how long ago an item was posted to Hacker News. This information depends on the current date, using the `Date.now` method. This could be a problem. A snapshot generated today might include the text *posted 3 minutes ago*. When you run the tests tomorrow, without changing any code, it would render the text *posted 1 day ago*. The snapshot test would fail even though the component hasn't changed. To avoid this unnecessary notification, you need to mock the `Date.now` method so that it always returns the same time, to make your snapshot test deterministic.

Open src/components/__tests__/Item.spec.js. Add the test from the next listing to the `describe` block.

Listing 12.5   Writing a snapshot test for a dynamic component

```
test('renders correctly', () => {
  const dateNow = jest.spyOn(Date, 'now')
  const dateNowTime = new Date('2018')

  dateNow.mockImplementation(() => dateNowTime)      ⟵  Mocks the date so that Item
                                                        always renders the same time

  const item = {                    ⟵  Creates the mock data
    by: 'eddyerburgh',                  for Item to render
    id: 11122233,
    score: 10,
    time: (dateNowTime / 1000) - 600,
    title: 'vue-test-utils is released',
    type: 'story',
    url: 'https://vue-test-utils.vuejs.org/'
  }
  const wrapper = createWrapper(Item, {      ⟵  Creates a wrapper with
    propsData: {                                an item prop
      item
    }
  })
  dateNow.mockRestore()                            Generates
  expect(wrapper.element).toMatchSnapshot()   ⟵  the snapshot
})
```

Run the tests with `npm run test:unit` to generate the snapshots. This will create another snap file with the output from the test in Item.spec.

If you look at the code in src/components/Item.vue, you'll see that there is a `v-if` statement. You'll write another snapshot test to capture this conditional *branch*.

DEFINITION   Branches are the different routes that a program can take, depending on the conditions of a control statement. For example, an `if/else` statement produces two branches, and an `if/else/else if` statement produces three branches.

The `v-if` statement checks for a type of `job`. The first snapshot test did not have a `type` property, so the next snapshot should have `type` set to `job` to render with the content inside the `v-if` branch. Add the following code to src/components/ __tests__/Item.spec.js.

Listing 12.6   Mocking `Date.now`

```
test('renders correctly as job', () => {
  const dateNow = jest.spyOn(Date, 'now')
  const dateNowTime = new Date('2018')

  dateNow.mockImplementation(() => dateNowTime)

  const item = {                              ◁─┐  Creates an item object
    by: 'eddyerburgh',                            with a job type
    id: 11122233,
    score: 10,
    time: (dateNowTime / 1000) - 600,
    title: 'vue-test-utils is released',
    type: 'job'
  }
  const wrapper = createWrapper({
    propsData: {
      item
    }
  })
  dateNow.mockRestore()
  expect(wrapper.element).toMatchSnapshot()
})
```

Run the tests. You'll see that Jest writes a new snap file. If you open the snap file src/ components/__tests__/__snapshots__/Item.spec.js.snap, you can see that Jest has generated two snapshots for Items.spec.js. These two snapshots cover all the branches of the component output.

Ideally, you would cover all the branches of component output with snapshot tests, but this isn't always possible, or even desirable. Lots of snapshot tests for one component means lots of *failing* snapshot tests each time you make a change to that component. If you have too many failing snapshot tests, it can become overwhelming to update all the failing tests, and you might accidentally save a buggy snapshot. As a general rule, I don't write more than three snapshot tests for a component.

That's all there is to writing snapshot tests. You just need to provide a component that you're testing with the correct input to render.

Now that you've learned how to write snapshot tests, let's talk about how to add them to your workflow.

12.2   *Adding snapshot tests to your workflow*

Snapshot tests are like meetings. Used effectively, they can boost productivity, but too many will slow you down.

Earlier in this book, you wrote unit tests. Unit tests are great for testing logic in a component, but they aren't useful for testing static component output. Luckily, snapshot tests work really well at testing static output!

My workflow is to write unit tests to cover the core component functionality. After I have unit tests, I style the component without any extra tests and manually test the style in the browser. When I'm happy with the component style, I add a snapshot test (see figure 12.3). I've found this system works well. I get good coverage from unit tests, but I'm free to quickly change the style.

When you style components, there's always an element of manual testing. Unless you're a CSS prodigy, after you add CSS to a component you need to test the application manually in the browser to make sure it's applied correctly.

You can take advantage of the manual-testing phase of styling by capturing the manual test in a snapshot. A snapshot test freezes the manually tested output like Han Solo was frozen in carbonite. If your team is strict and commits snapshot tests only for components that they've tested in the browser, snapshot tests tell you that somebody has manually tested the component and it works correctly. With good snapshot tests, if you decide to make a large refactor to your codebase, you can run the snapshot tests and be sure that your refactor hasn't changed the component output.

What if a snapshot does fail? A failing snapshot test prompts you to look at the markup

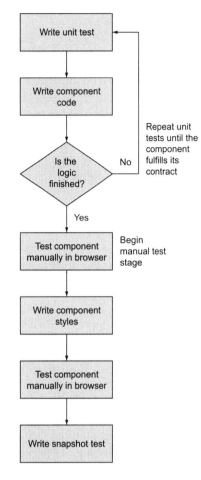

Figure 12.3   A testing workflow with snapshots

rendered by a component and decide whether the change is acceptable. If you're unsure whether the component will be styled correctly with the changed output, you can open the application in a browser and check manually that the component still looks correct.

Because you're putting trust in snapshot tests, it's important to treat the snapshots as part of your codebase. When you review a pull request that includes new or changed snapshot tests, you should read through the snapshot code with the same diligence as if you were reviewing any other code changes.

Now you understand where snapshot tests fit into your workflow. As I said at the beginning of the chapter, I'm a big fan of these tests. After reading this chapter, I hope that you're as excited as I am about snapshot tests!

In the next chapter, you're going to learn how to test server-side rendered code.

Summary

- Snapshot tests safeguard against unintentional changes by comparing a current version of your code against a saved version.
- Snapshot tests are written after you manually test a component.
- Jest includes snapshot testing as part of the framework.

Exercises

1   How many snapshot tests should you write for static components?

2   Why do you need to mock the Date object in a snapshot test?

3   Write a snapshot test for the following static component:

```
// TestComponent.vue
<template>
  <div>
    Hello, World!
  </div>
</template>
```

Testing server-side rendering

This chapter covers

- Understanding server-side rendering
- Unit testing server-side rendered Vue components
- Testing HTTP response codes from a server

Server-side rendering (SSR) is when you render the HTML code of an application on the server before returning it to the client. It's common to use Vue for SSR, so to be a versatile Vue tester you should learn the techniques to test server-side rendered apps.

SSR is a big topic—too big to go over in a book on testing—so this chapter won't teach you the specifics of how to add SSR to an app. Instead, I've converted the Hacker News app into an SSR app by following the official guide (https:// vuejs.org/v2/guide/ssr.html). That way, you can focus on testing, rather than adding boilerplate.

> **NOTE** To follow along with this chapter, you need to switch to the chapter-13 branch of the Git project. If you've forgotten how to do that, you can go to appendix A for instructions. You're going to use Node in

this chapter to serve the application, so you'll need an understanding of serving applications with Node.

Although I'm not going to teach the technical details involved in setting up a SSR app, I'll give you a high-level overview of SSR. You don't need to be familiar with SSR to follow along with this chapter and learn some useful skills.

The fundamental difference between testing SSR code and client-side code is that it runs on the server rather than in a browser. All the tests you've written so far have been for code that runs in a browser. That's going to change in this section.

The first section of this chapter is about understanding SSR. The second part is about writing unit tests for server-side rendered components.

The final part is about testing the status codes returned from a server. When you add SSR to an app, you become responsible for the server and sending the correct HTTP codes to the user. You can test HTTP codes by writing an integration test, which is a kind of test you haven't seen yet. I'll show you how to test status codes returned by SSR apps. This section isn't Vue specific and can be applied to any SSR app, but it's a useful testing technique that I don't often see covered.

The first thing to do is learn about what server-side rendering is and why it's useful.

13.1 Understanding server-side rendering

With Vue SSR, a server generates the initial HTML of an application using Vue. When the code runs on the client, Vue *hydrates* the static HTML to make it interactive.

> **NOTE** Hydrating a server-side app is the process of making an app interactive by adding event listeners to the HTML. It's much faster to hydrate an app, instead of rerendering the HTML client side. Vue hydrates a server-side rendered app automatically when mounting on the client side.

SSR offers some benefits, as well as some drawbacks. First let's look at the benefits.

13.1.1 The advantages of SSR

SSR has the following two big advantages over client-side rendered apps:

- Improved search engine optimization (SEO)
- Improved time to content

A typical client-side rendered Vue app is an HTML page with a `<div>` and a `script` element, as shown in the next code. When the JavaScript is loaded and evaluated, the app is rendered into the `<div>`.

Listing 13.1 HTML response for a client-side app

```
<head>
...
</head>
<body>
  <div id="app" />          Root div that the app
                            will be rendered into
```

```
<script src="/dist/app.js"></script>
</body>
```

◁───┐ **Links to the script that will mount the Vue app and render it into the div**

This works fine. But serving web pages like this can cause problems for search engines like Google and Bing. Search engines use crawler bots to index sites. The bots make a request to a web page and then index the response. Search engines then use the indexed response to decide whether a page contains relevant information to show to users, so it's important that the response contains the rendered page content.

Search engines *can* execute JavaScript on a page before they save the HTML, but it doesn't always work. For example, if data is fetched in an asynchronous call, the search engines might index the site before the asynchronous call has finished and the data has rendered.

If a site isn't fully rendered when a crawler indexes it, the site's page ranking, otherwise known as SEO, will be negatively affected. For most websites, SEO is vital, so any chance that client-side rendered content will harm SEO is avoided. Server-side rendering ensures that search engines correctly index the page content, because it's returned as static HTML from the server.

The other benefit of SSR is that it improves the *time to content*. When you request a web page with client-side rendering, the page is empty until the JavaScript downloads and executes (figure 13.1). On a slow connection, this can take a long time!

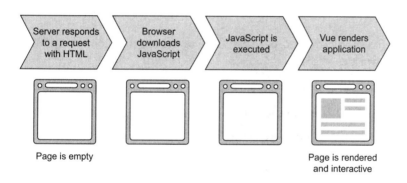

Figure 13.1   The process of a client-side rendered app

A SSR response, shown in the next listing, would contain all the HTML of an app, so the browser can render content as soon as it has parsed the HTML (figure 13.2).

Listing 13.2   HTML response for a server-side app

```
<head>
...
</head>
<body>
```

```
<div id="app">
  <header class="header">
    ...
  </header>
  <div class="view">
    ...
  </div>
</div>
<script src="/dist/app.js"></script>
</body>
```

The script that hydrates the Vue application on the client side

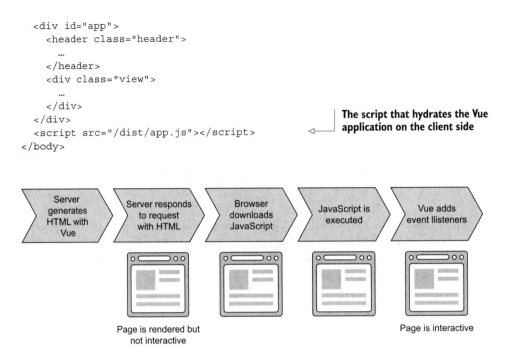

Page is rendered but not interactive

Page is interactive

Figure 13.2   The process of a server-side rendered app

So the benefits of SSR are improved SEO and improved time to content. But there are also some downsides to SSR.

13.1.2 *The disadvantages of SSR*

SSR isn't all rainbows and kittens. It has some serious downsides:

- SSR makes your code more complex.
- SSR requires a server.
- SSR increases the server-side load.

The first downside is that it makes the code more complex. When you write code to run on both the client side and server side, you need to consider which environment the code will run in. For example, on the client side, document is a global object. You can set the title of the page with document.title. You can't do this on the server side, because in Node there is no document object. If you try to access document.title in your application code—for example, in a mixin—Node will create an error, and the application won't be served.

The second downside is that SSR requires a server. For a normal Vue.js app, all the content could be served as part of a static site. With server-side rendering, you need to manage your own server to render the application. This makes hosting and deploying an application more complex and probably more expensive.

> **DEFINITION** A static site is a site that contains only static assets, like HTML files, JavaScript files, and CSS files. You can use services to host static websites on your behalf, which means you don't need to manage a server.

If you already use a server to serve your site, you can update the server-side code to render the application before it serves it. Unfortunately, rendering on the server uses more CPU than sending back a static asset, which will increase the server response time. You need to make sure you cache your pages effectively so you don't increase memory consumption too much.

> **NOTE** You can create the server using any server-side language that supports a JavaScript sandbox. That means you can write your server in PHP, Ruby, or Python.

Now that you know the advantages and disadvantages of SSR, it's time to take a look at your application and how you can test it.

13.2 Testing server-side rendered components

Unit testing server-side rendered components presents some challenges, but the techniques are pretty simple.

> **NOTE** I'm not going to teach you the steps for adding SSR to a project, but I've updated the Hacker News app to use SSR; you can find it in the chapter-13 branch. It follows the conventions that are laid out in the Vue SSR docs. If you want a good understanding of SSR, I recommend reading those docs—https://ssr.vuejs.org/en.

You can't use Vue Test Utils to test server-side rendered components, because Vue Test Utils needs to be run in a browser environment. The way Vue Test Utils works under the hood is that it mounts a component, which creates DOM nodes. Server-side rendered code is different: it returns a string of HTML without creating DOM nodes.

To create a string of HTML from a Vue instance, you use the `vue-server-renderer` package. The `renderToString` method returns a string that contains the HTML generated from a Vue instance, as shown in the next listing.

Listing 13.3 Rendering a Vue instance to a string

```
const { createRenderer } = require('vue-server-renderer')
const renderer = createRenderer()          ← Creates a renderer
const vm = new Vue({                        ← Creates an instance
  template: '<div />'
})
renderer.renderToString(vm)                 ← Renders an instance to a string
```

When you write unit tests for server-side rendered code, you do something similar. You can generate a string and then assert that the string is correct.

Throughout this book, I've discussed how you should provide an input in a test and assert against an output. The output of server-side rendered components is almost always a string, so the technique to test these components is relatively straight-forward: You provide a component with the correct input and then assert that the string generated from the component either contains the correct HTML or matches a snapshot.

I'm going to be honest: I don't write many unit tests for server-side rendered components. I write unit tests for the components using the client-side Vue Test Utils. That way, I can interact with the component instance. I rely on end-to-end tests to catch problems with server-side rendered components. But I know that other developers do unit test server-side rendered components. Some large companies even unit test every single component on both the server and the browser, so it's a valid test approach.

Two compelling reasons to write unit tests for server-side rendered components follow:

- The component behaves differently on the browser than the server.
- You only rely on unit tests and snapshot tests (no end-to-end tests).

To test server-side rendered components, you can use the Vue Server Test Utils library.

13.2.1 Using Vue Server Test Utils

Vue Server Test Utils is a testing library for server-side rendered Vue components. It shares the same mounting API as Vue Test Utils and accepts the same options to create a component instance, but instead of returning a wrapper object containing a mounted instance, Vue Server Test Utils returns a string of rendered HTML (see listing 13.4).

> **NOTE**   Under the hood, Vue Server Test Utils uses the `vue-server-renderer` package. You can read about the API in the docs—https://ssr.vuejs.org/en/api.html.

> **Listing 13.4   Writing a snapshot test with `renderToString`**

```
import { renderToString } from '@vue/server-test-utils'
import Component from './Component.vue'

test('renders correctly on server ', () => {
  const str = renderToString(Component, {          ◁─┐ Creates a string using the
    propsData: { msg: 'Hello, World!' }                Vue Server Test Utils
  })                                                    renderToString method
  expect(str).toContain('<p>Hello, World!</p>')    ◁─┐ Asserts that the rendered
})                                                      string contains a <p> element
                                                        with the text "Hello, World!"
```

To practice writing tests for server-side rendered components, you're going to write a snapshot test for a `NotFound` view component. The `NotFound` component is rendered when Vue Router can't find a matching route.

NOTE The Hacker News app with SSR uses Vue Router on the server and the client.

First, add Vue Server Test Utils as a dev dependency to the project:

```
npm install --save-dev @vue/server-test-utils
```

Create a file in src/views/__tests__/NotFound.server.spec.js. The .server file extension helps differentiate between client-side tests and server-side tests.

To create a snapshot test, generate the HTML string of the page, and pass it to the Jest toMatchSnapshot matcher. Add the code from the next listing to src/views/__tests__/NotFound.server.spec.js.

Listing 13.5   Writing a snapshot test with `renderToString`

```
import { renderToString } from '@vue/server-test-utils'
import NotFound from '../NotFound.vue'

describe('NotFound', () => {
  test('renders correctly on server ', () => {
    const str = renderToString(NotFound)      ◁──┐ Renders the NotFound component
    expect(str).toMatchSnapshot()                │ to a string with Vue Server Test Utils
  })
})
```

Before you run the tests, add a beforeCreate method to the NotFound component. Then add the following code to the options object inside the <script> block of src/views/NotFound.vue:

```
beforeCreate() {
  document.title = 'hello'
}
```

Now run the unit tests with the npm run test:unit command. The test will pass, and the snapshot test will be written. The thing is, this test shouldn't pass. Build and start the server as follows:

```
npm run build && npm run start
```

Now navigate to localhost:8080/does-not-exist. You'll see that the application is broken in production and returns a 500 error. The reason it's broken is that you're trying to set document.title when you render the code on the server, but document is undefined when you render the component in Node. Makes sense, but why is the unit test passing?

NOTE   If you get an EADDRINUSE error, that means a process is already listening to port 8080. You need to stop the process from listening to 8080, or add a PORT environment variable in front of the start command: npx cross-env PORT=1234 npm run start.

The problem is that Jest runs tests inside a jsdom environment by default, which means DOM properties like `document` are defined when you run the test. This can lead to false positives where your unit tests pass but the code fails in production when you render the component on the server.

When you write unit tests for server-side rendered components, you should run the tests in a Node environment, not a jsdom environment. In Jest, you can set this in the test file, by adding a comment to the top of the file. Add the following code to the top of src/views/__tests__/NotFound.server.spec.js.

Listing 13.6 Setting a Jest test file to run in a Node environment

```
/**
 * @jest-environment node
 */
```

Run the tests again. You should see a warning that `document` is `undefined`, and the test will fail because the snapshots don't match. Perfect—now your tests are running in a realistic environment, and the tests fail correctly. You can remove the `before-Create` hook and run the tests again to make sure they're passing.

You've just seen the problem with running tests for server-side rendered components in a jsdom environment. This is another reason that you should split server-side tests and client tests into separate files. You can run each test file in only one environment. I use the convention of adding a .server extension to identify test files for server-side rendered code. A server-side test file for `ItemList` would be ItemList.server.spec.js, for example, and a client-side test file would be ItemList.spec.js.

> **NOTE** When you use Vue Server Test Utils, `VUE_ENV` is set to server. This is fine when you separate tests into client-side and server-side tests and use Jest, because Jest runs each test in a new process. But this setup could be a big problem if you use other tests runners that don't run test files in separate processes. If you use a different test runner, you should use one script to run tests for client-side code and another script to run tests for server-side code.

The `renderToString` method you used returns a string of HTML. But what if you want to traverse the server-side rendered markup? Vue Server Test Utils also exports a method to traverse the rendered output—`render`.

13.2.2 *Traversing server-side rendered markup with render*

Vue Server Test Utils exposes two methods—`renderToString` and `render`. `render-ToString` returns a string of the rendered markup. You can run only a few assertions on a string. If you want to traverse the server-side rendered markup, you should use the `render` method.

The Vue Server Test Utils `render` method returns a wrapper object similar to the normal Vue Test Utils wrapper object, which I'm sure you're familiar with now. The Vue Server Test Utils wrapper has methods to traverse and assert the rendered string, but the API is slightly different from the Vue Test Utils wrapper. The difference is that the `render` method returns a *Cheerio* wrapper object. Cheerio is a Node implementation of the jQuery API, so it should feel familiar if you've used jQuery before. If not, you can find extensive docs at https://cheerio.js.org.

Using the `render` method with the Cheerio API can make your test code easier to read, and you can write assertions that are difficult to write when you're just using the `renderToString` method. Add `render` to the `import` statement in src/views/__tests__/NotFound.server .spec.js as follows:

```
import { renderToString, render } from '@vue/server-test-utils'
```

You'll add a new test to the `NotFound` component that uses the `render` method. The test will check that `NotFound` renders an `<h1>` element that contains the correct text by calling `find` on the wrapper with an `h1` selector and calling a `text` method to return the text of the `<h1>` element.

Add the code from the following listing to the `describe` block in src/views/__tests__/NotFound.spec.js. This test will pass, because the code already exists.

Listing 13.7   Using `render` to assert against server-side rendered code

```
test('renders 404 inside <h1> tag', () => {          Generates a
  const wrapper = render(NotFound)        ⟵——        Cheerio wrapper
  expect(wrapper.find('h1').text()).toBe('404')   ⟵  Finds an <h1> tag, and asserts
})                                                    that it contains the text "404"
```

You can check that the tests pass with `npm run test:unit`. If you want to be extra careful, you should edit the 404 page to make sure it fails for the correct reason.

> **NOTE**   To see the full list of methods available for the Cheerio wrapper, visit the Cheerio docs—https://cheerio.js.org.

That's how you can unit test server-side rendered components with Vue Server Test Utils. Server-side rendered component unit tests are normally simple, because you're not asserting against a running instance, but you can use the same techniques that you use when you write normal unit tests. The main difference is that SSR tests need to run in a node environment using the Vue Server Test Utils library.

One other useful technique for testing SSR is to check that a server responds with the correct status codes. You can write tests to check that using SuperTest.

13.3   *Testing status codes with SuperTest*

When you add SSR to your app, you're responsible for responding to requests with the correct HTTP status codes. Normally, there's some logic involved in how you respond with status codes, so it can be beneficial to write tests to check that you're responding with them correctly.

You can test that your server responds with the correct status codes using SuperTest. SuperTest is a library used to test HTTP responses.

> **NOTE** In this section, you're going to test HTTP responses. I'll talk about the response body and the response headers. If you aren't familiar with response bodies, response headers, or HTTP, read MDN's excellent primer on HTTP: http://mng.bz/0WWW. If you're familiar with HTTP but need to refresh your knowledge of HTTP responses, read this MDN page on HTTP responses: http://mng.bz/K11E.

This process is a departure from the tests you've written so far. The focus of this book is on frontend tests—unit tests, end-to-end tests, and snapshot tests. The tests I'm about to teach you are *integration tests*.

Integration tests are tricky to define. Different people have different definitions, and there isn't a definitive answer. Roughly, though, integration tests examine parts of an application that work together, but they don't test the entire system.

For example, the tests I'm going to teach you will make a request to a server, and check that the server responds with the correct status code. They don't test the client-side code, just that the server response is correct.

First, you should write a basic sanity test that makes a request to facebook.com to be sure the setup works correctly. Install SuperTest as a dev dependency by running the following command:

```
npm install --save-dev supertest
```

Now create a server.spec.js file in the root of the project. You'll add all your SuperTest tests in this file. Add the code from the next listing into server.spec.js to be a request to facebook.com and assert that it responds with a 200.

Listing 13.8   Testing an HTTP request with SuperTest

Imports SuperTest as a request; this is
the convention for importing SuperTest.

```
import request from 'supertest'

test('returns 200', () => {
  return request('https://www.facebook.com')
    .get('/')
    .expect(200)
})
```

Because SuperTest is asynchronous, you need to return the promise that it returns.

Makes a get request to the root of the base URL

Asserts that the HTTP status code is a 200

Run the unit tests with npm run test:unit. Jest will pick up server.spec.js and run the new test. The test you added should pass, although it might fail if you're in a country where Facebook forces redirects. Don't worry—a test that fails because Facebook returned a 302 rather than a 200 still proves that SuperTest is set up correctly.

You might have noticed that the tests take slightly longer to run now. Tests that use SuperTest take longer than normal unit tests because they make HTTP requests. If you have hundreds of tests using SuperTest, your test suite could take minutes to run. Minutes are years in unit test time, and you shouldn't slow down your unit tests. Instead, you should separate unit tests and integration tests to make sure your unit tests are fast.

To do that, open your package.json file. Edit the `test:unit` script to run tests only in the src directory as follows:

```
"test:unit": "jest src --no-cache"
```

NOTE   Here the `--no-cache` flag is added to fix bugs with older versions of Windows. If you're using macOS or Linux, you can omit the `no-cache` flag.

Now create a new `test:integration` script that runs the SuperTest tests. Because SuperTest creates a running app using the client-side JavaScript bundle, you need to create a new bundle for the server to use each time you run the tests. If you don't create a new bundle, you'll be testing old code. To build the bundle, you can run the `build` script before you run the tests. Unfortunately, this slows down the tests even more!

SuperTest tests need to run in a Node environment, like the server-side rendered unit tests. In your package.json file, add to the `scripts` field a new `test:integration` script that runs the server.spec.js file with Jest using a Node env:

```
"test:integration": "npm run build && jest --testEnvironment node --forceExit
    server.spec.js"
```

Add the integration script to the test script in the package.json file like so:

```
"test ": "npm run lint && npm run test:unit && npm run test:integration"
```

Run the integration tests with the command `npm run test:integration`. This is how you'll run the tests that use SuperTest.

You've seen that you can use SuperTest to request a URL and assert that the response from the URL was correct. You don't want to assert against Facebook, though; you want to check that your own app works correctly. To do that, set the server running in your tests. It's easy to create a running server with SuperTest—import the application express app, and pass it in to SuperTest. Refactor server.spec.js to include the code in the next listing.

Listing 13.9   Testing a 200 response with SuperTest

```
import app from './server'

describe('server', () => {
  test('/top returns 200', () => {          ◁─── Creates the server by passing
    return request(app)                           the app to SuperTest
      .get('/top')                      ◁─── Makes a get request
      .expect(200)        ◁───                    to the /top route
  })               Asserts that the server
})                 responds with a 200
```

Checking 200 responses is great, but you can implicitly test 200s with end-to-end tests (which you'll write in the next chapter). Instead of testing 200 errors, let's write some tests for a 404-error response.

To check that you get a 404-error response, you can make a GET request to a route that you know doesn't exist. Copy the code from the following listing into server.spec.js.

Listing 13.10   Testing that the server responds with 404 when the page isn't found

```
test('returns a 404 when page does not exist', () => {
  return request(app)                              Makes a GET request to
    .get('/does-not-exist')                        a route that doesn't exist
    .expect(404)          Asserts that the server
})                        responds with a 404 error
```

This test will pass; the app already handles 404-error responses. You can change the HTTPStatusCode property in src/views/NotFound.vue to make sure the test fails with an assertion error.

> **NOTE** The project uses a mixin that uses the HTTPStatusCode property to set the status code. This isn't a standard Vue feature!

I recommend having one SuperTest for each error-status code the server should return, normally a 200, a 404, and a 500. The main benefit of SuperTest is how easy it is to test the server response, so you can check that you have the correct HTTP headers, like cache-control or link.

You should avoid testing markup in SuperTest tests. When you have lots of tests that use SuperTest, they take a long time to run. You can test the markup of components in your unit tests or snapshot tests instead.

The main reason I use SuperTest is to check HTTP status codes. With other end-to-end tests, it's not always possible to determine whether the code you're testing was returned by the server as part of the HTTP request or whether it was rendered by the script executing after the server returned the code. With SuperTest, you can test explicitly that the server-side rendered code has been included in the HTTP response.

Now that you've seen how to write unit tests and integration tests for server-side tests, I want to cover testing SSR implicitly and why it's often more valuable than explicitly unit testing server-side rendered code.

13.4 *Testing SSR implicitly*

I've written in this book about testing implicitly and testing explicitly. *Explicit testing* is writing tests that assert that some functionality is working correctly. Writing unit tests for SSR code is explicit testing. *Implicit testing* is testing functionality as part of another test by relying on that functionality for the test to pass. If you test some functionality implicitly, the test will break if the functionality isn't working correctly, but the test isn't asserting it directly.

For example, end-to-end tests are tests that start up an application and run through user journeys. These tests do a lot of implicit testing, as well as checking that all the units of your application work together correctly.

It's useful to have a mixture of implicit and explicit tests. Implicit tests are good because you can test more functionality with fewer tests. The downside is that when an implicit test fails, it's difficult to pinpoint which part of the code is causing the problem. There's no explicit assertion that says, "Hey, here's what's wrong with your code"; you'll have to debug the stack trace to see what went wrong. The benefit of testing code implicitly is that you don't need to spend time writing tests, and you can refactor the code easily.

You won't explicitly test a lot of the code used to set up the server-side rendering. For example, in the server-side Hacker News app you have two entry files, one for the server and one for the route. You shouldn't write unit tests that check that the entry files are set up correctly. The files will be tested implicitly by end-to-end tests that load a page and run through a user journey. If the configuration is incorrect, the end-to-end tests won't be able to run through the user journeys, and the tests will fail.

Similarly, a lot of SSR code can be implicitly tested by end-to-end tests, without writing separate unit tests. Often, with SSR code, the cost of writing explicit unit tests outweighs the benefits. But there are cases where writing a unit test for SSR code is beneficial. I'll leave that to your discretion.

In the next and final chapter, you'll learn how to write end-to-end tests to finish off your test suite.

Summary

- You can test server-side rendered code with the Vue Server Test Utils library.
- You can traverse the string output of a server-side rendered component with the Vue Server Test Utils `render` method.
- You should write server-side unit tests in a separate file from client-side unit tests, so that you can run them in a Node environment, instead of a jsdom environment.
- You can test HTTP status codes with the SuperTest library.

Exercises

1 What comment can you use to make Jest run tests in a Node environment?
2 What is the difference between `render` and `renderToString`?

Writing end-to-end tests

As they say, all great things must come to an end. This is the final chapter of the book, and the last part of your quest to create a frontend testing suite. In this closing chapter, you'll learn how to test a running application by writing end-to-end tests.

In this book you've learned how to write unit tests and snapshot tests. They're both effective at testing individual units, but they have one glaring problem—they don't check that the units of code work together. End-to-end tests solve this problem by performing tests against a fully operational application.

The first section of this chapter is about what end-to-end tests are, how they fit into a testing workflow, and how to write effective ones. After you've learned about end-to-end tests at a high level, I'll show you how to write them.

You can use a few different tools to write end-to-end tests and automate a browser, but in this book I'll show you how to write tests with a framework called Nightwatch that uses the WebDriver API under the hood.

In the main part of this chapter, you'll learn how to write end-to-end tests that cycle through user journeys by automating Chrome. After you have some end-to-end tests running in Chrome, I'll show you how to set them up to run in multiple browsers.

Before you write any end-to-end tests, you need to know what end-to-end tests are and how they fit into the frontend testing pyramid.

14.1 Understanding end-to-end tests

End-to-end tests check that an application behaves correctly by automating a browser to interact with the running application. In chapter 1, I compared end-to-end testing to manual testing. When you're testing an app manually, you open the app, click through some actions, and make sure the app responds correctly. End-to-end tests are the same, except a program—not a human—interacts with the app.

Imagine you wanted to test that the Hacker News app renders a new list when you click the New link in the header. If you were testing manually, you would run the application server, open the application in a browser, click the New link, check that the route changes, and check that the list updates. An end-to-end test would automate a browser to perform exactly the same actions.

End-to-end tests are awesome, but they do have some downsides. To overcome the downsides, you need to write these tests effectively.

14.1.1 Using end-to-end tests effectively

End-to-end tests are a vital part of a frontend testing suite. Without end-to-end tests you wouldn't know that an application was working correctly! But there are some downsides to end-to-end tests: they're slow, they're difficult to debug, and they can be flaky.

The key to using end-to-end tests effectively is to use them sparingly. Instead of writing all your tests as end-to-end tests, you should write only a few that run through core user journeys. That's what the frontend testing pyramid describes (figure 14.1).

Think of end-to-end tests as supplements for unit tests and snapshot tests. Unit tests and snapshot tests thoroughly check the components and functions that make up an application. End-to-end tests check that these components and functions work together correctly.

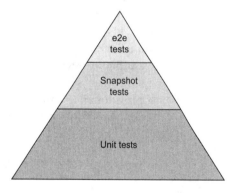

Figure 14.1　The frontend testing pyramid

Works on my machine!

Works on my machine (WOMM) is an infamous response to a bug report. It happens when a developer fails to reproduce a bug locally. When they can't reproduce the bug, they reply with the infamous words: *I don't know what's wrong—it works on my machine.*

End-to-end tests are difficult to debug, but the task becomes even more frustrating if you can't reproduce the bug on your machine.

You can avoid the WOMM problem by running your application and tests in a reproducible environment, like a Docker container. It's beyond the scope of this book to teach you how to set up and use Docker, but if you want to take your tests to the next level, I recommend learning how to run your application and end-to-end tests in a Docker container.

Now that you understand end-to-end tests at a high level, it's time to look at how you implement them. In this book, you'll use Nightwatch and the WebDriver API.

14.1.2 *Understanding Nightwatch and WebDriver*

Nightwatch is a JavaScript framework for automating browsers. Under the hood, Nightwatch uses WebDriver to control the browser. It's important to understand Web-Driver to be able to set up Nightwatch tests.

WebDriver is an interface for automating browsers. The most popular way to use WebDriver is with Selenium Server—a Java servlet with a REST API for applying the WebDriver protocol.

> **NOTE** A REST API is an interface that use HTTP requests to perform actions on a server.

To run end-to-end tests, start Selenium Server to listen for incoming HTTP requests. You can automate a browser by sending HTTP requests to Selenium Server. For example, if Selenium Server was listening on port 4444, a POST request to http://localhost:4444/wd/hub/session/1352110219202/element/0/click would cause the Selenium Server to click an element in a browser.

It's difficult to write tests that communicate with Selenium directly. You need to manage browser sessions, and the request URLs make tests difficult to read. Night-watch provides an abstraction over the WebDriver API.

In the next listing, you can see an example of using Nightwatch to enter a search in Google and assert that "Nightwatch" is included in the results.

Listing 14.1   Testing that Google displays results

```
module.exports = {
    'displays result correctly' : function (browser) {
        browser
```

Tests are defined as methods on an object, with the property name used as the specification name.

```
                .url('http://www.google.com')
                .waitForElementVisible('body', 1000)
                .setValue('input[type=text]', 'nightwatch')
                .click('button[name=btnG]')
                .pause(1000)
                .assert.containsText('#main', 'Nightwatch')
                .end();
    }
};
```

Enters a value into an input field → `.setValue('input[type=text]', 'nightwatch')`

Automates the browser to visit www.google.com ← `.url('http://www.google.com')` `.waitForElementVisible('body', 1000)`

Clicks a button ← `.click('button[name=btnG]')`

Asserts that the page contains the text "Nightwatch" ← `.assert.containsText('#main', 'Nightwatch')`

Nightwatch communicates with Selenium Server using HTTP requests. Selenium Server then forwards commands to the browser to execute (figure 14.2). Luckily, you don't need to know the REST endpoints for Selenium Server; all you need to do is start a Selenium Server and tell Nightwatch what URL Selenium Server is running on.

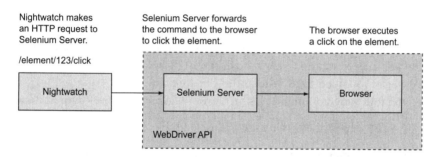

Figure 14.2   Clicking an element with Nightwatch

Now that you've looked at how Nightwatch works, it's time to add it to your project.

14.2   *Adding Nightwatch to a project*

Setting up Nightwatch can seem difficult when you don't understand what you're doing. In this section, I'll walk you through the process of installing the dependencies and configuring Nightwatch to run against the correct port on localhost.

You will do the following four things to get Nightwatch running:

1   Install Nightwatch dependencies.
2   Add the Nightwatch configuration.
3   Add a sanity test.
4   Write a script to start the server and run Nightwatch.

14.2.1   *Installing dependencies*

Dependencies can be a nightmare. When I write non-JavaScript apps, I'm always amazed at how difficult it can be to download a project, install its dependencies, and set it running locally. npm takes a lot of this pain away for us lucky JavaScript developers—you run `npm install`, and the dependencies are installed for you. npm is a natural fit for JavaScript dependencies, but you can use it for non-JavaScript dependencies too.

Nightwatch uses Selenium Server, which is a Java applet. Even though Selenium Server is written in Java, you can install it with npm. This ensures that you can still download a project, run `npm install`, and have the test and development scripts work correctly. You should always make it a goal of your project that running `npm it` (aliases for `npm install && npm run test`) will install all dependencies and run the test script.

> **NOTE** You need to have the Java Development Kit (JDK) installed to run Selenium Server; the minimum required version is 7. You can read how to do this in appendix A.

Install Selenium Server and Nightwatch as a dependency with the following command:

```
npm install --save-dev nightwatch selenium-server
```

You also need to add *browser-specific drivers*. Browser drivers are programs used by Selenium Server to execute the tests in the different browsers. For now, you'll run the tests in Chrome, so you need to download the Chrome driver.

Run the following command to save ChromeDriver as a development dependency:

```
npm install --save-dev chromedriver
```

With Selenium Server and the ChromeDriver binary files installed in npm packages, the next step is to configure Nightwatch to start Selenium Server and communicate with it.

14.2.2 Configuring Nightwatch

Nightwatch runs Selenium Server and ChromeDriver for you. For Nightwatch to run these programs, you need to add a Nightwatch configuration file to tell Nightwatch the location of the binary files.

So far in this project, you've kept unit tests and snapshot tests in the src directory next to the code that they're testing. For end-to-end tests, you'll create a separate e2e directory in the root of the project. The end-to-end tests check the running application—they don't focus on one particular file, so there's no need to house them next to a file they are testing as with unit tests and snapshot tests.

Create an e2e directory in the project root. Now create an e2e/nightwatch.conf.js file, and add the code from the next listing.

Listing 14.2   Nightwatch configuration file

```
module.exports = {
  src_folders: ['e2e/specs'],        ⟵──┐ The directory that
  output_folder: 'e2e/reports',            │ the test files are in
  selenium: {                          ⟵──┘
```

The directory that the test files are in

The directory to which Nightwatch should output test reports

```
                     start_process: true,
                     server_path: require('selenium-server').path,
                     host: '127.0.0.1',
                     port: 4444,
                     cli_args: {
                       'WebDriver.chrome.driver': require('chromedriver').path
                     }
                   },

                   test_settings: {
                     chrome: {
                       desiredCapabilities: {
                         browserName: 'chrome'
                       }
                     }
                   }
                 }
               }
```

4444 is the default Selenium Server port.

The Selenium Server binary path; this is exported by the selenium-server npm package.

Sets Nightwatch to start the Selenium process with the ChromeDriver path. You're using the path exported by the chromedriver package, which handles the installation of ChromeDriver.

Settings for the chrome test environment. The test environment is configured by passing the --env argument to Nightwatch.

Now that Nightwatch is configured, you can write a sanity test to make sure the setup is working.

14.2.3 Adding a sanity test

When you finish cooking a delicious soup, it's always a good idea to try a spoonful before you serve it to your guests, just to make sure it tastes fine. In the same way, you should always add a sanity test when you add a new test setup. You don't want to spend hours debugging a test only to find out your setup was wrong.

Like other tests you've written in this book, you should split the end-to-end tests into their own script. Open the package.json file, and add a `test:e2e` script to run Nightwatch using the Nightwatch configuration file, as follows:

```
"test:e2e": "nightwatch --config e2e/nightwatch.conf.js --env chrome",
```

You should include the `test:e2e` script in the complete `test` script. Open package.json, and update the `test` script to run the end-to-end tests like so:

```
"test": "npm run lint && npm run test:unit && npm run test:integration && npm
    run test:e2e",
```

This is a momentous occasion! You finally have a complete test script to run against the application.

Next you need to add the sanity test to check that the runner and configuration are set up correctly. Create a new file e2e/specs/journeys.js. Open the file, and add the following code.

Listing 14.3 Nightwatch test that visits localhost:8080

```
module.exports = {
  'sanity test': function(browser) {
    browser
      .url('http://localhost:8080')
```

```
        .waitForElementVisible('.item-list', 2000)
        .end();
  }
}
```

To run Nightwatch tests against your app locally, the application must be running. Enter the following command in the command line to build the JavaScript files and start the server:

```
npm run build && npm run start
```

Open a new tab in the command line, and run the test script with the command `npm run test:e2e`. Nightwatch will find the test file, open a browser, navigate to localhost :8080, and wait for the `.item-list` element to be visible.

> **NOTE** On Windows you might see a warning dialog asking you to allow Selenium to run. You should accept.

The test should pass. This is great, except there's a problem with this setup. You had to run two processes in two separate terminal tabs for the server and the tests to run.

> **NOTE** If the test isn't passing, it will be because the server isn't running on port 8080. You might need to stop another process from listening to port 8080 for the server to run.

The test suite should run from a single script. You can't rely on somebody starting the server manually. The solution is to create a runner script that starts the server for you and then runs Nightwatch in a separate process.

14.2.4 *Writing an end-to-end test script*

You're going to write a file that starts the server and then spawns a *child process* that runs Nightwatch with the correct arguments. That way, you can run one script to start the server *and* run Nightwatch.

> **NOTE** If you aren't familiar with child processes, you can read about them at https://nodejs.org/api/child_process.html.

The runner file will import the project's Express app; then it will start the server listening by calling the `listen` method. When a server starts listening, the process will run until it's stopped by either a signal or an error. You'll use Node event emitters to attach to these events and stop the process if the server exits.

> **NOTE** If you aren't familiar with Node event emitters, you can read about them at https://nodejs.org/api/events.html#events_events.

When the server has started listening, you'll create a child process to run Nightwatch. When the tests finish running, you will close the server and exit the script. Create a file called e2e/runner.js, and add the following code to the file.

Listing 14.4   Starting a server and running Nightwatch

```
const app = require('../server')
const spawn = require('cross-spawn')

const PORT = process.env.PORT || 8080

const server = app.listen(PORT, () => {
  const opts = ['--config', 'e2e/nightwatch.conf.js', '--env', 'chrome']
  const runner = spawn('./node_modules/.bin/nightwatch', opts, { stdio:
    'inherit' })

  runner.on('exit', function (code) {
    server.close()
    process.exit(code)
  })

  runner.on('error', function (err) {
    server.close()
    throw err
  })
})
```

Gets the port number from the environment variable if it's set, or defaults to 8080

Starts the server listening on the port, and calls the callback once the server is running

Spawns a subprocess that runs the nightwatch binary with the config path and env set to chrome. This is the equivalent of running nightwatch --config e2e/nightwatch.conf.js --env chrome in an npm script. This spawns a child process that runs that command, which will start Nightwatch running. The stdio inherit option tells the subprocess to log everything to the main process, so you will see the output in the terminal when you run the script.

spawn creates a stream. You can use the on method to listen to events from the process and close the server and the process when Nightwatch finishes running.

This callback will run when the server creates an error. You should close the server and create the error in this process.

Now you have the runner file you need to update the `test:e2e` script. Open the package.json file, and update the script to run the runner file with Node:

```
"test:e2e": "node e2e/runner.js",
```

Run the test script: `npm run test:e2e`. This will start the server, run the test, open a browser that navigates to the app, wait until the .item-list element is visible, close the browser, and report whether the test passed or failed.

You've seen how to add Nightwatch to server-side projects. The next step is to write some tests.

Running tests on a client-side rendered project

Adding a script to run Nightwatch end-to-end tests to a client-side project is slightly more complicated than it is for a server-side rendered project.

The difference between a client-side rendered project and a SSR project is that an SSR project already includes a server that can serve your app locally. With client-side projects, you normally don't have a server in the project to run the application.

Luckily, most client-side rendered Vue projects use webpack to bundle the code. Webpack has a development server package that runs a Node server to serve a project. You can use the webpack development server in the runner script to serve your file and run the tests against the file running on the development server.

14.3 *Writing end-to-end tests with Nightwatch*

It's time to get your hands dirty and write some end-to-end tests in Nightwatch. Before you write the code, you need to decide which tests you are going to write.

14.3.1 *Deciding which end-to-end tests to write*

Deciding which tests to write and which not to write is a fine art. It's important to write as few end-to-end tests as possible, because an end-to-end test script quickly becomes slow and flaky.

It's not realistic to write end-to-end tests for every possible user journey. There are too many combinations of actions that the user could take. Instead, you need to be selective and write tests that check only core user journeys.

The key to effective end-to-end tests is to use them mainly to perform actions. A common mistake I see is people checking page HTML. For example, they will check that a page renders a list with the correct items. This is an expensive duplication of unit tests and snapshot tests. If you wrote tests for each piece of HTML on a page, your test suite would take years to run. Of course, sometimes you will need to check HTML, but keep it to a minimum.

In the Hacker News application, you have several lists. There are the top, new, show, ask, and jobs lists. You could write end-to-end tests for each of these lists, but that would mean testing the same functionality five times.

In tests, time is a valuable resource. You should be frugal about the number of end-to-end tests you write. With that in mind, the following are a few core journeys for the Hacker News app that you will test:

- Clicking Comments takes the user to the item page.
- Clicking a username redirects to a user page.
- Clicking a list in the header refreshes the list items.
- The page paginates correctly.

The first tests you write will check that the app routing is working correctly.

14.3.2 *Writing end-to-end tests for routes*

Routing is difficult to test with unit tests, which makes it a good candidate to write end-to-end tests for. One of the difficulties of end-to-end tests is deciding what you should assert to tell you that a journey is working correctly. If you manually tested that *clicking Comments takes the user to the item page,* you would open the browser, click a Comments link, and check with your eyes that the page updated. You would see visually that the page was correct, but how do you tell a program that the page is correct? You could make sure that each of the correct elements was rendered, but that would lead to long tests. Instead, you need to compromise and choose something that gives you enough confidence that the code is working correctly. For example, you could check that a single element is rendered that's unique to the new page.

In the test to check that *clicking Comments takes the user to the item page,* you'll check that the URL has updated and that an element with the class `item-view` is visible after you click a Comments link. Replace the sanity test in e2e/specs/journeys.js with the code from the next listing.

Listing 14.5 Testing that a link navigates correctly

```
'takes user to the item page': function(browser) {
  browser
    .url('http://localhost:8080')                              Navigates to the
    .waitForElementVisible('.news-item', 1)                    running app
    .click('.comments-link')
    .assert.urlContains(`/item`)                               Waits for an item with the
    .waitForElementVisible('.item-view', 15000)                news-item class. This
    .end();                                                    makes sure the items are
}                                                              rendered before you try to
                                                               click the Comments link.
```

Clicks the Comments link → `.click('.comments-link')`

Asserts that the item-view component is visible

Asserts that the URL now contains /item. This means the route has worked correctly.

Run the tests: `npm run test:e2e`. The test will fail. The problem is that the items did not load fast enough, so the `waitForElementVisible` command failed. You can fix the problem by increasing the time that `waitForElementVisible` waits. The second argument in `waitForElementVisible` is the number of milliseconds it should wait before throwing an error. In the file, increase the time of the first `waitForElementVisible` call to 15000 (15 seconds) as follows:

```
.waitForElementVisible('.news-item', 15000)
```

Now run the tests again; they will pass if your internet connection is fast enough. If you have a poor connection, you can increase the milliseconds value that `waitForElementVisible` will wait.

Flaky tests

End-to-end tests suffer from a problem known as *flaky tests*. Flaky tests are tests that fail regularly even though the code is working correctly. Tests can become flaky for many reasons. For example, if part of the user journey calls an API that takes a long time to respond, the test will time out and fail.

When you have a flaky test in your test suite, you will start to ignore failing tests. It's easy to slip into a habit of thinking a failing test suite is just another flaky test. This makes your test suite much less effective. In an effective test suite, any failing test tells you there's a bug in the application.

You can avoid flaky tests by adding long timeouts to your end-to-end tests. If an API call takes longer than expected, the test won't fail. It's difficult to completely avoid flaky tests. The best way is to write as few end-to-end tests as possible, while still testing core journeys.

The next test to write checks that *clicking a username redirects to a user page*. This test will be similar to the previous test. You'll open the app in the browser, wait until the items have loaded, click a user link, and then assert that the browser navigates to the correct route.

To check that the browser navigates to the next route, the test will check that the route has updated and that an element with a `user-view` class is visible. Add the test from the next listing to the object in e2e/specs/journeys.js.

Listing 14.6   Checking that a route has updated

```
'clicking on a user redirects to  the user page': function(browser) {
  browser
    .url('http://localhost:8080')
    .waitForElementVisible('.news-item',  15000)        Clicks
    .click('.by a')                                     the link
    .assert.urlContains(`/user`)                        Asserts that the URL now
    .waitForElementVisible('.user-view',  30000)        contains /user in the path
    .end();
}                                                       Asserts that the user-view
                                                        element is rendered
```

Run the tests to watch them pass: npm run test:e2e. As long as you have a good internet connection, the test will pass.

The tests you just wrote checked that the URL was updated and that the app rendered the correct element. You didn't check that the values are correct. Checking values can be difficult when the page has dynamic data.

14.3.3   *Writing end-to-end tests for dynamic data*

It's difficult to check apps that use dynamic data. For example, the Hacker News app will display different items over time. You can't hardcode a value into a test; if you assert that an item has the title *Some HN item title*, when you run the test a week later, the title will have changed and the test will fail.

In the Hacker News app, you need to test that pagination works correctly. You can do this by asserting that the URL updates when you click a pagination link. But that isn't a rigorous test. It doesn't verify that the page content has changed.

One way to test that page content has changed is by saving the previous page content as a variable and comparing it against the new page content. This test still isn't perfect, but it does tell you that the content has changed.

You'll write a test that saves the list text as a variable. Then you'll navigate with the pagination links and assert that the current list text has changed from the previous value. That way, you can know that the list values have been updated.

Add the following code to e2e/specs/journeys.js.

Listing 14.7   Changing the list by clicking through the navigation

```
'paginates items correctly': function(browser) {
let originalItemListText;
```

```
browser
  .url('http://localhost:8080')
  .waitForElementVisible('.news-item',  15000)
  .getText('.item-list', function(result)
    originalItemListText = result.value
  })
  .click('.item-list-nav a:nth-of-type(2 )')
  .waitForElementNotPresent('.progress',  15000)
  .perform(() => {
    browser.expect.element('.item-
      list').text.to.not.equal(originalItemListText)
  })
  .getText('.item-list', function(result) {
    originalItemListText = result.value
  })
  .click('.item-list-nav a')
  .waitForElementNotPresent('.progress',  15000)
  .perform(() => {
    browser.expect.element('.item-
      list').text.to.not.equal(originalItemListText)
  })
},
```

Waits until the items have loaded

Gets the text of the .item-list element, and stores it in the originalItemListText variable

Clicks the More link

Waits until the progress bar has disappeared (until the new items have loaded)

Perform is a command that gives you a callback in which to execute commands. Here, you're using the callback to perform an expect assertion to make sure the text in the .item-list element is not the same as the original text. This assertion checks that the .item-list has updated.

Updates the originalText value

Clicks the Prev link

Asserts that the text has changed again

You can use the same technique to check that the list is updated when the user clicks different list types in the navigation. Add the following code to e2e/specs/journeys.js.

Listing 14.8 Checking a user journey with an end-to-end test

```
'changes list by clicking through nav': function(browser) {
  let originalItemListText;
  browser
.url('http://localhost:8080')
    .waitForElementVisible('.news-item',  15000)
    .getText('.item-list', function(result) {
      originalItemListText = result.value
    })
    .click('.inner a:nth-of-type(2)')
    .waitForElementNotPresent('.progress',  15000)
    .perform(() => {
      browser.expect.element('.item-
    list').text.to.not.equal(originalItemListText)
    })
    .getText('.item-list', function(result) {
      originalItemListText = result.value
    })
    .click('.inner a:nth-of-type(4)')
    .waitForElementNotPresent('.progress',  15000)
    .perform(() => {
      browser.expect.element('.item-
    list').text.to.not.equal(originalItemListText)
    })
  },
```

Waits until the items have loaded

Gets the text of the .item-list element, and stores it in the originalItemListText variable

Clicks a link to load a new list

Asserts that the .item-list has updated by comparing the new text to the old text before loading a new list

Stores the current list text

Loads a new list by clicking a link

Asserts that item-list has updated

Run the test script: npm run test:e2e. You've written tests to check the core use journeys. The tests will fail if the units of the app aren't connected correctly. These end-to-end tests are implicitly testing that the application is configured correctly.

Now that you've got end-to-end tests written and passing in Chrome, it's time to run them in another browser. You can do this without editing the test code. All you need to do is add some extra configuration.

14.4 *Running end-to-end tests in multiple browsers*

Cross-browser testing is an important part of any large application, but it's time-consuming. One of the benefits of writing end-to-end tests with Nightwatch is you can run them in multiple browsers with a little extra configuration. In this section, you'll look at how to run tests in Firefox as well as Chrome.

> **NOTE** Remember, Nightwatch uses the WebDriver API, which is a W3C standard. That means most browsers support the WebDriver protocol.

You're going to run your tests in Firefox, so you need to download the Firefox driver—geckodriver. Remember, drivers are WebDriver implementations for different browsers. You'll use an npm package to manage the downloading of the driver binary, so the first step is to install geckodriver and save it as a dependency. Run the following command in the command line:

```
npm install --save-dev geckodriver
```

You need to set Nightwatch to pass the geckodriver binary path to the Selenium process. You do this in the Nightwatch config file. Open the e2e/nightwatch.conf.js file, and, in the selenium.cli_args object, add the following extra line:

```
'WebDriver.gecko.driver' : require('geckodriver').path
```

Now you can update the runner script to call Nightwatch with a new environment. That way, Nightwatch will run tests in both the Chrome and Firefox environments. Open the e2e/runner.js file. In this file is an opts array that contains the command-line options you pass when you call the Nightwatch process. You need to update the line to pass chrome,firefox as the env argument. Replace the line with the following code:

```
const opts = ['--config', 'e2e/nightwatch.conf.js', '--env', 'chrome,firefox']
```

When you run the runner script, Nightwatch will run tests in the Chrome environment and the Firefox environment. If you run the test:e2e script, you'll get an error that Nightwatch is passed an invalid test environment—you need to add the Firefox environment in the Nightwatch config file.

You'll add the option in the e2e/nightwatch.conf.js file. This option tells Nightwatch to use the Firefox browser when running the Firefox environment. Open e2e/nightwatch.conf.js, and add the code from the next listing to the test_settings object.

Listing 14.9 Defining a Firefox environment Nightwatch config

```
firefox: {
  desiredCapabilities: {
    browserName: 'firefox'          ◁────┐  Sets Nightwatch to use the Firefox browser
  }                                        when running the Firefox environment
}
```

That's all the setup you need to run tests in Firefox. Run the end-to-end script: npm run test:e2e. You'll see that Nightwatch now runs the tests in Firefox and Chrome.

You can add extra browsers by following the same steps, although you will need to use an operating system that supports the browser. For example, you must be using Windows 10+ to run tests in Edge.

Great—now you have tests running in Chrome and Firefox with Nightwatch, which uses the WebDriver API.

Alternative end-to-end testing frameworks

Most end-to-end testing frameworks use WebDriver. The reason I've taught you how to use Nightwatch is that WebDriver is the most popular solution. But there are alternatives to WebDriver. The two most promising are TestCafe and Cypress.io. They are both faster than WebDriver solutions and require less configuration to set up. The downside to these alternative frameworks is that they are new and have a smaller community than the WebDriver API.

The best place to learn about TestCafe is its Getting Started Guide: http://mng.bz/nxn5. Cypress.io also has a good Getting Started guide at http://mng.bz/vOgp.

Now you have unit tests, snapshot tests, integration tests, and end-to-end tests running against the Hacker News application. You can run them all from the following script:

```
npm t
```

Congratulations! You've finished the Hacker News application, and you've developed a test suite that effectively tests that the application is behaving correctly.

Summary

- You can write end-to-end tests to test that user journeys work correctly.
- You can use the Nightwatch framework to write end-to-end tests.
- You can set up Nightwatch to run for SSR apps and for client-side rendered apps,

Where to go from here

Your testing quest has come to an end. You've gained experience points, leveled up your skills, and achieved the sought-after title of Vue Test Master.

It's been a long journey from the first test back in chapter 2. You've learned to write unit tests for Vue components. You've learned to use snapshot tests to test static output of components. Finally, you've learned to write end-to-end tests to check that a running application behaves correctly.

Of course, like a student graduating from college, your Vue testing journey has only just begun. Out there in the wide world you'll encounter innovative code bases and unforeseen problems that will challenge your testing prowess. But I'm confident that, armed with the techniques you learned in this book, you will find solutions and overcome these unknown challenges.

As you increase your testing skills and experience, you may decide to contribute to the Vue testing community. There are many ways that you can help push the community forward. You could create a library, write a blog post, or teach other developers. You'll be surprised at the impact your actions can have and the good they can bring other developers.

Whatever your future holds, I'm glad that I could teach you my approach to testing and that there's one more Vue testing master in the world.

Happy testing!

appendix A
Setting up your environment

To follow along with this book, you need to have some programs installed on your machine.

A.1 Choosing a text editor

You can choose from many great editors. Most of the popular ones have add-on Vue plugins that add syntax highlighting to .vue files.

I use WebStorm because it makes debugging a breeze. Some other good editors include Visual Studio Code, Sublime Text, and Atom. You can even use Notepad if you're feeling old school.

For .vue file highlighting in VSCode, Sublime, or Atom, you need to install a plugin (table A.1).

Table A.1 Editors and plugins

Editor	Plugin	URL
Sublime	vue-syntax-highlighting	https://github.com/vuejs/vue-syntax-highlight
Atom	language-vue	https://github.com/hedefalk/atom-vue
vim	vim-vue	https://github.com/posva/vim-vue
Visual Studio Code	vetur	https://github.com/vuejs/vetur

This book is text-editor agnostic. For example, when I teach you how to debug tests, I'll use a method that works for all text editors and IDEs using Node Debugger and Chrome DevTools.

A.2 Using the command line

You're going to use the command line a lot in this book. You won't write any complex scripts, but you'll regularly enter commands to run tests with npm scripts, start

231

servers, and clone repositories with Git. You need to be able to navigate the filesystem with `cd` and create directories with the `mkdir` command.

> **TIP** If you need to improve your command-line skills, you should read *Getting to Know the Command* Line by David Baumgold: www.davidbaumgold.com/tutorials/command-line.

Throughout this book, I'm going to instruct you to *enter the following command*. When I tell you to *enter the following command*, I mean that you should add the code that follows to a command-line interface in the project root directory, and press Enter.

You should use a UNIX command-line interface. Linux and macOS users can use your favorite terminal program. For Windows users, I recommend using Git Bash. Git Bash is a UNIX terminal emulator that is installed by default by the Windows Git installer.

Make sure you're in the Hacker News project root directory. If you're using a UNIX terminal, you can check the current working directory with the `pwd` command.

A.3   *Installing Chrome*

You should use Chrome as your browser for this project. It makes it easier for me to teach you what commands to enter if we're both using the same browser. Plus, Chrome has an awesome Debugger that I'll show you how to use in chapter 2.

If you don't have Chrome installed, you can install it following the instructions on the Chrome install page—https://support.google.com/chrome/answer/95346.

A.3.1   *Using Chrome DevTools*

In this book, I'll sometimes ask you to open the Chrome DevTools. Chrome DevTools are a collection of tools built into Chrome that make debugging easier. There are a huge number of tools, but the only ones you'll use in this book are the Console and the Debugger. There's a detailed guide on using the Debugger in chapter 1.

To use the Console, you need to open the DevTools. Use Ctrl-Shift-J (or Cmd-Opt-J on Mac) to open the DevTools and bring focus to the Console. Try typing a sum into the Console as follows:

```
1 + 1
```

You'll see the output in the Console (figure A.1). This is a great way to get quick feedback on your JavaScript—I write little functions in there all the time.

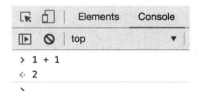

Figure A.1 Using the Chrome Console

In the book, when I tell you to write something in the Console, this is the Console I'm talking about.

A.4 Installing the Vue.js devtools Chrome extension

The Vue.js devtools extension for Chrome is a tool that makes debugging Vue components, events, and Vuex easier. To install the Vue.js devtools in Chrome, go to the Chrome webstore page—http://mng.bz/1Qxn.

The Vue devtools add a new tab to the Chrome DevTools window. You can use it to inspect the Vue component tree and see the state of each component (figure A.2).

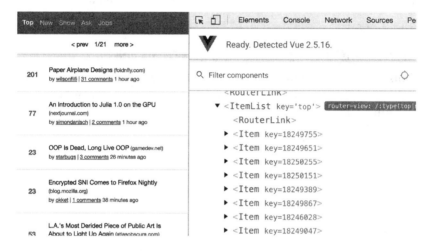

Figure A.2   Using Vue developer tools to inspect the Hacker News app

I won't instruct you to use it in the book, but if you're confused with the application or want to debug the component tree, Vue devtools are useful. For a full guide on using the Vue developer, read the article, "Using the Vue.js Devtools" by Joshua Bemenderfer (https://alligator.io/vuejs/vue-devtools/).

A.5 Installing Node and npm

In this book, you'll run tests in node and use npm to manage packages, so you need to have both installed on your machine. npm is bundled with Node. If you already have both installed, fantastic, you can skip to the next section.

You can install Node in a few different ways:

- One-click installer
- Homebrew or MacPorts (OSX only)
- Using the Linux package management system (Linux only)
- Using NVM

A.5.1   *Installing Node with the one-click installer*

This is the easiest way to install Node. If you're on Windows or macOS, a one-click install method is available online. Visit the Node website, and follow the instructions to download Node using the installer—https://nodejs.org/en/download.

A.5.2   *Installing Node with Homebrew (macOS only)*

Homebrew is a package manager for macOS. If you already have Homebrew installed, you can use it to install Node. If you don't have Homebrew, you can install it from the website—https://brew.sh. I recommend installing using the Mac one-click installer if you are not familiar with Homebrew.

To install Node with Homebrew, enter the following command in your terminal:

```
brew install node
```

A.5.3   *Installing Node with Linux package managers (Linux only)*

Most Linux distributions have Node in their package repositories. You need to enter the correct command for your Linux distribution into the command line.

In Ubuntu, you can use `apt-get`:

```
sudo apt-get install -y nodejs
```

In Arch Linux, you can use `pacman`:

```
pacman -S nodejs npm
```

In CentOS, you can use `yum`:

```
sudo yum -y install nodejs
```

The Node website has a list of all known package managers that include Node in their repositories and instructions on how to install using them—https://nodejs.org/en/download/package-manager.

A.5.4   *Installing with NVM*

NVM is a script that helps install and manage node versions. It provides a way to manage multiple node versions on the same machine.

I won't give detailed instructions on using NVM; you can read about installation and usage on the GitHub repository—https://github.com/creationix/nvm. But I recommend using it if you use Node regularly.

A.5.5   *Verifying that Node and npm are installed*

To check whether Node is installed on your machine, enter the following command in the command line:

```
node -v
```

This should output the version number, something like `v8.1.1`. If the command displays an error, node isn't installed. To install node, you can try a different method. Next check whether npm is installed as follows:

```
npm -v
```

Again, this should output a version number, like `5.0.3`. Node comes with npm by default, so if you have Node installed, you should also have npm. If not, you can follow the guide on the npm site—https://www.npmjs.com/get-npm.

A.6   Installing Git

To work along with this book, you need to clone Git repositories from GitHub, so you need Git installed. To check that Git is installed on your machine, enter the following command:

```
git --version
```

You should see a version number, like `git version 2.11.1`. The command line will display an error if you don't have Git installed.

If Git is not installed, you can install it by following the official instructions on the Git website: http://mng.bz/Waad.

A.7   Starting a new chapter

In this book, you'll work on a Hacker News application. This is available on GitHub at https://github.com/eddyerburgh/vue-hackernews.

Most chapters in this book have a corresponding branch in the Git repository for you to use. To make it possible for you to jump into a chapter and work along with the code examples, you can change to the relevant branch for the chapter using Git.

> **NOTE** Branches are different versions of a code base in a Git project. You can read more about Git branching on the Git website: http://mng.bz/jOOV.

To get started, download the project using `git clone`, as follows:

```
git clone git@github.com:eddyerburgh/vue-hackernews.git
```

If you do not have SSH set up with GitHub, use the HTTPS version, shown next:

```
git clone https://github.com/eddyerburgh/vue-hackernews.git
```

To get the correct code for the chapter, you need to change to the chapter branch. To do this, change into the Git repository, like so:

```
cd vue-hackernews
```

Then change branches with `git checkout`:

```
git checkout chapter-2
```

If you're dropping into a chapter, you should change to that chapter branch. For example, if you've jumped into chapter 4, `git checkout` the chapter-4 repository when you're inside the Git project, as follows:

```
git checkout chapter-4
```

NOTE There is no chapter-5 or chapter-6 branch.

A.8 *Starting chapter 5*

Chapter 5 uses a different project to learn how to test events in Vue apps. To get started, download the project using Git clone as follows:

```
git clone git@github.com:eddyerburgh/vue-email-signup-form-app.git
```

Or use HTTPS, as shown next:

```
git clone https://github.com/eddyerburgh/vue-email-signup-form-app.git
```

Change into the Git repository like so:

```
cd vue-email-signup-form-app
```

Then change to the starter branch with `git checkout`:

```
git co starter
```

A.9 *Installing the Java Development Kit*

In chapter 13, you run Selenium Server, which requires the Java Development Kit (JDK). The minimum Java version is 7 (the full version string is 1.7.0). You can check your Java version from the command line as follows:

```
java -version
```

If you don't have the minimum version installed, follow the instructions for your operating system on the Java website: http://mng.bz/8JJW.

appendix B
Running the
production build

In this appendix, you'll learn how to get the production build of the Hacker News application running locally.

B.1 Understanding the production build

The Hacker News application has two build pipelines—production and development. The two different build pipelines exist because you want to produce different files depending on whether you're developing or serving the app over HTTP.

The development build creates JavaScript files with source maps and hot module replacement. You can run the development build on a dev server by using the `serve` npm script as follows:

```
npm run serve
```

> **DEFINITION** Hot module replacement updates modules in the browser without losing state when you make changes to the code. You can read about hot module replacement on the webpack website: http://mng.bz/NAAx.

The production build minimizes the JavaScript to make the final bundle size as small as possible. This app is designed to be served over HTTP, so the fewer bytes the better. There isn't a server to serve the production files, so to run the production build you need to generate the build files and serve it over HTTP.

B.2 Running the Hacker News production build locally

To build the Hacker News app for production, you need to run the npm `build` script. In the Hacker News directory, run the following command in the command line to create the production build:

```
npm run build
```

This will bundle your project with webpack. The built files including index.html are generated in the dist folder.

You can create a server using the `http-server` Node module. The first thing to do is install `http-server` globally:

```
npm install http-server -g
```

Change into the dist folder with `cd`. Then run the simple server as follows:

```
http-server
```

This will start a server listening on port 8080. If you get an `[Errno 48]` error, port 8080 is busy. You can change the port number to something else and try again, as shown next:

```
http-server -p 1234
```

When the server is running, you'll see a `Starting up http-server, serving ./` message. Open a browser and go to http://localhost:8000. This is your application!

Deploying the application to production is beyond the scope of this tutorial. You could choose hundreds of ways to host your application, and choosing a provider is up to you.

appendix C
Exercise answers

This appendix provides the answers to the end-of-chapter exercises.

Chapter 2

```
1 test('renders Hello, World!', () => {
    const wrapper = shallowMount(TestComponent)
    expect(wrapper.text()).toContain('Hello, World!')
  })

2 shallowMount
```

Chapter 3

```
1 test('renders item.author, () => {
    const item = {
      author: 10
    }
    const wrapper = shallowMount(Item, {
      propsData: { item }
    })
    expect(wrapper.text()).toContain(item.author)
  })

  test('renders item.score, () => {
    const item = {
      score: 10
    }
    const wrapper = shallowMount(Item, {
      propsData: { item }
    })
    expect(wrapper.text()).toContain(item.score)
  })

2 import Child from 'child'

  test('renders Child', () => {
    const wrapper = shallowMount(TestComponent)
```

```
      expect(wrapper.find(Child).props().testProp).toBe('some-value')
   })
```

3 ```
  test('renders a tag with correct href', () => {
    const wrapper = shallowMount(TestComponent)
    expect(wrapper.find('a').attributes().href).toBe('https://google.com')
  })
```

4 ```
  test('renders p tag with correct style', () => {
    const wrapper = shallowMount(TestComponent)
    expect(wrapper.find('p').element.style.color).toBe('red')
  })
```

Chapter 4

1 ```
  test('styles the bar correctly when fail is called', () => {
    const wrapper = shallowMount(ProgressBar)
    expect(wrapper.classes()).not.toContain('error')
    wrapper.vm.fail()
    expect(wrapper.classes()).toContain('error')
  })
```

2 ```
  test('sets the bar to 100% width when fail is called', () => {
    const wrapper = shallowMount(ProgressBar)
    wrapper.vm.fail()
    expect(wrapper.element.style.width).toBe('100%')
  })
```

3 ```
  test('calls $bar.fail when load unsuccessful', async () => {
    const $bar = {
      start: () => {},
      fail: jest.fn()
    }
    fetchListData.mockImplementation(() => Promise.reject())
    shallowMount(ItemList, { mocks: { $bar }})
    await flushPromises()

    expect($bar.fail).toHaveBeenCalled()
  })
```

## Chapter 5

1 Using the wrapper `trigger` method
2 By emitting an event on the child component instance with the `$emit` method

## Chapter 7

1 You need to mock lots of Vuex functions. This can lead to tests that pass but are incorrect due to the mock behaving differently than the real function.

2 The tests are less specific. If a test fails, it can be difficult to find out where the test failed and how to fix it.

3 ```
  test('mounts correctly', () => {
    const localVue = createLocalVue()
```

```
    localVue.use(Vuex)
    const store = new Vuex.Store(storeConfig)
    shallowMount(TestComponent, {
      localVue,
      store
    })
  })
```

Chapter 8

1 Don't repeat yourself.

2 Factory functions avoid repetition and provide a pattern to follow.

Chapter 10

1
```
test('calls injectedMethod with the route path', () => {
  const $route = { path: '/some/path' }
  const injectedMethod = jest.fn()
  shallowMount(TestComponent, { mocks: { $route, injectedMethod } })
  expect(injectedMethod).toHaveBeenCalledWith($route.path)
})
```

2 vuex-router-sync

Chapter 11

1
```
test('calls myMethod beforeMount', () => {
  const Component = {
    methods: {
      myMethod: jest.fn()
    },
    mixins: [testMixin]
  }
  shallowMount(Component)
  expect(Component.methods.myMethod).toHaveBeenCalled()
})
```

2
```
function capitalize (string) {
    return string.charAt(0).toUpperCase() + string.slice(1);
}
```

3
```
// test-setup.js
import Vue from 'vue'
import uppercase from './uppercase'

Vue.filter('uppercase', uppercase)

// TestComponent.spec.js
test('renders a capitalized name', () => {
  const wrapper = shallowMount(TestComponent, {
    propsData: {name: 'edd'}
  })
  expect(wrapper.text()).toContain('Edd')
})
```

Chapter 12

1 1, because a static component has only one branch of logic

2 Because the date changes over time, which will cause your snapshot test to fail even if the code hasn't been changed. A snapshot test must be deterministic.

3
```
test('renders correctly', () => {
  const wrapper = shallowMount(TestComponent)
   expect(wrapper.element).toMatchSnapshot()
})
```

Chapter 13

1
```
/**
 * @jest-environment node
 */
```

2 render returns a Cheerio wrapper object; renderToString returns a string.

index

RELATED MANNING TITLES

Vue.js in Action
by Erik Hanchett with Benjamin Listwon

    ISBN: 9781617294624
    304 pages, $44.99
    September 2018

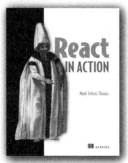

React in Action
by Mark Tielens Thomas

    ISBN: 9781617293856
    360 pages, $44.99
    May 2018

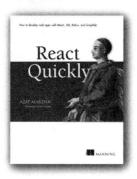

React Quickly
Painless web apps with React, JSX, Redux, and GraphQL
by Azat Mardan

    ISBN: 9781617293344
    528 pages, $49.99
    August 2017

Secrets of the JavaScript Ninja, Second Edition
by John Resig, Bear Bibeault, and Josip Maras

    ISBN: 9781617292859
    464 pages, $44.99
    August 2016

For ordering information go to www.manning.com